CONFERENCES

CONFERENCES

A Twenty-First Century Industry

TONY ROGERS

ADDISON WESLEY LONGMAN

Harlow, England ● Reading, Massachusetts ● Menlo Park, California

New .York ● Don Mills, Ontario ● Amsterdam ● Bonn ● Sydney ● Tokyo

Madrid ● San Juan, Milan ● Paris ● Mexico City ● Seoul ● Taipei

Addison Wesley Longman Limited
Edinburgh Gate
Harlow, Essex CM20 2JE, England
and Associated Companies throughout the world.

Published in the United States of America
by Addison Wesley Longman Publishing, New York

© Addison Wesley Longman Limited 1998

First published 1998

ISBN 0 582 31930–7

British Library Cataloguing-in-Publication Data

A catalogue record for this book is
available from the British Library.

Set by 35 in 9.5/12pt Garamond Light
Produced by Addison Wesley Longman Singapore (Pte) Ltd.,
Printed in Singapore

DEDICATION

To my wife, Jane, and to my daughters Joanne, Helen and Katie.
Also to my mother, and in memory of my father.
And a special mention for my mother-in-law, Edna.

Contents

Preface

When, in 1989, I was applying for my first job in the conference industry with what was then the British Association of Conference Towns (BACT), I endeavoured to prepare for my interview by reading up on the industry. I managed to find almost no information, apart from one trade magazine. And so I consider myself very fortunate to have been appointed to the position I still enjoy with BACD (British Association of Conference Destinations, as it now is), despite my relative ignorance. In the ensuing years, through my efforts to respond to requests for information from colleagues, students and many others, I have been made painfully aware of the general dearth of literature about this great industry.

This book is an attempt, therefore, to fill something of this void. It tries to paint a broad picture of the scope and composition of the industry, its structure and value, its activities and personnel, and its characteristics and trends. The book also looks ahead to the development of the industry into the twenty-first century. I very much hope that it will be of interest to students and lecturers, to those working in the industry as well as to those who may be looking to make a future career in the industry, to politicians (local and national), to consultants, and to anyone else seeking an overview of this dynamic, fascinating, endearing but under-recognised sector of the national and global economies.

Each chapter follows a similar pattern with an introduction, main theme, summary, review and discussion questions, and references. In the text I have, for stylistic simplicity, used 'he' rather than '(s)he' where appropriate, but such uses should be interpreted as applying equally to both genders. Indeed, I should perhaps have used 'she' throughout as women are represented very strongly at all levels of the industry, probably outnumbering men in many sectors.

The book would not have been possible without the unstinting help, advice and provision of data and information that I have received from colleagues across the world. One of the delights of the conference industry, for me, is this very openness and willingness to share that I have experienced at every turn. To everyone who has helped in any way, I owe an enormous debt of gratitude. I hope they will understand if I do not mention all of them individually (which would certainly take several pages, with the risk of offending someone by accidentally omitting their name).

I would like, however, to acknowledge publicly the assistance received from the following, who have gone much more than the 'extra mile':

- Robin Anderson, of Robin Anderson and Associates, for reading the whole of my draft text and making innumerable suggestions for improvements. His experience and knowledge of the industry, as well as his creativity, attention to detail and mastership of his craft as a 'wordsmith' have been absolutely invaluable.
- Peter Glover of the British Tourist Authority for surviving, and always responding equably to, my requests for advice and information.
- Ian Banks, of Banks Associates, for advice on research and statistics.
- Geoffrey Smith, of Geoffrey V. Smith Associates, for information on a number of the European and international trade associations.
- Sally Greenhill, of The Right Solution Limited, for information on research findings and on the design of conference facilities.
- Penny Hanson, of The Hanson Organisation, for checking my references to the exhibition sector.
- Eddie Friel, Eddie Friel Associates (now with Greater Glasgow and Clyde Valley Tourist Board), and Martin Peters (Leicester Promotions) for reading through and commenting on passages in the book.
- Mary Tack, International Association of Convention and Visitor Bureaus, for information on the US scene.
- Kevin Fields, Birmingham College of Food, Tourism and Creative Studies, for encouraging me to write the book in the first place.
- Ian Little, Addison Wesley Longman, for constant advice, help and encouragement throughout the writing period.
- The BACD Management Committee for supporting my wish to put pen to paper!
- The BACD Secretariat (Tracy Johnson, Brian McNidder, Sarah Smart, Paula Deenah) for all sorts of practical help, advice and support.
- And, finally, my family for their support, patience and tolerance during the 'burning of the midnight oil'!

Tony Rogers

Chapter 1

A Global Industry

Introduction

The conference industry is a young, dynamic industry which is growing and maturing at a rapid rate. From origins in Europe and North America, it is now a truly international industry witnessing huge investments across all continents. Its youthfulness, however, does mean that it lacks some of the necessary characteristics of more established industries, such as well-defined terminology, adequate market intelligence, appropriate education and training structures and clear entry routes. Conferences are part of the business tourism sector, a major though often undervalued sector of the tourism industry.

Objectives

This chapter looks at:

- the origins of the conference industry
- the foundations of a proper industry
- the industry's recent globalisation
- world rankings of the leading cities and countries
- certain industry shortcomings
- industry parameters and definitions
- business tourism and leisure tourism
- the benefits of conference and business tourism.

The Origins of the Conference Industry

Napoleon Bonaparte may well be the unwitting founder of the modern conference industry. His military exploits across Europe and beyond at the end of the eighteenth and beginning of the nineteenth centuries led, on his downfall, to what was perhaps the first truly international conference, the Congress of Vienna, held from September 1814 to June 1815. The Congress was called to re-establish the territorial divisions of Europe at the end of the Napoleonic Wars, and representatives included all of the major world powers of the day (with the exception of Turkey).

It is tempting to imagine what the 'delegate spend' must have been like, with delegates such as Alexander I, Emperor of Russia, Prince Karl August von Hardenberg from Prussia, and Viscount Castlereagh and the Duke of Wellington as the principal British representatives. Each representative would have been accompanied by a substantial delegation of support staff and partners, requiring accommodation, social programmes, lavish corporate entertainment, ground handling, not to mention state-of-the-art conference facilities. The Vienna Convention Bureau no doubt celebrated long and hard its success in attracting such a high-profile, high-spend event to the city.

The peace of Europe remained relatively undisturbed for 40 years after the Congress of Vienna, a testament to the Congress's achievement in re-establishing the balance of power among the countries of Europe. While a few other international conferences, mostly of a political and scientific nature, took place during the remainder of the nineteenth and first half of the twentieth centuries, these were relatively infrequent and certainly not sufficient to warrant any reference to a conference 'industry'.

During this period too, business organisation was autocratic and hierarchical in character: the manager's word was to be obeyed and implemented, not questioned. It was not in the regular order of things to seek employees' views, to 'confer' with colleagues in a structured way off company premises.

The situation was somewhat different in North America during the latter half of the nineteenth century, particularly across the eastern seaboard of the USA where various trade and professional associations, as well as religious groups, were being formed and, as they became more established, beginning to hold conventions for their membership. Gartrell (1994) records that, in due course, a number of committees were also created to 'lure the growing convention business from these expanding and thriving associations'. As more and more cities became aware of the value of convention business, Gartrell suggests that it was

> inevitable that the solicitation of these conventions would be assigned to a full-time salesperson; and, while this might have happened in any one of many major cities, history records that it first happened in Detroit, Michigan, when a group of businessmen decided to place a full-time salesperson on the road to invite conventions to their city. Thus, in 1896, the first convention bureau was formed, and an industry emerged.

Detroit was shortly followed by other US cities which established their own convention bureaus: Cleveland (1904), Atlantic City (1908), Denver and St Louis (1909), Louisville and Los Angeles (1910). Now many cities around the world have their own convention bureau, or convention and visitor bureau.

The Foundations of a Proper Industry

The origins of today's conference industry lie in the political and religious congresses of earlier centuries, as well as the trade and professional association conventions in the USA during the latter part of the nineteenth century. However, the development and recognition of a proper 'industry' is a much more recent phenomenon, in Europe especially, effectively dating from the middle to latter part of the twentieth century.

The foundation of trade associations is often a useful, objective way of marking the real formation of an industry. Some of the principal conference industry associations were founded as follows:

- Association Internationale des Palais de Congrès (AIPC)   1958
- International Congress and Convention Association (ICCA)   1963
- European Federation of Conference Towns (EFCT)   1964
- International Association of Professional Congress Organisers (IAPCO)   1968
- British Association of Conference Destinations (BACD)   1969
- Association for Conferences and Events (ACE)   1971
- Meetings Industry Association (MIA)   1990

The International Association of Convention and Visitor Bureaus, on the other hand, with a predominantly North American membership, was founded as long ago as 1914.

Since the 1960s there has been a very rapid growth in the whole infrastructure that supports conferences, meetings and related events, with UK cities such as Birmingham and Glasgow epitomising the huge scale of investment that has taken place (see Case Study 1.1 – Glasgow). Table 1.1 lists the major, purpose-built convention centres which have been opened in the United Kingdom since 1990. This list does not include other substantial investments in buildings which, though not purpose-built for the conventions industry, are capable of staging very large conferences, such as the Sheffield Arena (12 000 seats, £45 million), Birmingham's National Indoor Arena (13 000 seats, £51 million), Manchester's £42 million Bridgewater Hall and the 19 000-seat Nynex Arena, and the Newcastle Arena (10 000 seats, £10.5 million) in Newcastle upon Tyne (see also Figure 1.1, overleaf).

Name of centre	Year of opening	Cost (m)
International Convention Centre (Birmingham)	1991	£180
Plymouth Pavilions	1992	£25
Cardiff International Arena	1993	£25
North Wales Conference Centre, Llandudno	1994	£6
Edinburgh International Conference Centre	1995	£38
Belfast Waterfront Hall (Conference Centre and Concert Hall)	1997	£32
Clyde Auditorium at the Scottish Exhibition and Conference Centre (Glasgow)	1997	£38
Millennium Conference Centre (London)	1997	£35

Table 1.1
Investments in major UK conference centres since 1990

Figure 1.1
Belfast
Waterfront Hall
Conference and
Concert Centre.
Built at a cost
of £32 million
and opened in
January 1997,
the Centre can
seat up to 2235
delegates.

(*Source:* Belfast City Council)

Case Study 1.1 Glasgow

The economy of Glasgow was, until the 1960s, heavily dependent upon shipbuilding and manufacturing industry. As a city, it was the antithesis of a traditional tourism destination. The decline of its industrial base by the 1970s led to a need to diversity the economy and tourism, especially conference and business tourism, was seen as a major potential contributor to Glasgow's economic revival and regeneration.

So successful has the city been that, in the remarkably short period of 15 years, tourism is now worth around £650 million per year to Greater Glasgow and the neighbouring Clyde Valley, supporting 47 500 jobs. Between 1983 and 1994 the number of overseas tourists to Glasgow grew by 123 per cent, compared with a growth of 55 per cent for Scotland as a whole and 35 per cent for the UK in the same period. Glasgow is now the third most popular UK destination for overseas visitors, after London and Edinburgh.

The area currently attracts 1.2 million overnight visitors a year, and 25 million day visitors. The Greater Glasgow and Clyde Valley Tourist Board is aiming for a 10 per cent growth in tourism to the area between 1995 and 1999. Expenditure on tourism-related projects in this period will be £500 million, including £38 million on a new 3000-seat auditorium for the Scottish Exhibition and Conference Centre.

Conferences are now worth over £50 million per year to the destination, having increased in value by 34 per cent between 1991 and 1995. Since its inception in 1987, Glasgow's Convention Bureau has secured over £200 million of conference business. The historical development of the Convention Bureau is shown below. An organisational chart showing its structure within the Greater Glasgow and Clyde Valley Tourist Board is given in Chapter 5.

▷

Convention Bureau Development within the Evolution of the Glasgow Tourism Product

1983: Greater Glasgow Tourist Board was established to market the Greater Glasgow area as a tourism destination.

1984: Opening of the Burrell Collection housing art and historical treasures. It attracted over one million visitors in its first year.

1985: Opening of the Scottish Exhibition and Conference Centre as Scotland's largest, purpose-built centre.

1987: The Convention Bureau division was established within the Tourist Board in order to undertake conference marketing activities and position Greater Glasgow as a leading meetings destination.

1988: The Glasgow Garden Festival was staged, and played a part in attracting such large-scale conferences as the World Baptist Youth Congress (10 000 delegates) and Round Tables of Great Britain and Ireland (6000 delegates).

1989: The Convention Bureau was voted 'Best UK Convention Bureau' in the Meetings and Incentive Travel Awards.

1990: Glasgow was 'Cultural Capital of Europe' in 1990. This accolade helped to attract major Arts conferences during the year, heightened the profile of the destination, and led to the securing of new conference business.

1991: Glasgow's 'Ambassador Programme' was launched, with the objective of identifying leading representatives from the area's academic, medical, scientific, professional and business communities and encouraging their participation in attracting new conference business. Subsequent research has shown that around 80 per cent of association conferences to Greater Glasgow and Clyde Valley have been influenced by local 'Ambassadors'.

1993: The Convention Bureau again won 'Best UK Convention Bureau' award. Conferences held included: World Orchid Society (2000 delegates), International Union of Physiological Sciences (4000 delegates), and the International Congress of Virology (4000 delegates).

1994: The Convention Bureau again won 'Best UK Convention Bureau' award.

1996: The new Greater Glasgow and Clyde Valley Tourist Board was established, expanding the area represented to cover the Clyde Valley. Conferences staged included the International Society of Hypertension (6000 delegates).

1997: Conferences held included Rotary International World Convention (24 000 delegates) and the American Society of Travel Agents World Congress (5000 delegates). The Clyde Auditorium (nicknamed 'The Armadillo'), a new purpose-built 3000-seat auditorium at the Scottish Exhibition and Conference Centre, was opened.

Major conferences confirmed for Glasgow for future years include:

● the European League Against Rheumatism – 6000 delegates, 6–12 June 1999, expected to generate around £3 million for the local economy

● the International Society of Magnetic Resonance in Medicine – 3000 delegates over five days in 2001; the conference and exhibition will be worth an estimated £2.5 million to the area

● the 30th International Geographical Congress – up to 3000 delegates over five days in 2004, expected to inject over £1.4 million into the local economy.

Case Study 1.2 The Philippines

The Philippines is a relative veteran among Asian convention countries, having launched itself to the international meetings industry as long ago as 1976 with the opening of the continent's first purpose-built convention centre, the Philippine International Convention Center (PICC) in Manila. Since that date its share of international events has continued to grow to the point where Manila was ranked thirty-seventh in the UIA rankings of leading convention cities of the world for events staged in 1996. For the same year the Philippines as a national destination was also well up in the top 50 countries, hosting a 'significant number of international' conferences, according to UIA figures.

Since the mid-1970s investments have continued apace, developing an infrastructure of de luxe accommodation, efficient transport, and modern telecommunications to support a versatile range of meeting facilities. Manila's international airport is undergoing a major refurbishment and two new terminals are planned to cater for an expected annual growth of 7 per cent in passenger traffic. A further international airport (in Cebu, Southern Philippines) and six new domestic airports (in central Philippines) are also being developed to help boost tourism on a national scale.

The new 3000-seat Cebu Convention Centre is due for completion by November 1997, which will be accompanied by major hotel developments. The PICC in Manila also underwent substantial renovations and refurbishments in 1996. The PICC has a multi-level Plenary Hall seating 4000, a 55 700-square foot Reception Hall, 14 meeting rooms of varying capacities, and over 80 000 square feet of exhibition space. Manila's other new facilities include the World Trade Center Manila, which offers a total exhibition space of 8300 square metres, with a 22-storey hotel also planned alongside the Center. Pan Pacific will open a 250-room hotel in Manila in 1998, and Sheraton a 250-room property in 1999. Major hotel developments are under construction elsewhere in the Philippines, including the US$25 million expansion of Shangri-La's EDSA Plaza Hotel in Mandaluyong where a 14-storey wing will house an additional 218 rooms as well as 6560 square feet of meeting space.

A Tourism Infrastructure Development Fund has been established with the backing of the World Travel and Tourism Council, World Bank, Asian Development Bank, and other funding institutions to make funds readily available to speed up infrastructure developments in the Philippines. A 20-year Tourism Master Plan specifically underlines Manila's focus as the hub of international meetings and conventions. The Philippine Convention and Visitors Corporation launched a campaign ('Convention City Manila') in 1995 to encourage local associations, who form the backbone of the convention industry, not only to bid for and host international and regional events, but to create new ones as well.

Out of a total of just over 2 million overseas visitors to the Philippines in 1996, 1.7 per cent were convention visitors and a further 18.9 per cent were business visitors. Overseas visitors spent on average US$151.61 per capita per day, and stayed for an average of almost ten nights each.

Case Study 1.3 Durban

The City of Durban, situated on South Africa's Indian Ocean coastline and with a population of 2.75 million, recognised a growing demand for conference and convention facilities during the 1980s. Tourism Durban, the organisation tasked with the promotion of the City as a tourism destination and with increasing the numbers of both international and domestic tourists, formalised the operation of a conference bureau in March 1994 (Durban Metropolitan Convention and Visitors Bureau, whose main function is to market Metropolitan Durban as the 'Convention Capital' of South Africa).

Prior to this date, Durban City Council had already decided to build the International Convention Centre (ICC), which was officially opened in August 1997. Capital funding of R260 million (approximately £38 million) for the project was provided wholly by the Metropolitan Authority, which ▷

has also undertaken to meet any excess operational costs for the period until the Centre becomes operationally viable (which is expected to be within four years of opening). The ICC is a state-of-the-art meeting place with three halls, the largest seating up to 3000 delegates. There is a second hall with a raked (or tiered) auditorium to seat 1800 delegates. The third hall can seat up to 2440 delegates, and there are a further 23 meeting rooms seating between 20 and 350 delegates. By June 1997, 31 confirmed conference bookings had been secured up to the end of 1998, projected to generate 18 290 delegates and 1 551 140 room nights. Further confirmed bookings have been achieved up to 2008. The development of the ICC enables Durban to compete on equal terms with the world's other leading convention cities.

The public sector investment in the ICC has stimulated private sector investments in the construction of a new Hilton Hotel (alongside the ICC) and the refurbishment of two existing hotels, developments which, alone, have exceeded the initial investment by the Metropolitan Authority. Durban's infrastructure also includes a purpose-built exhibition centre, some 50 conference venues apart from the ICC, 17 000 beds along the City's famous four-mile long Golden Mile, and its own international airport just 15 minutes from the Central Business District.

The table below gives an activity analysis for Durban Metropolitan Convention and Visitors Bureau (as at July 1997). It measures the value of events to Durban as economic impact (see Chapter 4). This is the *new* spending brought to, and generated by, the event itself in the region, and excludes travel to and from the region and pre- and post-conference tours. The basis of calculation and input data are those published by the International Association of Convention and Visitor Bureaus, adjusted to reflect the purchasing power of the Rand:

Year	Value of bids handled (R)	Won (R)	Lost (R)	Potential annual impact (R)	Confirmed annual impact (R)
1994	720 872 100	250 519 068	197 000 000	153 595 638	153 595 638
1995	481 545 354	266 248 530	60 261 700	186 977 400	169 325 100
1996	862 700 284	232 658 640	483 238 400	210 702 900	166 667 100
1997	233 165 000	267 655 000	–	299 679 300	107 828 400

Note: All values are in Rand

But it is not just in Europe and North America that major investments are being made. In the past five to ten years, large-scale infrastructure projects have been undertaken throughout much of Asia and the Pacific rim, in the former East European countries such as Hungary and the Czech Republic, and in a number of African countries, particularly South Africa (see Case Study 1.2, the Philippines, and Case Study 1.3, Durban).

There appear to be a number of reasons for these investments, many of which are paid for out of central government and other public sector funds:

1. Such countries and destinations are probably already active in the leisure tourism sector and have developed much of the infrastructure for it, which is the same infrastructure (airports and other communications facilities, 3-star/4-star/5-star hotels, attractions, trained staff, for example) as that required to attract international conference business. Although additional investment in purpose-built conference and exhibition facilities may not be an insignificant cost, it is likely to be a relatively small additional amount compared with the total infrastructure investments already made.

2. Such destinations quite rightly see conference business as complementary to leisure tourism business, in the same way that the longer-established destinations do.

3. Conference and business tourism, being at the high quality, high yield end of the tourism spectrum, brings major economic benefits for developing as well as for developed countries. Such benefits include year-round jobs and foreign exchange earnings. There is also the potential for future inward investment from conference delegates who have liked or been impressed by what they have seen of a country while attending a conference there and return to set up a business operation, or persuade their own employers to do so.

4. There is undoubted prestige in being selected to host a major international conference and some less developed countries would see this as a way of gaining credibility and acceptance on the international political stage. There is perhaps an element of conferences and conference centres being developed as status symbols, signs of having 'arrived' as destinations to be taken seriously.

Such huge infrastructure investments are driven by a number of demand factors, both economic and social (analysed in further detail in Chapter 4). The challenge for those planning major new purpose-built convention centres (usually local authorities and public sector organisations) is to anticipate future demand accurately. Lead time from the initial idea for a convention centre until its opening can be as much as ten years. The process involves, inter alia, identification of a suitable site, design and planning stages, assembly of the funding package, construction of venue and related infrastructure, recruitment and training of staff. In such a period, substantial changes in the wider marketplace may have occurred.

There is less of a risk for hotel and smaller venue developments, where the period between initial concept and completion is much shorter (typically three to five years), but the same principles apply. Many venues conceived, for example, in the boom times of the late 1980s found that they were opening in a very different market in the early 1990s, with the economy in full recession, and many of the venues struggled or foundered as a result.

The Industry's Recent Globalisation

Conference and business tourism is a very important sector of the tourism industry, an industry which, in all its guises, is forecast to become the world's largest by the beginning of the new millennium. Conference tourism is now a truly global industry, as evidenced by the scale of international investments described earlier in this chapter. But there is much other evidence to substantiate such a claim. Nowhere is its truth better demonstrated than in the evolution of one of the industry's major trade shows, the European Incentive and Business Travel and Meetings Exhibition (EIBTM), which is held in Geneva in May each year. In 1988 54 countries were represented as exhibitors at EIBTM, a number which had almost doubled by 1997 to 105 countries. In the same period the number of visitors increased from 2850 in 1988 to 6958 in 1997, with 67 different countries supplying visitors to the show in 1997.

And yet, while competition is increasing from countries seeking to act as suppliers to the conference industry, the markets from which to win business still remain relatively few in number: 98 per cent of the visitors to EIBTM '97 were drawn from just 11 countries (see Table 1.2).

Country	%	Country	%
Austria	2	Italy	9
Benelux	11	Switzerland	14
France	9	United Kingdom	21
Germany	19	USA/Canada	8

Source: EIBTM Holdings Ltd

Table 1.2
Markets supplying visitors to EIBTM '97

There are a number of reasons for this:

- the national economies of many of the emerging nations are not yet sufficiently strong for their corporate sector organisations to be planning events overseas (sales meetings, product launches, incentive events, for example), although this will no doubt change in the near future in view of the rapid growth now being enjoyed by a number of countries, particularly in South-East Asia

- the headquarters of many international associations and intergovernmental organisations are located in Western Europe and North America. Such headquarters are also where those organising events on behalf of these bodies are based

- market intelligence is much better developed in respect of the 'buyers' (conference organisers) in the most experienced conventioneering countries. Quite sophisticated databases exist detailing the buying requirements and preferences of conference organisers in the more established North American and European markets. Such data do not yet exist, either in quantity or quality, for many of the newer markets.

World Rankings of Leading Cities and Countries

The global nature of the conference industry is also very well illustrated by figures produced annually by the International Congress and Convention Association (ICCA), from its headquarters in Amsterdam, and by the Union of International Associations (UIA), which is based in Brussels. Such figures record the staging of international conferences and conventions by country and city. They enable trends to be monitored and give an indication of which countries and cities are gaining market share and which may be losing it.

International Congress and Convention Association (ICCA) rankings

ICCA maintains a database which holds information on the location of international meetings. All meetings in the ICCA database must meet the following criteria:

- be organised on a regular basis
- rotate between at least four different countries
- attract a minimum of 100 participants.

The database allows ICCA to provide rankings (by country and city) showing market share in respect of such meetings. ICCA's figures for 1994–96, published in May 1997, and given in Table 1.3 (overleaf), show market share for the top 20 countries by number of events in that three-year period, and include a forecast for 1997. When the same

Table 1.3
Market shares of the top 20 countries by number of events in the period 1994–96, with a forecast for 1997 (ranking based on 1996 performance)

	Country	1997	1996	1995	1994
1	USA	6.41	7.06	7.50	8.53
2	United Kingdom	7.27	6.08	6.76	5.59
3	Japan	3.61	5.06	5.37	4.63
4	Australia	5.33	4.72	3.15	3.24
	Netherlands	5.10	4.72	5.78	5.02
6	France	3.95	4.59	5.61	6.33
7	Germany	4.30	4.55	4.59	5.25
8	Italy	4.07	4.42	4.26	4.55
9	Denmark	2.69	4.25	3.03	2.78
10	Spain	4.41	4.00	4.42	4.28
11	Austria	2.58	3.27	2.95	3.28
12	Israel	1.95	3.10	2.34	1.20
13	Finland	3.32	3.02	2.50	2.31
14	Hungary	1.26	2.76	1.76	1.39
15	Belgium	2.81	2.68	2.46	1.66
16	Sweden	2.86	2.64	2.25	2.28
17	Canada	2.92	2.47	2.70	3.90
18	Switzerland	1.89	2.34	1.93	1.77
19	Hong Kong	2.35	1.83	1.56	1.20
20	Norway	2.29	1.74	1.84	2.47
	Market Share top 20	**69.07**	**73.55**	**70.91**	**69.17**

Source: ICCA DATA (International Congress and Convention Association, May 1997)

Figure 1.2
Market shares of the top 10 countries by number of events, 1994–96, with a forecast for 1997.

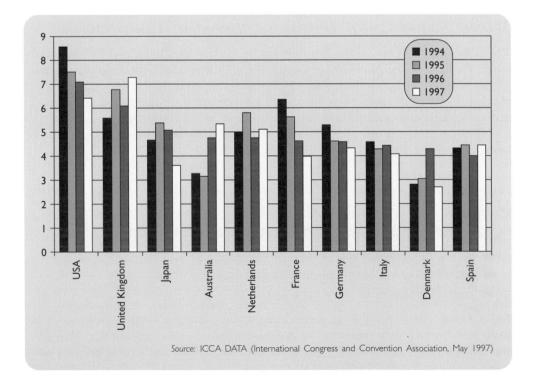

Source: ICCA DATA (International Congress and Convention Association, May 1997)

	Country	1996	1995		Country	1996	1995
1	USA	166	183	33	Philippines	19	15
2	United Kingdom	143	165		Thailand	19	16
3	Japan	119	131	35	Chinese Taipei	15	14
4	Australia	111	77	36	India	14	14
	Netherlands	111	141		Turkey	14	20
6	France	108	137	38	Iceland	13	9
7	Germany	107	112	39	Poland	12	16
8	Italy	104	104	40	Argentina	11	22
9	Denmark	100	74	41	Venezuela	10	5
10	Spain	94	108	42	New Zealand	8	11
11	Austria	77	72	43	Slovenia	7	9
12	Israel	73	57	44	Egypt	6	8
13	Finland	71	61		Monaco	6	7
14	Hungary	65	43		Romania	6	3
15	Belgium	63	60		Slovak Republic	6	6
16	Sweden	62	55		Tunisia	6	4
17	Canada	58	66	49	Chile	5	14
18	Switzerland	55	47		Russia	5	10
19	Hong Kong	43	38	51	Costa Rica	4	1
20	Norway	41	45		Zimbabwe	4	5
21	Korea Rep.	33	24	53	Cyprus	3	6
22	Greece	32	28		Ecuador	3	4
23	Portugal	28	28		Jordan	3	0
	South Africa	28	20		Latvia	3	1
25	Ireland	26	27		Luxembourg	3	7
26	China-PR	25	32		Morocco	3	4
27	Czech Republic	24	38		Panama	3	1
	Malaysia	24	13		Trinidad & Tobago	3	0
29	Singapore	22	45		Uruguay	3	5
30	Indonesia	21	20		Other Countries	61	102
31	Brazil	20	33				
	Mexico	20	18		Total	2352	2441

Table 1.4
Number of events per country, 1995–96

Source: ICCA DATA (International Congress and Convention Association, May 1997)

information is presented graphically in bar chart format (Figure 1.2), certain trends in market share are highlighted, such as the consistent decline in market share of the USA and France, contrasting with the steady growth being achieved by Australia as one of the newer destinations.

ICCA's analysis of the number of events per country (Table 1.4) further underlines the global nature of conferences, including as it does many countries which would not have appeared at all, even just a few years ago, such as China, Malaysia and Poland.

Although international conventions are tracked by country, as shown in Tables 1.3 and 1.4, the events are actually won by individual destinations (normally cities) through a bidding process, and ICCA's record of where events were held on a city basis in 1996 (see Table 1.5, overleaf) provides a challenging test to anyone's knowledge of world geography. As well as confirming the strength of international competition for convention business, it also suggests that London's pre-eminence among British destinations is being strongly contested by Edinburgh, Birmingham and Glasgow.

Table 1.5
Number of events per city in 1996

	City	1996		City	1996
1	Copenhagen	76	35	Cape Town	14
2	Vienna	55		San Francisco	14
3	Budapest	54	37	Zurich	13
4	Jerusalem	48		Taipei	13
5	Barcelona	44		Montreal	13
	Amsterdam	44		Florence	13
7	Hong Kong	43		Jakarta	13
8	Paris	39	42	Nice	12
9	Stockholm	36		Osaka	12
10	Melbourne	32		Glasgow	12
11	Helsinki	29		Atlanta	12
	Sydney	29		Washington, DC	12
13	Edinburgh	28		Tel Aviv	12
14	Seoul	27		Geneva	12
15	Dublin	24		Rio de Janeiro	12
16	Munich	23	50	Brisbane	11
17	London	22		Milan	11
	Prague	22		Adelaide	11
	Singapore	22		Orlando	11
	Brussels	22		Reykjavik	11
21	Athens	20		New York City	11
22	Beijing	19	56	Göteborg	10
	Oslo	19	57	Tampere	9
24	Manila	18		The Hague	9
	Antwerp	18		Nagoya	9
	Berlin	18		Graz	9
27	Kuala Lumpur	17		Veldhoven	9
	Madrid	17	62	Hamburg	8
29	Lisbon	16		Rotterdam	8
	Tokyo	16		Aarhus	8
	Bangkok	16		Maastricht	8
	Vancouver	16		Sevilla	8
33	Rome	15		Boston	8
	Yokohama	15		Tsukuba	8
				Turku	8

Source: ICCA DATA (International Congress and Convention Association, May 1997)

Union of International Associations (UIA) statistics

Since 1949 the Union of International Associations has undertaken annual statistical studies on international meetings taking place worldwide. The statistics are based on information collected by the UIA Congress Department and selected according to very strict criteria. Meetings taken into consideration include those organised and/or sponsored by the international organisations which appear in the UIA's *Yearbook of International Organisations* and *International Congress Calendar*, i.e. the 'sittings' of their principal organs, congresses, conventions, symposia, regional sessions grouping several countries, as well as some national meetings with international participation organised by national branches of international associations. Under this last category are included meetings which are

Year	Number of events worldwide	Number of events in Europe	Europe share of world market as %	Number of events in UK	UK share of the European market as %
1983	4864	3147	64.7	460	14.6
1984	5840	3797	65.0	511	13.5
1985	6232	3952	63.4	598	15.1
1986	6742	4183	62.0	606	14.5
1987	7370	4399	59.7	701	15.9
1988	8394	5001	59.6	750	15.0
1989	8207	4945	60.3	700	14.2
1990	8559	5225	61.0	722	13.8
1991	8251	5107	61.9	660	12.9
1992	8703	5299	60.9	577	10.9
1993	8871	5269	59.1	633	12.0
1994	9068	5294	58.4	645	12.2
1995	8802	5106	58.0	637	12.5
1996	8991*	5146	57.9	588	11.4

Note: * The overall total includes 96 conferences of unknown location
Source: Union of International Associations (July 1997)

Table 1.6
Europe's market share of international organisation conferences, 1983–96 (also showing the UK share of the European market)

not collected systematically but which have been brought to UIA's knowledge and which meet the following criteria:

- minimum number of participants: 300
- minimum number of foreigners: 40 per cent
- minimum number of nationalities: five
- minimum duration: three days.

These more stringent criteria for inclusion account, in large measure, for the differences in rankings between the UIA and ICCA figures.

The UIA figures for 1996 (published July 1997) include almost 9000 international meetings organised worldwide in no fewer than 187 different countries. The total number of meetings represents an overall increase of 2.14 per cent on the 1995 figures, with just South America recording a slight decrease. The increase experienced in other regions was as follows: Asia: 0.91 per cent, Australasia: 0.73 per cent, Europe: 0.47 per cent, North America: 0.40 per cent, Africa: 0.03 per cent.

These figures provide further evidence of the growing market share being won by countries in the Asia/Pacific region, to which reference has already been made, and which results from their major infrastructure investments, aggressive marketing, as well as perhaps the normal human desire, which conference delegates reflect, to experience places that are new and different.

Despite the small net increase in the number of meetings held, Europe's overall share of the market continues to decrease, a trend which must be of concern to European convention destinations. The fall may, at least in part, be a result of the world economic recession which was in full swing during the early 1990s, a time when many of the international meetings which took place in 1996 were being planned. Europe's declining market share is, however, part of a long-term trend, as confirmed by the figures shown in Table 1.6. They reveal that Europe had 64.7 per cent of international association meetings

Table 1.7
Leading countries
hosting
international
organisations
meetings in 1996,
as a percentage
of the worldwide
total

	Country	Meetings of international organisations	Meetings of national organisations	Total
1	USA	9.40+	2.39−	11.79+
2	France	5.37−	1.85−	7.22−
3	United Kingdom	5.34+	1.27−	6.61−
4	Germany	3.81−	1.54+	5.35−
5	Italy	3.78−	0.44+	4.22−
6	Netherlands	2.82=	0.32−	3.47−
7	Belgium	2.97=	0.65−	3.29−
8	Austria	2.75=	0.46−	3.21−
9	**Spain**	**2.43+**	**0.54+**	**2.97+**
10	Switzerland	2.74−	0.22=	2.96−
11	**Australia**	**1.95+**	**0.67+**	**2.62+**
12	Japan	1.76+	0.83−	2.59−
13	Canada	1.81−	0.52=	2.33−
14	**Denmark**	**1.76+**	**0.31+**	**2.07+**
15	**Hungary**	**1.52+**	**0.29+**	**1.81+**
16	Finland	1.42+	0.28+	1.70+
17	**Sweden**	**1.38+**	**0.25+**	**1.63+**
18	Singapore	1.09+	0.44−	1.53+
19	Israel	0.95+	0.58+	1.53−
20	Norway	1.32+	0.19−	1.51+
21	Hong Kong	0.70+	0.60+	1.30+
22	**Russia**	**0.90+**	**0.29+**	**1.19+**
23	China	0.91+	0.22=	1.13+
24	Czech Republic	1.05+	0.03−	1.08+
25	**Greece**	**0.91+**	**0.13+**	**1.04+**

Notes: The +, − and = signs next to each figure represent changes compared with 1995. Countries in bold have improved their ranking compared with 1995

Rankings by international organisation meetings, column 1

Source: Union of International Associations (July 1997)

in 1983, but just 57.9 per cent in 1996. In the same period the United Kingdom's share of the European market dropped from 14.6 per cent to 11.4 per cent, with its share of the world market declining from 9.5 per cent in 1983 to 6.6 per cent in 1996.

Table 1.7 gives the UIA rankings of the leading countries hosting international organisations' meetings in 1996 as a percentage of the worldwide total, distinguishing between the meetings of international organisations and the meetings of national organisations which had a minimum of 40 per cent of delegates attending from overseas. Other countries hosting a significant number of international meetings in 1996 were: South Africa, India, Republic of Korea, Thailand, Poland, Argentina, Portugal, Brazil, Malaysia, Mexico, Ireland, Turkey and the Philippines.

Table 1.8 gives the UIA rankings of the leading cities in 1996, and it should be remembered that it is the cities which are the actual 'destinations' for the meeting, conference or convention. Other cities hosting a significant number of international events, but not in the top 23, were (in order): Strasbourg, Tokyo, Montreal, Buenos Aires, Munich, Kuala Lumpur, Bangkok, Melbourne, Oslo, Dublin, Moscow, Orlando, Lisbon, Manila, San Francisco, San Diego, Chicago, Athens, Trieste, Vancouver, Antwerp, Edinburgh, Cairo,

	City	Meetings of international organisations	Meetings of national organisations	Total
1	Paris	2.09–	1.06–	3.15–
2	Vienna	1.89–	0.20–	2.09–
3	London	1.75+	0.26–	2.01–
4	Brussels	1.90+	0.10–	2.00=
5	Geneva	2.01–	0.05–	1.61–
6	**Copenhagen**	**1.39+**	**0.25+**	**1.64+**
7	Singapore	1.09+	0.44–	1.53–
8	**Budapest**	**1.18+**	**0.22–**	**1.40+**
9	Washington, DC	1.09–	0.21+	1.30+
10	Amsterdam	1.06+	0.23–	1.29+
11	Hong Kong	0.70+	0.59+	1.29+
12	New York	1.04–	0.20+	1.24–
13	Berlin	0.66–	0.30+	0.96–
14	**Jerusalem**	**0.55+**	**0.39+**	**0.94+**
15	Rome	0.80–	0.12+	0.92–
16	Madrid	0.65+	0.27–	0.92=
17	**Stockholm**	**0.73+**	**0.13+**	**0.86+**
18	**Helsinki**	**0.68+**	**0.17+**	**0.85+**
19	Prague	0.82+	0.02–	0.84+
20	**Barcelona**	**0.70+**	**0.12=**	**0.82+**
21	Beijing	0.68+	0.12+	0.80+
22	Seoul	0.50–	0.25+	0.75–
23	**Sydney**	**0.73+**	**0.27+**	**0.73+**

Notes: The !, – and = signs next to each figure represent changes compared with 1995. Cities highlighted have improved their ranking compared with 1995

Rankings by international organisation meetings, column 1

Source: Union of International Associations (July 1997)

Table 1.8
Leading cities hosting international organisations' meetings in 1996, as a percentage of the worldwide total

New Delhi, Warsaw, Atlanta, The Hague, Maastricht, Luxembourg, Nice, Toronto, Istanbul, Birmingham and Cambridge.

Certain Industry Shortcomings

Lack of market intelligence

It has been seen that, in comparison with many other industries, the conference industry is still very young, less than 50 years of age in Europe and even younger in most of the rest of the world. Although it is maturing at a very rapid rate, it is indisputable that one of the legacies of its relative immaturity is a lack of reliable statistics and regular research to provide a base of intelligence and information on trends and on the size and value of the industry (the ICCA and UIA statistics quoted in this chapter are something of an oasis in what is generally a rather bleak statistical landscape). This, in turn, has meant that governments have not taken the industry seriously as a major benefactor to national economies because it has been impossible to demonstrate clearly the economic impact that conferences can have (except in some of the so-called less developed countries, who have very quickly realised its potential and invested accordingly).

At the time of writing (September 1997) the author has received details of an initiative spearheaded by the Union of International Associations and the European Union Statistics Unit (Eurostat) to develop an integrated methodology for conference sector statistics, using Eurostat and World Tourism Organisation (WTO) methodological frameworks on tourism and service statistics. The objective is to establish a common methodology by which, through the creation of criteria and definitions, greater coverage and statistical comparability may be guaranteed. It is hoped that this initiative will make a real contribution to addressing the conference industry's hunger for a comprehensive statistical base.

Non-standardised terminology

One of the reasons for the limited statistics on the size and value of the industry is the lack of an accepted and properly defined terminology. Words such as 'conference', 'congress', 'convention', 'meeting' even, are often used synonymously or indiscriminately. Other words are also used with similar but more specialised connotations, such as 'symposium', 'colloquium', 'assembly', 'conclave', 'summit', though it is probably only the last of these for which it might be easy to reach a consensus on its precise meaning (namely, a conference of high level officials, such as heads of government).

Arguments still rage over whether to describe conferences as a sector of the 'business tourism' or 'business travel' industry, although the author inclines firmly to the belief that business tourism is a more appropriate generic term.

A first attempt was made by a number of industry professionals in 1990 to produce a 'Meetings Industry Glossary'. A finished version of the Glossary was published in 1993 under the auspices of the Convention Liaison Council and the Joint Industry Council as the 'International Meetings Industry Glossary'. It is revealing to see how the definitions changed from the first draft to the final version. Both are given below, with the draft version followed by the published definition (in bold type):

Conference

Conferences can be used as an appropriate tool by any organisational group, private or public body, corporation, trade association, scientific or cultural society wishing to confer, exchange views and, consequently, to convey a message, open a debate or give publicity to some area of opinion on a specific issue. Most conferences are for 'study' purposes, generally involving some sort of special research input or conveyance of findings and require an active contribution from the participants. Compared with a congress, a conference is on a smaller scale and this gives a somewhat higher social connotation and makes it easier to exchange information. An example of the latter can be seen in a meeting of heads of state, ministers or official representatives of various states to examine, discuss and resolve, preferably by mutual agreement, political, economic or juridical problems of common interest. By and large, conferences are intended to facilitate communication and establish position reports or papers as a result of exchange of views. No tradition, continuity or periodicity is required to convene a conference. Although generally limited in time, conferences are usually of short duration with specific objectives.

An event used by any organisation to meet and exchange views, convey a message, open a debate or give publicity to some area of opinion on a specific issue. No tradition, continuity or periodicity is required to convene a conference. Although not generally limited in time, conferences are

usually of short duration with specific objectives. Conferences are generally on a smaller scale than congresses.

Congress

The regular coming together of several hundreds, even thousands, of individuals on a representational basis belonging to one professional, cultural, religious or other sphere, who are generally united in associative groups. A congress is often convened to discuss a particular subject. Contributions to the presentation and discussion of the subject matter come only from members or the promoting associative group. A congress will often last several days and have several simultaneous sessions. The length of time between congresses is usually established in advance of the implementation stage, and can be either pluri-annual or annual. Most international or world congresses are of the former type while national congresses are more frequently held annually.

The regular coming together of large groups of individuals, generally to discuss a particular subject. A congress will often last several days and have several simultaneous sessions. The length of time between congresses is usually established in advance of the implementation stage, and can be either pluri-annual or annual. Most international or world congresses are of the former type while national congresses are more frequently held annually.

Using this definition, it may be considered that the Congress of Vienna, to which reference was made at the beginning of this chapter, should more accurately have been called the 'Convention' of Vienna.

Convention

A general and formal meeting of a legislative body, social or economic group in order to provide information on a particular situation and in order to deliberate and, consequently, establish consent on policies among the participants. Usually of limited duration with set objectives, but no determined frequency.

Unchanged.

Meeting

A general term indicating the coming together of a number of people in one place, to confer or carry out a particular activity. Can be on an ad hoc basis or according to a set pattern.

Unchanged.

The descriptions listed above help to shed some light on the nature of different kinds of 'communications' events, but it is perhaps not surprising that they have not as yet been adopted as succinct, easy-to-remember definitions for the modern conference industry.

It could be argued that the variety of available vocabulary is more a reflection on the rich diversity of the English language than a symptom of an industry with myriad events, each with its own distinct characteristics. It may not really matter whether an event is called a 'conference' or a 'convention', and certainly there are as many misuses of these terms as there are correct interpretations, if indeed such a thing as a correct interpretation really exists.

What is important, however, is the need to ensure that statistics are being collected and interpreted in a standardised way on a worldwide level, as befits a truly global industry. This will enable the real size and value of the conference industry to be established and monitored. This is critical to the national and international recognition and support which the industry now deserves and demands.

Under-developed educational framework

One of the other reasons for the lack of a standardised terminology is that, for many of those now working in the industry, it is a second or even third career. They have come into conference work from related disciplines such as hotel and catering, travel, sales and marketing, public administration, but also from what might appear superficially to be unrelated spheres of employment. Whereas many, if not most, other professions have a formal induction and training process for new entrants which provides opportunities for them to be educated in the use of the accepted, clearly defined terminology, such opportunities and structures do not yet exist within the conference industry (although this is beginning to change with the advent of university and college courses providing modules on the conference industry).

Professional qualifications specific to the industry have existed for some years in North America. Such qualifications are now emerging elsewhere (see Chapter 7) and it is likely that, within the next five years, an appropriate range of educational courses and qualifications will have been established within the United Kingdom, and probably other countries. Such a development will provide an overdue support and recognition for what is a highly sophisticated industry but, nevertheless, one in which many conference organisers have received no formal training or obtained recognised qualifications to prepare them for their event management responsibilities. Conference organising may only be a small part of their job, undertaken for just a limited period of time. These are again factors which help to explain the problems sometimes experienced with semantics and the lack of clear, well understood terminology.

Industry Parameters and Definitions

Even if precise definitions are not yet in regular use, it is important, at the beginning of a book on the conference industry, to set out certain parameters for the measurement of conference events and facilities, and it is hoped that these might become widely accepted as appropriate criteria.

The sponsors of the 'British Conference Market Trends Survey' (British Tourist Authority, British Association of Conference Destinations, British Universities Accommodation Consortium, Conventions Great Britain, International Congress and Convention Association, Meetings Industry Association, and the Scottish Tourist Board) agreed in 1993 to use the following minimum criteria in respect of the Survey, and the author believes that these provide a good basis for the industry at large:

1. *A conference*: 'A conference or meeting is an event that involves 15 or more people and occupies a venue for six or more hours during the course of one day, or six or more hours on any one day if the event is for more than one day.' (*It is possible that the minimum number of participants will be reduced from 15 to 10 from 1998 onwards.*)

2. *A conference venue*: 'A conference venue must be able to seat 20 or more participants theatre-style.'

This is not to imply, of course, that events with fewer than 15 delegates are not 'conferences', or indeed that a venue with a conference room capacity of less than 20 cannot be active in the conference market, but such limits as those outlined above seem to offer a reasonable minimum base from which measurements of the size and value of the industry can be made, both realistically and consistently. In practice, to be taken seriously as a significant player by conference organisers, a conference venue will need to be able to offer far more than simply a 'room' to seat at least 20 people, and organisers' expectations continue to rise.

The conference industry forms one sector within 'business tourism', itself a sub-sector of the overall tourism industry which comprises both leisure tourism and business tourism. Apart from conferences, the other main components of business tourism are: exhibitions and trade fairs, incentive travel, corporate hospitality and individual business travel (also referred to as 'corporate travel').

One useful definition of a business tourist is: *a traveller whose main purpose for travelling is to attend an activity or event associated with his/her business or interests.*

Conferences, exhibitions and trade fairs, incentive travel and corporate hospitality are the four business tourism sectors which are the prime focus of marketing activities by venues and destinations, because decisions about where the events take place are open to influence. The organisers of the event may have great flexibility in deciding where it is to be held, and are able to use their own judgement or discretion. For this reason these four business tourism sectors are sometimes described as 'discretionary'.

Individual business travel or corporate travel relates to those whose work regularly involves travel within their own country or overseas, such as a lorry driver or sales representative, as well as to people who may have to travel away from their normal place of employment from time to time (a management consultant, for example, or an engineer responsible for installing a new piece of equipment in a client's factory). In all such business travel, which represents a major portion of business tourism, the opportunities to influence where the individual travels to are minimal, and this sector is consequently referred to as 'non-discretionary'.

Research into business travel in the USA in 1994 suggested that the primary purpose of 49 per cent of business trips was to attend a convention, meeting or trade show (US Travel Data Center survey findings, reported in *IACVB News*, 1994/95). An additional 11 per cent of those surveyed cited attending these events as a secondary purpose for their trip.

Business Tourism and Leisure Tourism

Reference has already been made to the broad division of tourism into the two sectors of business tourism and leisure tourism, although these two sectors share much common ground. As Davidson (1994) points out,

> *business tourism, in particular, can involve a substantial leisure element. Incentive travel, for example, may consist entirely of leisure, sport and entertainment. But, even for conference delegates, visitors to trade fairs and individual business travellers, excursions to local restaurants and places of entertainment, or sightseeing tours, can be a way of relaxing at the end of the working day. Socialising in this way can be an important part of the business tourism experience for groups, as it gives delegates or colleagues the opportunity to unwind together and get to know each other on a less formal basis.*

Figure 1.3
Eastnor Castle,
Herefordshire.

Source: Eastnor Castle Estates Office

This is why bidding destinations sell the concept of 'destination' and place great emphasis on everything from leisure, cultural and entertainment assets to shopping, sports and dining attractions.

Davidson also makes clear that

> *the distinction between the two categories of tourism is further blurred by the presence of 'accompanying persons' alongside many business tourism events. Incentive travel often includes the husbands or wives of those selected for such trips. But also, it is not uncommon for those travelling to exotic destinations for conferences or trade fairs and exhibitions to take their spouses along and make a short holiday out of the trip. In such cases, the couple may prolong their stay in order to have the time to tour around the destination after the business part of the trip is over.*

Business tourism and leisure tourism rely on the same, or a very similar, infrastructure to take place successfully. Both sectors need accommodation (hotels, guest houses), transport and communications (airports, railway stations, good road networks, coach and taxi services, modern telecommunications links), entertainment (shopping, bars and restaurants, night clubs/casinos, visitor attractions), as well as information and advisory services, emergency medical services and an attractive and welcoming environment. Figure 1.3, Eastnor Castle (near Ledbury, Herefordshire) is a good example of a tourism product catering equally well for both the business and leisure tourism sectors by focusing on several niche markets: conferences and board meetings, private dinners, team-building and activity days, plus a limited number of Open Days for the general public.

But conference and business tourism has additional infrastructure needs, such as appropriate venues, specialist contractors (audio-visual suppliers, exhibition contractors, interpreters, for example), and, perhaps most importantly, staff who are trained to be aware of and to respond to the particular needs of conference organisers and delegates. It is in the provision of this latter service that venues and destinations most frequently fall down, a theme which is further developed in later chapters of this book.

The Benefits of Conference and Business Tourism

Although business tourism and leisure tourism rely on a similar infrastructure, the former brings with it a number of significant extra benefits which makes it particularly attractive to destinations.

Greater profitability

Conference and business tourism caters for the high quality, high cost and, therefore, high yield end of the market. In 1996, for example, conference visitors to the United Kingdom from overseas spent an average of £151.10 per day compared with an average of just £55.50 per day for all categories of visitors (Office for National Statistics, 1997). The greater spending power of business tourists means increased economic benefits for the host destination and a greater return on its investment in infrastructure and marketing.

All-year-round activity

Conference and business tourism takes place throughout the year. Spring and Autumn are the peak seasons of the year for conferences (with most of the larger, high profile association and political party conferences taking place at these times), but many smaller conferences and meetings are also held during the winter months. July and August are the months of least activity which, for many resort-type destinations, is an added benefit because it means that there is no clash between the demands of leisure and business tourism, but rather they are complementary.

The all-year-round nature of conference and business tourism also leads to the creation and sustenance of permanent jobs, as opposed to the seasonal, temporary jobs which are a frequent characteristic of the leisure tourism sector. This, in turn, ensures that 'careers' rather than simply 'jobs' can be offered to new entrants, with clearly defined structures and opportunities for career progression being established.

Future inward investment

Those organising a conference or incentive travel trip will always be very keen to make sure that it is as successful as possible. One of the ways in which this can be achieved is by giving delegates and participants a pleasant, positive experience of the destination in which the event is being held. This usually means showing delegates the most attractive, scenic parts of the destination in the hope that creating a memorable experience for them will encourage many to return.

Some will return as leisure visitors, perhaps bringing their partners and families for a holiday or short break. Some, it is hoped, will have been so impressed that they may decide to re-locate their business to the destination or look to set up a subsidiary operation there. As Davidson (1994) says, 'a business visitor who leaves with a good impression of the conference, trade fair or incentive destination becomes an unpaid ambassador for that place . . . these are often influential people, whose opinions of the destination will be instrumental in determining its image in the minds of others who have not visited it'.

'Green' tourism

Conference and business tourism has far fewer negative impacts on the environment than mass leisure tourism. It is concerned with smaller numbers, but much higher spend. It is characterised by the use of coach transfers and public transport (or Shanks' pony) within a destination, minimising traffic congestion and environmental pollution.

Conference delegates are together as a group, so that it is possible to inform and educate them about the local community in which their conference is being held in order to maximise the enjoyment of their stay but also to minimise any disruption and possible inconvenience to the local resident population. It is very much harder to manage, in the same way, the impact of individual leisure travellers on a destination.

Summary

- The USA was the first country to recognise the potential economic benefits of conference business for a city or local destination. Detroit was the first US city to establish a convention and visitor bureau in 1896, followed by a number of other US cities in the early years of the twentieth century. Europe did not follow suit until the latter half of the twentieth century, and it was at this time also that conference tourism came to be recognised as an industry in its own right.

- The final two decades of the twentieth century have witnessed spectacular investment in the infrastructure which supports both leisure and conference/business tourism. Such investments are taking place not only in the more established conference destinations of Western Europe and North America, but in every continent and region.

- The conference industry is now a truly global industry, with almost 200 countries vying for a share of the lucrative international conferences and meetings market. A greater market share is now being won by countries in Eastern Europe and in the Asia/Pacific region in particular.

- The conference industry is still young, though maturing at a rapid rate. Symptomatic of the industry's youthfulness, yet contributing to its lack of proper recognition in commercial and political circles, is the lack of a comprehensive statistical base to measure its true size and value. Its relative immaturity is also shown in its use of terminology.

- Conference/business tourism and leisure tourism are closely intertwined, relying on similar infrastructure and support services. However, conference tourism also has a number of unique characteristics and advantages, which can bring additional benefits to those destinations successful in attracting conference business.

> ## Review and discussion questions
>
> 1. Analyse the three case studies in this chapter (Glasgow, Durban and the Philippines) and identify the principal features which they have in common and which are contributing to their success as conference destinations. Then compare these with a destination which has been less successful and put forward reasons why it has fared less well in the international conference marketplace.
>
> 2. Summarise the main changes in international convention market share experienced by Western Europe over recent years, giving examples of national and city destinations, and drawing comparisons with one of the emerging areas (Asia or Australia, for example). Suggest strategies for increasing Western European market share.
>
> 3. Compare and contrast the conference industry with another young industry (for example, computing and information technology, the fitness and health food industry). Draw conclusions on which has progressed further, and give reasons why.
>
> 4. Choose a seaside resort destination active in both the leisure and conference/business tourism sectors. Identify the best niche markets for both sectors (see also Chapters 2 and 4) and produce the 'ideal calendar' of business for a year which maximises use of its facilities and generates the highest level of economic benefit.

Acknowledgements

- ICCA DATA are used by permission of the International Congress and Convention Association, Entrada 121, 1096 EB Amsterdam, The Netherlands.
- UIA statistics are used by permission of the Union of International Associations, Congress Department, Rue Washington 40, B-1050 Brussels, Belgium.

References

- Gartrell, Richard B. (1994) *Destination Marketing for Convention and Visitor Bureaus*, 2nd edn, International Association of Convention and Visitor Bureaus, Kendall/Hunt Publishing Company.
- *Meetings Industry Glossary* (1993) Convention Liaison Council and Joint Industry Council.
- Davidson, Rob (1994) *Business Travel*, Addison Wesley Longman.
- *IACVB News* (1994/95) International Association of Convention and Visitor Bureaus, p. 8.
- Office for National Statistics (1997) *International Passenger Survey – Overseas Conference Visitors to the UK 1996*, Office for National Statistics and BTA/ETB Statistical Research.

Further Reading

- *International Conferences in Britain 1998–2008* (1998) British Tourist Authority, Thames Tower, Black's Road, London W6 9EL.

Chapter 2

A Complex Industry

Introduction

The conference industry is highly complex, comprising a multiplicity of buyer and supplier organisations and businesses. For many conference organisers ('the buyers'), the organisation of conferences and similar events is only a part of their job, and often one for which they have received little formal training and may only have an ephemeral responsibility. Suppliers include conference venues and destinations, accommodation providers and transport companies, agencies and specialist contractors. Both buyers and suppliers are welded together and supported by national bodies and associations, trade press and educational institutions, each contributing to the overall structure of this fast developing, global industry.

Objectives

This chapter looks at the roles and characteristics of:

- the buyers (corporate, association, government)
- the suppliers (venues, destinations, other suppliers)
- agencies and intermediaries
- other important organisations (trade associations, trade media, national tourism organisations, consultants, educational institutions).

The Buyers

In common with other industries, the conference industry comprises 'buyers' and 'suppliers'. The buyers in this case are conference organisers and meeting planners who buy, or more accurately, hire conference venues and related services in order to stage their events.

Most people working within the conference industry refer to two broad types of buyer: 'corporate' and 'association'. However, in some cases 'government' buyers are treated as a separate entity, rather than being included within the 'association' category. All three of the above types may also employ the services of various kinds of 'agency' to assist them in the staging of their events.

The corporate buyer

Definitions

The term 'corporate' is used to describe conference organisers who work for corporate organisations. Corporate organisations are companies established primarily to generate a profit and thus provide a financial return for their owners, whether these are the proprietors of a family-run business or the shareholders of a large publicly quoted company. They can be manufacturing or service companies.

Corporate organisations are to be found in most, if not all, industry sectors. The sectors which are particularly prominent in generating corporate conference business include:

- oil, gas and petrochemicals
- medical and pharmaceuticals
- computing and telecommunications
- engineering and other manufacturing
- financial and professional services
- retail and wholesale distibution
- travel and transport.

Identifying the corporate buyer

Relatively few companies have a dedicated conference or event management department. Indeed, during the recession of the early 1990s, this was an area where many companies opted to make savings by closing down their event management departments and putting the work out to agencies on a contract basis. In some cases, they contracted the employees from their former event management departments to continue to organise their events, but such employees now worked on a freelance basis and so were not a direct overhead to the company.

The larger corporate organisations are, of course, multi-division entities located on a number of different sites, often in a number of different countries. Staff involved in organising meetings and conferences appear in a whole range of guises and job titles. Research carried out by the Meetings Industry Association (1997) found that, in 500 of the leading companies in the UK, no fewer than 33 different job titles/types were being used by staff engaged in meeting planning and conference organising. Table 2.1 (overleaf) gives further details of this research.

In broad terms, however, most corporate events will fall within the ambit of the following departments: sales and marketing, training and personnel/human resources, central administration including the company secretarial activities.

Staff involvement in organising events often varies considerably. At one extreme, their task may simply be to obtain information on potential venues for an event, while at the other they will be given complete responsibility for planning and running the event. It is estimated that around 80 per cent of corporate organisers have received little formal training in conference and meeting planning, such activities account for just a part of their overall responsibilities, and their responsibility for conference organising may only be of a short-term nature.

Table 2.1 Job titles or type of staff engaged in corporate meeting planning (including an analysis of the size of companies participating in the Survey)

Administration	26	Travel Manager	13
Sales/Marketing	95	Corporate Events/Hospitality	9
Corporate Communications/Affairs	12	Manager	17
Customer Liaison	2	Public Relations	18
Communications Manager	19	Exhibition Manager/Coordinator	7
Promotional Services	1	Human Resources/Personnel	8
Conference/Events Manager/Coordinator	23	Director	6
Operations Manager	1	Conference Organiser	16
Management Assistant	1	PA/Secretary	182
Training	23	Office Manager	1
Community Relations	1	Purchasing	1
Publicity Services	1	Operations Manager	2
Projects Manager	1	Booking Assistant	1
Commercial Assistant	2	Business Development Manager	1
Internal Affairs	3	Services Manager	3
Facilities Manager	1	Customer Support	2
Managing Director	1		

Notes: Size of companies in the UK Conference Market Survey, 1996 (by number of employees):

Employee numbers	Number of companies
1–10	10
11–50	28
51–100	26
101–200	32
201–500	91
501–1000	62
1001–5000	146
over 5000	90
no answer	15

Total number of respondents 500

Source: UK Conference Market Survey, 1996

Identifying the corporate buyer is, therefore, a major and continuous challenge for those organisations wishing to market their facilities and services to him. The transience of many corporate conference organisers also makes it difficult to provide an effective education and training framework for them, and thus develop their expertise and increase their professionalism. It is only when such support systems are in place that proper recognition can be given to the role of the corporate conference organiser as a crucial component of any company's communications strategy.

Corporate buying patterns

Decisions about the conference or meeting (choice of venue, budget, size of event, visiting speakers, programme content, and so forth) will be taken by the corporate conference organiser or a line manager or the managing director, or by a group of such people in consultation. The decision-making process is relatively straightforward and more-or-less immediate.

Corporate events can be of many different types and sizes. The most common of these events are shown in Table 2.2.

The majority of corporate conferences and meetings are held in hotels. Some take place in purpose-built conference centres and management training centres. Incentive

annual general meetings (AGMs)	product launches
board meetings	sales conferences
corporate hospitality/entertainment	team-building activities
exhibitions	technical conferences
incentive travel	training courses and seminars

events and corporate entertainment will often make use of unusual venues. Civic venues and town halls tend to attract relatively few corporate events because of a perception that they may be staid and 'basic', which is often far from the reality, and the same is true of university and academic venues unless they have invested in dedicated conference facilities with high quality, en suite accommodation (as, indeed, an increasing number are doing).

Corporate events often have a fairly short 'lead time', especially compared with association conferences, with just a matter of weeks or a few months available to plan and stage them. The majority of such events involve small delegate numbers (e.g. ten to 100). Delegates are told to participate by the company, they are often not given a choice.

Corporate conferences and events take place throughout the year, peaking in Spring and Autumn. July and August are the months of least activity because of holidays, although the corporate hospitality sector is buoyant at this time with its links to major sporting events such as Wimbledon, Henley Regatta, and the British Open Golf Championship.

The budget for corporate conferences, expressed in terms of expenditure per delegate, is generally much higher than that for many 'association' conferences as it is the company which pays for delegate attendance, not the delegates themselves.

The costs can be incorporated into a company's marketing or staff training budgets, for example, and the selection of an attractive, quality venue coupled with a professionally produced conference will reinforce the importance of the event in delegates' minds and contribute to the successful achievement of its objectives, whether these be motivational, information sharing, team-building, or other.

Corporate conferences are now more intensive, business-related events than was the case during the 1980s, when they were often seen as something of a 'jolly'. Return on investment (ROI) is one of the buzz phrases across the industry, emphasising the need to measure the effectiveness of all investments and activities, including those investments made in a company's workforce. Despite this, research suggests that around one-third of corporate conference organisers do not evaluate their events after they have taken place, a finding which calls into question their professionalism and the investment which the company is making in them as people who place a high value on the virtues of two-way communication.

In summary, therefore, the corporate sector of the conference industry is characterised by: events with fewer than 100 delegates, fairly short lead times, and high spend with costs being borne by the company. Conferences are one of the prime ways in which corporate organisations communicate with their employees and their customers, although the generic term 'conferences' may describe a variety of sizes and types of events. Conferences are a high profile communications vehicle conveying important messages about the company: it is vital, therefore, that conferences are successful in meeting the objectives set for them. This often means that the budget for the event will be a generous one, making it an attractive piece of business for venues and other suppliers.

Corporate buyer research findings

The Meetings Industry Association carries out an annual survey (*The UK Conference Market Survey* mentioned earlier) of 500 leading British companies. Principal findings from the 1996 survey, published in February 1997, were (with my comments in italics) that:

- approximately 11 per cent more events were held in 1996 than in 1995
- more management meetings were held than other types of meeting
- delegate numbers were higher, but events were shorter and fewer were residential.

  These findings in respect of the shorter duration and the smaller number of residential events are surprising in view of the more buoyant market for conferences in 1996. One explanation may be that conferences are now more intensive, work-based events, making it possible to achieve more in less time.

- lead times were slightly longer than in 1995.

  The greater volume of conference business meant that it was necessary to book earlier to secure a preferred venue. There is still much anecdotal evidence, however, of lead times being measured in days and weeks, rather than months.

- average delegate rates (both residential and non-residential) paid were higher
- London and Central England were the most popular destinations.

  There are a number of factors for this, which include location (i.e. centrality within England making the area accessible to delegates from different parts of the country), communications, and quality of facilities. It is also the area where the majority of businesses and trade associations are located, giving it a natural advantage over other regions of Britain.

- the majority of events still remain in the UK
- hotels, along with a company's own in-house conference facilities, and unusual venues were the most popular options
- more venues were being considered before selection (the majority considering three or more venues before making a decision).

  This may be a reflection of the explosion of information, both in traditional printed formats as well as via the new communications technologies (CD Rom and computer disk, e-mail, Internet, and fax) now available to conference organisers, including access to various venue finding agencies. It also suggests that organisers, faced with an ever-growing range of venues, are being more selective about what they want. From the venues' perspective, it means that they have to work harder to win the business, and business retention becomes even more important.

- 71 per cent of respondents return to a venue if they are happy with it
- 55 per cent of organisers interviewed were in favour of a classification and grading scheme for venues. To date, the most often used source of information is their own knowledge or word-of-mouth recommendation, although over 50 per cent consider hotel star ratings to be influential

- factors influencing venue selection were very similar to 1995, e.g. convenient location was more than twice as important as competitive price
- satisfaction levels with venues most recently used were above 80 per cent. The main causes of dissatisfaction were staff and service-related issues.

  It would be good to see more venues seeking feedback from conference organisers on the quality of facility and service which they have provided for an event. Regrettably, and inexcusably, such evaluation still happens all too rarely.

- more use of computer-based presentation equipment had been experienced than in 1995.

  This is almost certainly an inexorable trend as companies must match and surpass the quality of presentations which delegates experience daily at work and in their own homes from their television sets and computers.

- attendance at trade shows and the reading of trade publications were still low among respondents.

  Both of these points raise major issues for suppliers wishing to market to corporate organisers. They may also underline the work which remains to be done to improve the education and training of conference organisers.

- delegate profiles indicated that the majority of those attending meetings were male, middle or senior managers or sales staff, aged from 25 to 50, who attended between one and four events a year and were mostly satisfied with the venues in which their events were held.

The association buyer

Definitions
The term 'association' organiser or buyer covers those representing a wide range of organisations, including:

- professional and trade associations/institutions (whose members join because of their employment)
- voluntary associations and societies (whose members join primarily to further an interest or hobby)
- charities
- religious organisations
- political parties
- trade unions.

Very few, if any, of these organisations are established mainly to generate a financial return. They are non-profit making organisations which exist to provide a service to their members and to the community at large. There is, however, an equal need for association conferences, as with corporate conferences, to be run extremely professionally, not least because they are often in the public eye, through press and media exposure, in a way that corporate conferences are not. And, while the associations themselves may be 'not-for-profit', association conferences must cover their costs and, in some cases, be planned to generate a profit which can be re-invested in the administrative and promotional costs of future conferences.

Delegate characteristics

Delegates attending association conferences usually share a number of common characteristics:

- They normally choose to attend the conference or other event run by the 'association', rather than being asked to attend by their employer.

- They are often required to pay their own expenses to attend, which means that the conference organiser must keep the costs as low as possible if it is important to maximise delegate attendance. In certain cases, particularly where the delegate is attending as a representative of a group of colleagues or fellow workers, as with trade union conferences, the delegate will receive a daily allowance to cover his/her costs while attending the conference.

- A range of accommodation will usually be required, from guest house to 5-star hotel.

- The number of delegates attending the main annual conference will be typically much higher than for corporate events. Indeed, association conferences can attract hundreds and sometimes thousands of delegates, and frequently receive high media attention.

These general characteristics may apply across the association sector, but they should not be allowed to hide some important differences between different types of associations. For example, delegates attending an annual surgeons' conference would expect to stay in accommodation of at least 3-star hotel standard (a 1000-delegate conference with many delegates bringing spouses would require a destination with a substantial number of high quality hotels), whereas a charity or religious conference is likely to require more modest accommodation at the budget end of the spectrum.

Buying patterns

The association decision-making process is different from the corporate sector. Even though many of the larger associations have dedicated conference organisers and, in some cases, event organising units, the decision on where the annual conference is to be held will normally be taken by a committee elected by the membership. The conference organiser will do much of the research and related groundwork, producing a shortlist of the most likely destinations and venues from which the committee will choose, and even making recommendations.

Destinations will put forward detailed 'bid' proposals outlining how they could help the association to stage a successful event (and, indeed, will also do this for corporate buyers). Such a bid document is likely to contain a formal invitation, often signed by the Mayor or other civic dignitary, a full description of the destination highlighting its attractions, access and communications details (e.g. road and rail links, the number of scheduled flights from the local airport), information on the support services available in the destination (transport operators, exhibition contractors, interpreters, audio-visual companies, and so on), a list of the services provided by the convention and visitor bureau or conference office, details of hotel and other accommodation and, of course, full details of the venue being proposed to stage the conference. The convention and visitor bureau/ conference office, acting on behalf of the destination, may be invited to make a formal presentation to the selection committee of the association, in competition with other destinations similarly shortlisted.

Before a final decision is made, the selection committee may undertake an inspection visit to the destination to assess at first hand its strengths and weaknesses. The whole decision-making process can, therefore, be very protracted, sometimes taking many months to complete.

Lead times for association events are much longer than for corporate events. It is not uncommon for associations organising a 1000-delegate conference to have booked venues for several years ahead. In part, this is because there is a much more limited choice of venue, in part because there is significantly more work involved in staging a 1000-delegate conference than one for 100 delegates. Some of the larger, purpose-built conference centres have provisional reservations more than ten years ahead from association conference organisers.

UK associations tend to follow one of several patterns in the staging of their main annual conferences:

- some will adopt an alternate north–south rotation, holding the conference in the north of England/Scotland one year, and then in the south of England the next, returning to the north in year three
- some associations operate a three- or four-year rotation, moving to different regions of the country in order to be seen to be fair to their members who are probably drawn from most parts of the country
- other associations appear to be quite immobile, opting to use the same destination year after year
- and, finally, certain associations look for somewhere different each year.

For those destinations and venues seeking to win their business, it is clearly important to have an understanding of which pattern a particular association has adopted.

Many association conferences have both delegates and their partners attending, a characteristic much less frequently found with corporate events, unless they include an incentive element. The partners do not normally attend the business sessions of the conference but they will be fully involved in the social events which form part of the conference programme. Partner programmes are designed to entertain partners while the conference is in progress. Quite often destinations will work with the conference organiser to help in the planning of partner (or spouse) programmes, as well as in coordinating tours and activities both pre- and post-conference. Such activities, together with the attendance of partners, can add significantly to the economic benefits that the conference brings to the destination.

Table 2.3 summarises the similarities and differences between corporate and association buyers.

International association conferences

The characteristics of national (UK) associations given in Table 2.3 apply equally to those associations which are primarily international in nature. Destinations bidding to stage major international conferences have to be extremely professional in their approach and be prepared to begin working for such an event many years before it is due to take place. It is not unusual to find lead times of five years or more, necessitating a great deal of research by those destinations seeking to host the conference, particularly in their cost calculations. It could be all too easy to offer certain hotel rates and venue hire charges to the association which, because of the effects of inflation and other possible

Table 2.3
Characteristics of corporate and association buyers

Corporate buyers	Association buyers
Corporate buyers are employed by 'for profit' organisations	Association buyers are employed by 'not-for-profit' organisations
Corporate organisations are to be found in both the manufacturing and service sectors	Associations are to be found in both the manufacturing, service and voluntary sectors
Event decision-making process is straightforward and more or less immediate	Event decision-making process is prolonged, often involving a committee
Events have a relatively short lead time	Major conferences have a relatively long lead time
Corporate buyers may organise a wide range of events	Association buyers organise a more limited range of events
Delegate numbers are typically less than 100	Delegate numbers are often several hundred and, for the larger associations, can be several thousands
Mostly use hotels, purpose-built conference centres and unusual venues	Mostly use purpose-built conference centres, civic and academic venues
A higher budget per delegate, with the company paying	A lower budget per delegate, with the individual delegate often paying
Events are organised year-round	Major events primarily in the Spring and Autumn, with some in the Summer
Events typically last 1–2 days	Major conference typically lasts 3–4 days
Accommodation normally in hotels (3 star and upwards)	Wide range of accommodation required
Delegate partners rarely attend	Delegate partners quite frequently attend

changes in the macro-economic climate, bear little relation to what should be being charged when the event actually takes place.

Case Study 2.1 illustrates the lead time involved in the City of Birmingham's attempts to secure and stage The Lions International Convention, one of the world's largest conventions, expected to attract around 30 000 delegates and partners to Birmingham's National Exhibition Centre Group facilities for a nine-day convention in 1998.

Case Study 2.1 The Lions International Convention, Birmingham 1998

Birmingham's interest in staging the Lions International Convention began in the early 1980s. During the 1980s it tried on several occasions to join shortlists of would-be host destinations, but it failed to meet the selection criteria, especially the requirement to have 9000 bedrooms fully contracted for the event. When the destination did eventually have the necessary infrastructure to match the Lions' specifications, it made two unsuccessful bids to attract the Convention.

In 1992 it tried for a third time, and heard in 1993 that its bid had been successful and it was chosen to stage the event in 1998. Some 15 years will have elapsed between the initial expressions of interest by Birmingham in hosting the Lions International Convention and the event actually taking place in the City.

▷

Previous cities to host this annual convention have included Hong Kong, Minneapolis, Phoenix, Seoul, Brisbane and Montreal. This is the first time that the convention has been held in Europe since it was staged in Nice in 1962. When the event was held in Hong Kong in 1992, its economic benefit was calculated at £33 million (£1342 per conventioneer).

International associations also operate rotational patterns in the staging of their events, often on a continental basis: for example, an international conference held in Europe one year may well not return to a European country for at least another five years. The Union of International Associations (UIA) and the International Congress and Convention Association (ICCA) both devote considerable resources to tracking where international conferences and congresses are held (see Chapter 1).

Bids to host an international conference will often be channelled through the national member representatives of that organisation. For example, a small group of British members of an international association will form a committee to plan and present a bid to the selection committee. They are likely to get support and assistance from the destination which they are putting forward to stage the conference, while the British Tourist Authority may also play a part in helping to fund the bid and contributing to it in other material ways.

Association conferences, because of their larger size, are often held in purpose-built conference centres. Some will use town hall and civic venues, and others book university and college venues. Where hotels are used, this will often be over a weekend because the hotel is offering cheaper rates than for weekday bookings. The peak seasons for association conferences are Autumn and Spring, but some conferences take place over the Summer months and a limited number during Winter.

The government buyer

The 'government' sector has much in common with the association sector (and, indeed, is often subsumed within it), covering organisations such as local authorities, central government departments and agencies, educational bodies, and the health service. These organisations are all 'not-for-profit' organisations and are accountable for the ways in which they spend public funds. Although delegates from 'government' organisations will not normally be expected to pay their own expenses to participate in a conference, it is likely that the events will be run on fairly tight budgets, often using the less expensive venues such as civic facilities, universities and colleges, and hotels up to 3-star standard.

There is, even so, a discernible trend for such public sector organisations to book higher standard facilities. Delegates' expectations are rising constantly and, whereas sharing a room or staying in bedrooms which are not en suite might have been the norm some years ago, this is now becoming less and less acceptable. Such trends help to account for the major investments which university venues, in particular, are making to upgrade their accommodation stock to enable them to compete in this highly competitive marketplace.

Tables 2.4 and 2.5 (overleaf) show a classification system developed by the British Association of Conference Destinations (BACD) for its 'Conference Buyer Database'. The system differentiates between corporate and association buyers (and also has a section for Agencies – see later in this chapter) by industry sector (based loosely on the Standard Industrial Classification). It also gives numbers of records held for each buyer category (as at May 1997). A search on *Sector Type 04*, for example, would pull out all of the

Table 2.4
BACD
conference buyer
database sector
coding

Corporate		Non-Corporate		
Code	Nos	Code	Nos	Sector description
01	276	21	54	Mining, energy (gas, electricity), water companies, petroleum, chemicals
02	257	22	327	Pharmaceuticals, medical, cosmetics, toiletries
03	393	23	54	Engineering
04	450	24	29	Computer manufacturing and services, information technology, telecommunications
05	633	25	58	Manufacturing/processing
06	135	26	106	Building and construction, civil engineering, surveying, architecture, estate agency, housing associations
07	498	27	73	Communications-radio, newspapers, TV, PR/marketing consultancy, advertising, publishing
08	350	28	39	Commerce-retail and wholesale distribution, import/export
09	880	29	117	Financial and professional services-banking, insurance, building societies, finance/credit companies, solicitors, accountants, management consultants, training consultants
10	128	30	13	Service companies (e.g. couriers, security, cleaning)
11	1282	31	172	Leisure and entertainment, hotels and catering, transport, travel (including professional conference/event/exhibition organisers, venue finding agencies)
12	44	32	121	Agriculture/forestry/environment/animals
13	41	33	219	Education
14	62	34	438	Central and local government depts and agencies (not covered above), public bodies, charities, religious groups
15	61	35	224	Others
	5490		2044	**Total**

Source: British Association of Conference Destinations

corporate organisation contacts in the *Computing and Telecommunications Sectors*, while the inclusion of *Sector Type 24* would bring in all of the association contacts for the same industry sectors.

The Suppliers

The suppliers are those who make available for external hire the venues, destinations and many other specialist services without which today's conferences could not take place.

Suppliers to the conference industry have grown in quantity and diversity in tandem with the overall growth of the industry over the past 50 years. Relatively few of these suppliers are dedicated exclusively to the conference industry, however.

Table 2.5
BACD
conference buyer
database buyer
coding

Numbers held on the database	Buyer code	Buyer code description
		Corporate
229	10	Others
547	11	Conference/event/incentive organiser
45	12	Exhibition organiser
700	13	Secretary/PA, administration manager/ assistant
698	14	Training and personnel manager/assistant, training consultant
1815	15	Sales and marketing manager/executive, PR manager/executive
295	16	Company secretary, managing director, chief executive
4329	**Total corporate**	
		Agency
505	20	Other (e.g. incentive travel house, business travel agency)
500	21	Professional conference/event organiser, conference production company
98	22	Venue finding agency (only)
58	23	Exhibition organiser (independent)
1161	**Total agencies**	
		Association
374	30	Others
670	31	Professional or trade association/institution/ society
563	32	Voluntary assoc/society, charity, religious group, political party
74	33	Trade union
362	34	Local or central government, educational body, health authority, other public agency
2044	**Total associations**	
7534	**Grand total**	

Source: British Association of Conference Destinations

This summary will divide the supply side of the conference industry into three main categories:

1. venues
2. destinations
3. others.

Venues

Within the British Isles alone there are over 4000 venues being promoted as suitable for conferences, meetings, and related events. It is impossible to give a precise number because new venues are regularly becoming available for external hire. There has been discussion about the establishment of a grading or classification system for conference

Figure 2.1 The Manor House, Castle Combe, Wiltshire.

Source: The Manor House and Castle Combe Golf Club Ltd

venues but nothing of this kind is yet in place. In theory, therefore, almost any type of building could be promoted as a conference venue.

A clearer idea of which are the leading conference venues would no doubt emerge if it were possible to ascertain what proportion of their turnover is accounted for by conference business. There are probably fewer than 500 venues for which conference business contributes more than 40–50 per cent of their annual turnover.

What is certain, however, is that hotels make up around two-thirds of all conference venues, being particularly important to the corporate market sector. The main types of hotel active in the conference market are:

● city centre hotels
● hotels adjacent to the national and international communications infrastructure (airports and motorways especially)
● country house hotels (Figure 2.1, The Manor House at Castle Combe, near Chippenham, Wiltshire, is an example of a country house hotel which is very active in the conference sector).

In addition to the conferences which they stage as venues in their own right, hotels located close to large conference centres also benefit as providers of delegate accommodation when a major conference comes to town. Additionally, the bigger association conferences often choose one hotel as their 'headquarters' hotel, and there can be significant public relations benefits with the hotel being featured in national, and sometimes international, television and media coverage.

The larger hotel chains have, in recent years, invested very heavily in the design and equipping of their conference facilities, recognising that the standard multi-purpose

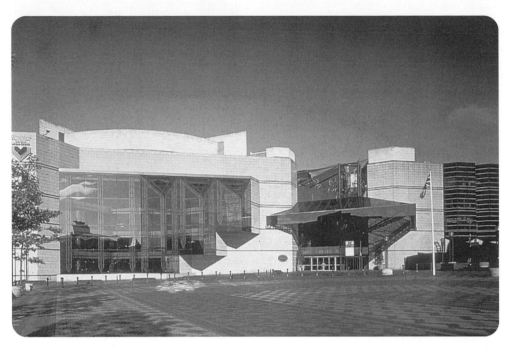

Figure 2.2 The International Convention Centre, Birmingham. Built at a cost of £180 million, the Centre has a number of large auditoriums, including a 3000-seat hall and the 2000-seat Symphony Hall.

Source: NEC Group Ltd

function room was no longer adequate for the needs of the contemporary conference organiser. Many have also branded their conference product (see Chapter 5) to assist in the promotion of these facilities and services, seeking to assure the buyer that he will receive the same level of service whichever hotel in the chain is used.

Alongside hotels, other principal types of venue include:

- *purpose-built centres* (residential and non-residential) – specifically designed to host meetings and conferences, whether they are the larger events for hundreds or even thousands of delegates (venues such as the International Convention Centre in Birmingham – see Figure 2.2 – the Harrogate International Centre, the Edinburgh International Conference Centre) or smaller, day and residential, events (venues such as Lawress Hall near Lincoln, Highgate House Conference Centre in Northamptonshire)

- *college, university and other academic venues* – there are around 150 academic venues, many only available for residential conferences during student vacation periods (but still staging some non-residential events during term time). An increasing number of academic venues have been investing in the construction of conference facilities which are available throughout the year, providing accommodation equivalent to a good 3-star hotel standard. The University of Warwick, UMIST in Manchester, and the University of Strathclyde are three very good examples of such investments. The East Midlands Conference Centre (see Figure 2.3, overleaf), located on the campus of the University of Nottingham, can seat up to 550 delegates in its main auditorium, complemented with exhibition or banqueting space and a range of syndicate rooms, and might equally be classed as a purpose-built conference centre

Figure 2.3 East Midlands Conference Centre, Nottingham.

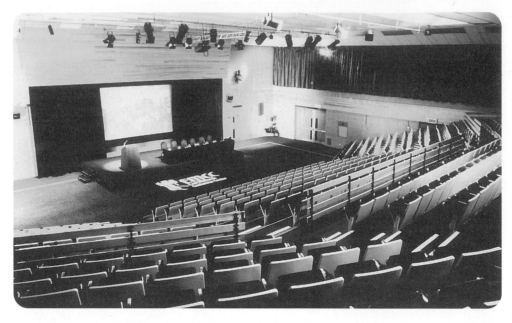

Source: East Midlands Conference Centre

Figure 2.4 Portsmouth Guildhall. The Guildhall has a seating capacity of 2000 and is popular with the association sector, in particular.

Source: Portsmouth City Council

Source: Kirklees Metropolitan Borough Council

Figure 2.5 The Alfred McAlpine Stadium, Huddersfield. Home of Huddersfield Town Football Club and Huddersfield rugby league team, and venue for conferences, corporate hospitality and exhibitions.

- *civic venues* – council chambers and committee rooms, town halls, and other civic facilities which are available for external hire, e.g. Perth City Hall, Portsmouth Guildhall (see Figure 2.4), Brangwyn Hall in Swansea

- *unusual venues* – this is a somewhat ill-defined term to describe a very wide range of venues which do not fit into the more common categories listed above. The attraction of unusual venues is they can give an event a special appeal and can make it memorable for years afterwards. Some have very high quality meeting and conference facilities, others may be quite limited in this respect but the setting in which the event is being held compensates for such shortcomings in the eyes of the conference organiser (and, it is hoped, of the delegates). Unusual options include sporting venues (football club facilities – see Figure 2.5, racecourses, leisure centres), cultural and entertainment venues (museums, theatres, television studios, stately homes), tourist attractions (theme parks, historical sites, heritage centres), transport venues (ferries, steam trains, canal barges), even a lighthouse or two!

Over 3000 of the 4000 plus venues in the British Isles are represented by members of the British Association of Conference Destinations (BACD). Figure 2.6 (overleaf) illustrates the proportions of the five different venue categories in the BACD Conference Venue Database. It can be seen from this that hotels account for around two-thirds of all venues, but the strong growth area is the 'unusual venues' category, which makes up almost a quarter (23 per cent) of venues.

The size of the largest conference venues, by seating capacity (theatre-style), in all the key British destinations is shown graphically in BACD's 'British Conference Destinations Directory', as reproduced in Figure 2.7 (pages 41–44).

Figure 2.6
BACD
conference
venues database
– proportions of
different venue
categories.

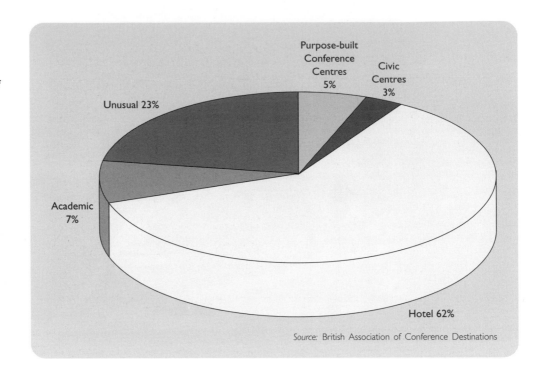

Source: British Association of Conference Destinations

Destinations

Conference organisers attach greater importance to 'location' than to any other single criterion when selecting their sites. Location may be expressed in terms of 'town', 'city', 'region of the country'. The widely accepted term to describe each of these is 'destination'. A destination may, of course, be an entire country (as a national destination), but within a country it is usually a discrete area with identifiable boundaries. Each conference destination must contain a range of venues, facilities, attractions, support services and appropriate infrastructure to help it to attract conference business.

Within the British Isles, the British Association of Conference Destinations represents all of the leading destinations active in serving the conference industry. Its 110 member destinations may be classified as follows:

- cities – 39
- towns – 46
- counties/regions – 21
- islands – 4.

A list of current BACD members is given in Appendix A.

Destination marketing organisations, often trading as 'convention and visitor bureaus' or 'conference desks' (see Chapter 5), bring the destination to the marketplace, offering a 'one-stop-shop' enquiry point to the conference and event organiser. Their role is to sell the destination, highlighting all its strengths and facilities, generating and converting enquiries into confirmed business. They are also involved in product development: identifying weaknesses in venues and facilities and in general infrastructure and working to rectify such faults.

Figure 2.7 Size of the largest conference venues, by seating capacity, in BACD member destinations.

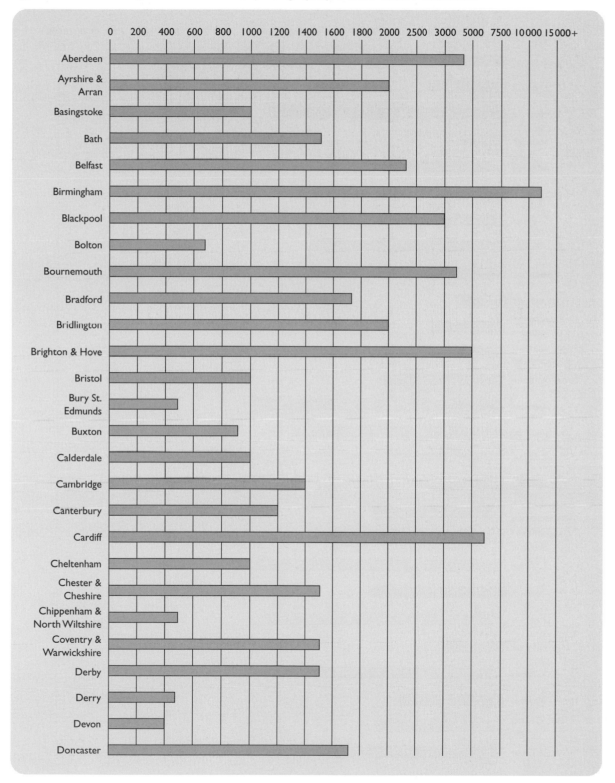

Figure 2.7 *(cont.)*

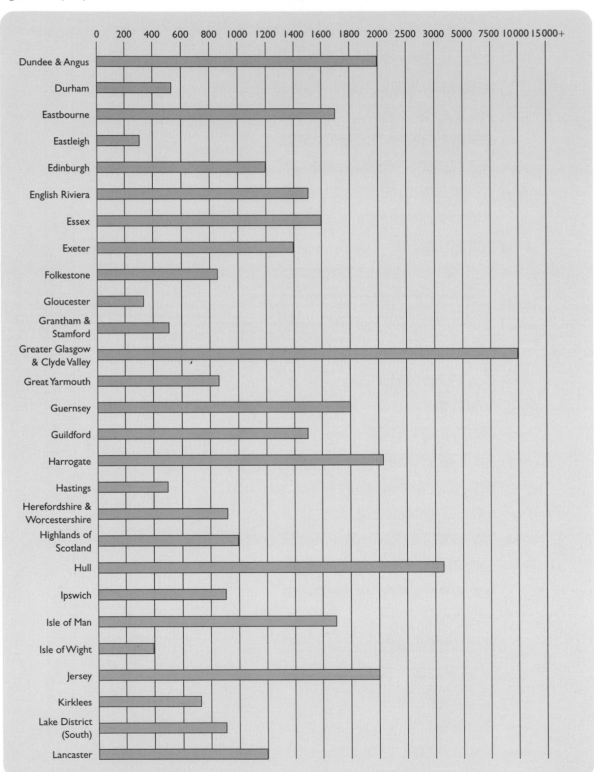

Figure 2.7 (*cont.*)

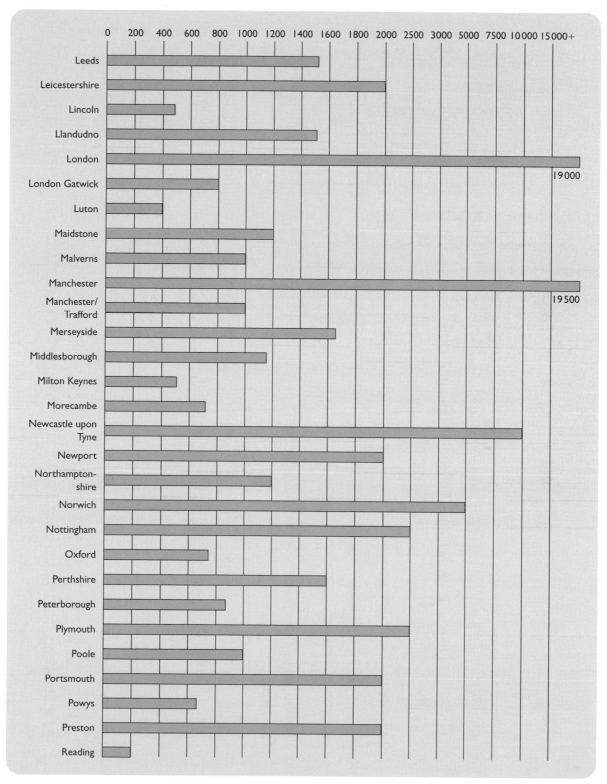

Figure 2.7 (*cont.*)

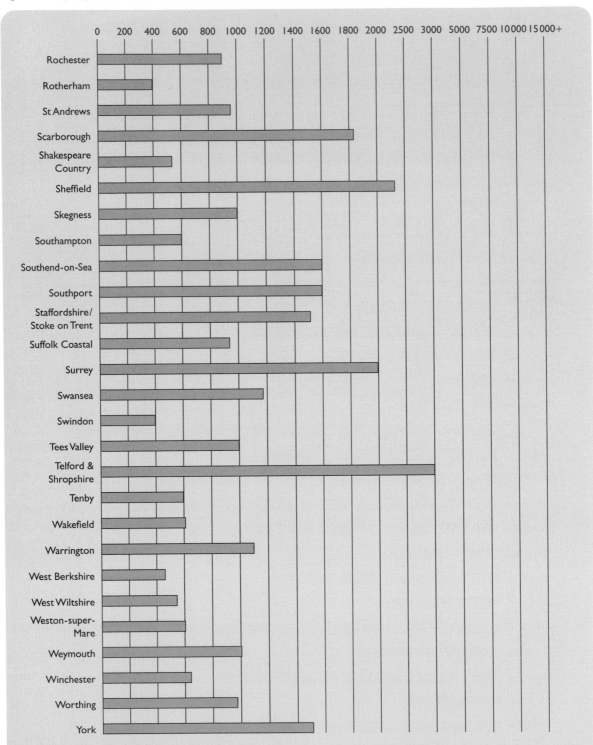

Source: British Conference Destination Directory, 1998

Other suppliers

The conference industry has to draw upon the services of many different supplier organisations in order to offer a complete service to its buyers. Those suppliers who fulfil a 'buying' role on behalf of corporate or association clients are described in the next section (Agencies). Examples of other key suppliers include the following, individually or in combination:

- audio-visual contractors (hire of specialist audio-visual equipment)
- telecommunications companies (video/tele/satellite conferencing)
- transport operators (airlines, coach and rail companies, taxi firms, ferry companies)
- interpreters and translators (for international conferences)
- after-dinner speakers, entertainers, corporate entertainment companies (e.g. companies running 'Murder Mystery' events), sports and outdoor activity organisers
- speciality caterers (banquets, receptions, buffets)
- floral contractors (flower displays for conference platforms, registration areas, exhibition stands)
- exhibition contractors
- venue-finding and event management software companies. There are several computer packages on the market which may be bought by organisers to assist them in researching venues or in the overall administration of their events (see Chapter 6).

Agencies and Intermediaries

'Agencies' is a generic term used to describe a range of different organisations which are both suppliers and buyers. They undertake a buying role on behalf of their clients, who may be companies or associations. They act as intermediaries or 'middlemen', and can be contracted to assist in the planning and running of a conference or similar event.

Agencies come in a number of forms, and the nomenclature can be somewhat confusing, but below are listed the principal kinds of intermediaries operating within the conference and events industry.

Professional conference organiser

The professional conference organiser, sometimes professional congress organiser, is often referred to simply as a PCO (but may also be described as an event management company). Employed to assist in the organisation of a conference, the PCO's role can include researching and recommending a suitable venue, helping to plan the conference programme including the social programme, booking accommodation for delegates, handling the financial arrangements and registration of delegates. The PCO will normally be paid a fee by the client organisation and may also charge a commission to the venue (usually 8–10 per cent of the value of the conference to the venue itself). Commission may also be charged on accommodation bookings and on other services provided.

Table 2.6 shows a typical portfolio of services offered by a professional conference organiser.

Table 2.6 A typical portfolio of services offered by professional conference organisers (PCOs)

- complete conference administration, including on-site registration of delegates
- budgeting and accounting for the conference
- design and print of conference programme and promotional materials
- distribution and mailings of delegate information
- sponsorship advice
- publicity and marketing
- correlation of scientific papers
- accommodation booking and catering arrangements
- poster sessions and exhibitions
- social programmes for delegates

Venue finding agency

As their name implies, such agencies offer a more limited service, restricted to researching and recommending a suitable venue for the event. They will normally put forward a shortlist of three potential venues to their client (or in some cases just one venue initially) and expect to receive a commission of 8–10 per cent of the value of the booking to the venue. Venue finding agencies may also get involved in booking accommodation for delegates, and again would expect to charge commission to the hotels and other accommodation providers. The agency's services to the client are usually provided free of charge.

Conference production company

Such companies specialise in the actual staging of the conference: designing and building conference sets, providing lighting, sound systems and special effects. Their expertise lies in audio-visual and communications technology, but they are required to match this to the needs of different clients. They also need creative and theatrical skills, recognising that conferences have to be professionally stage-managed and should be a memorable, striking experience for the delegates.

Incentive travel house

All-expenses-paid travel, often to overseas destinations, is still regarded as one of the best incentives a company can use to motivate and reward its employees, distributors and retailers. 'Incentive travel', as this has come to be known, is an important industry sector in its own right. Estimates of its global value suggest that it was worth some US$17 billion in 1990, which is likely to rise to US$56 billion by 2000. Incentive travel was worth approximately US$6 billion to European markets in 1997.

Research commissioned by the British Tourist Authority and others (*Incentive Travel Usage*, 1996) put the value of incentive travel to the United Kingdom (both inbound and domestic markets) at £180 million in 1995. Companies operating in the automotive, financial services and information technology sectors are among the leading users of outbound (overseas) incentive travel from the United Kingdom.

Incentive travel programmes should be tailored to the needs of each client company. An 'off-the-shelf' incentive programme is really a contradiction in terms. Incentive travel has been described as an 'extraordinary reward for extraordinary performance' (Paul Flackett, Managing Director, EIBTM Ltd). The definition of incentive travel used by the Society of Incentive Travel Executives (SITE) is as follows:

> *Incentive travel is a global management tool that uses an exceptional travel experi- ence to motivate and/or recognise participants for increased levels of performance in support of organisational goals.*

Incentive travel programmes are, therefore, designed to create an allure or dream which will make people want to produce that extra effort, achieve that exceptional performance, and strive to be the winners within a corporate organisation. From the company's per- spective, it is also about strengthening the loyalty of its best employees to the company, making them want to belong to the organisation, and giving them reasons to perform even better in the future.

Attention is now being paid to developing incentive travel as a tool for motivating achievers across the board. David Hackett, Chairman of The Travel Organisation, elabor- ated this point as follows (Conference and Exhibition Factfinder, June 1997):

> *League tables are frequently created in order to offer rewards and create motiva- tion at all levels. This can include lower targets to encourage first time qualifiers or graduated awards for top achievers to ensure they still strive to maximize their performance, even when they have qualified to participate in the travel programme. Individual benefits can include superior room allocation, upgraded flights and hosting allowances (for example, providing top achievers with budgets to host cock- tail parties in their suites).*

The specialised nature of the incentive sector has led to the growth of incentive travel houses, as these 'agencies' are generally known. Incentive programmes often involve travel to overseas destinations for UK-based companies, and there is a continuing need to discover new and exotic destinations and to create ever more memorable programmes. Likewise, many parts of the British conference and incentive travel product are attractive to companies based overseas.

Incentive travel programmes increasingly have an educational element for the parti- cipants. This can involve visits to factories and businesses in the same industry sector as that of the award winners, team-building programmes, and a conference-type session with an award presentation ceremony and announcements of corporate plans, designed to encourage the incentive winners to reach future performance targets.

Incentive travel is probably more susceptible to the ups and downs of the national and global economies than most other sectors of business tourism. In some cases, how- ever, an economic downturn in a particular industry or country can actually encourage incentive travel schemes. The beauty of incentive schemes is that they are totally self- funding, with the travel award being paid for by the success of the incentive travel pro- gramme. If no-one meets their sales targets, no-one wins. It is, therefore, one of the best promotional tools.

Perhaps even more important than economic factors in the health of this business sector is the national/international political situation. The Gulf War in 1990, for example, virtually wiped out the US incentive travel market, even to Europe. Similarly, one bomb planted on a transatlantic flight is likely to cause a steep fall in US incentive travel busi- ness to Europe. No company directors want to put their best employees or associates on an aeroplane and risk losing them all (in fact, as standard policy, they would normally use several different flights to transport the award winners to their incentive destination to minimise such risks).

Incentive travel houses charge a fee to their clients for the work they undertake on their behalf.

Destination management company

Destination management companies (or DMCs) are specialised ground-handlers operating in the incentive travel market. They have detailed knowledge and expertise of a specific destination, be this a city, an island or other discrete region, and sometimes even a whole country. They also have access to unusual venues such as private houses and stately homes which are not normally open to the general public. They have considerable buying power which makes them very useful to incentive travel houses situated in countries other than the one in which the incentive travel award is to be taken. Incentive travel houses and DMCs, therefore, work very closely together.

Where a client knows that he wants to hold an incentive event in a particular destination, he can employ the services of a DMC to locate a venue, to handle delegate accommodation, to assist with transport arrangements, and to put together itineraries and social programmes (for example, special interest visits, theme parties, unusual activities), even to provide 'pillow gifts' for award winners. DMCs are expected to develop tailor-made programmes within budget for their clients. They need to be creative and innovative and provide an experience which will give the participants an insight into a country or region which will be beyond the reach of the normal visitor or holidaymaker.

Most DMCs earn their income from commission, with the average commission figure being 15 per cent (1997). It can be seen that there is significant overlap between the work of a PCO and that of a DMC, as well as the work of a convention and visitor bureau. Nowadays, a DMC has to have some PCO or, at least, venue finding agency expertise.

Corporate hospitality company

Corporate hospitality companies are another specialist sector of the 'events' industry rather than conferences, but often there is only a thin dividing line between the two. Corporate hospitality and corporate entertainment often involve the exploitation of major sporting and cultural events to strengthen the links between an organisation, usually a corporate organisation, and its clients or potential clients – for example, inviting clients to spend a day watching tennis at Wimbledon, or being wined and dined at the British Grand Prix at Silverstone. Frequently, activities are arranged specifically for the company, and typically involve drinks receptions, dinners and banquets, dances and discos. Where such activities are provided for clients and potential clients, a formal presentation or short speeches will often be included in the event to ensure that the company 'gets its message across'.

Corporate hospitality/entertainment companies are also involved in corporate team-building exercises and activities, aimed at clients and/or employees. Such activities include golf days, clay pigeon shooting, off-road driving, go-karting, 'paint ball', and many, many more.

Skibo Castle, Dornoch, Sutherland (see Figure 2.8) is an unusual corporate hospitality venue, possibly unique in the British Isles, offering a wide range of corporate activities and entertainment through its exclusive Carnegie Club membership scheme.

Figure 2.8
Skibo Castle,
Dornoch,
Sutherland.

Source: Skibo Castle (Skibo Ltd)

Business travel agency

This is another form of travel agency, but one which seeks particularly to cater for the needs of business customers rather than the general public and which would not normally have a presence on the local High Street. The main thrust of their work is usually business travel: making air, rail, coach, and ferry as well as hotel reservations to meet the needs of people travelling nationally and internationally for business purposes. But they also get involved in sourcing venues for conferences and similar business events, and may contribute in other ways to the planning and organisation of such events.

Some of the larger business travel agencies have staff physically located in the offices of their major corporate clients. Such arrangements are referred to as 'agency implants'.

Exhibition organiser

Exhibitions are, of course, a major business tourism sector in their own right, but any clear divide between exhibitions and conferences which may have existed in the past has now been greatly eroded, especially as far as business-to-business exhibitions are concerned (less so for consumer exhibitions catering for the general public). Many exhibitions have a conference programme running alongside as a way of adding value to the exhibition and making it even more worthwhile for business people to visit. Similarly, many of the larger conferences and conventions have an exhibition running in parallel: for the exhibitors, the conference delegates are seen as important customers or potential customers, and for the conference organiser the exhibition is an important source of revenue which will help to offset the costs of the conference.

While some conference organisers undertake the organisation of the exhibition themselves, others prefer to employ the services of a specialist exhibition organising company.

There are around 500 exhibition organisers in the United Kingdom, represented by the Association of Exhibition Organisers. When contracting a specialist exhibition organiser, conference planners will either pay them a management fee for their work, or negotiate a payment based on the size of the exhibition itself (for example, the net exhibition area in square metres). A further alternative is for the exhibition to be contracted out for a set period to an exhibition organiser in return for a fee paid to the owner of the exhibition (i.e. the conference organiser).

Agreements or contracts may well include incentives or bonuses linked to the sale of space or cost savings achieved by the exhibition organiser, although this latter approach could encourage the cutting of corners and result in an exhibition of unacceptable quality.

The larger exhibition organising companies can bring added value to an event through their own network of contacts or simply via bulk purchasing power which would not be accessible to a conference organiser working independently. Exhibition organisers may already have links with airlines, hotel groups, stand and electrical contractors, carpet and furniture suppliers, as well as knowledge of the exhibition venue and specialist technical expertise. The services of such trade contacts can be made available to their conference organiser client at preferential rates, while first-hand knowledge and experience can be a further invaluable asset.

There is a very broad spectrum of relationships possible between conference and exhibition organiser, from just buying into certain specialist expertise to handling specific aspects of the exhibition (e.g. visitor badging and registrations, stand erection), right through to contracting out the organisation of an exhibition in its entirety. The reasons for such variations on the part of the conference organiser include: in-house staff resources (numbers of staff available and their experience and expertise), the need for a guaranteed financial return from the exhibition (minimise risk by opting for a known income, even if this is less than might have been possible), the overall profile of the event and the need to ensure its success, the benefits of having a well-known exhibition organiser working alongside thus giving confidence to potential exhibitors that the exhibition will be well organised and successful.

Other agencies

There are other companies who will undertake at least part of a conference organising role for their clients, although this would not usually be the main focus of their work. Such companies include: public relations and advertising consultancies (conferences and seminars, press launches, product launches, for example), management consultancies ('retreats', meetings, training events), and training companies (training, motivational, team-building events).

Other Important Organisations

As an industry emerges and matures it requires other bodies and structures to help it to function professionally, to establish standards and codes of practice, to represent the industry to other industrial sectors as well as to government departments and public agencies. Within the conference industry, such bodies include, inter alia:

- trade associations
- trade media
- national tourism organisations
- consultants
- educational institutions.

Trade associations

Trade associations are formed to serve the interests of their members. Their activities usually include lobbying and representation, establishing codes of practice, marketing and promotion, education and training, research and information.

Within the conference industry, some trade associations are international in the composition of their membership, others are strictly national. Among the leading international associations are:

- Association Internationale des Palais de Congrès (AIPC)
- European Federation of Conference Towns (EFCT)
- International Association of Convention and Visitor Bureaus (IACVB)
- International Association of Professional Congress Organisers (IAPCO)
- International Congress and Convention Association (ICCA)
- Meeting Professionals International (MPI)
- Society of Incentive Travel Executives (SITE).

The leading British trade associations include:

- Association for Conferences and Events (ACE)
- Association of British Professional Conference Organisers (ABPCO)
- Association of Exhibition Organisers (AEO)
- British Association of Conference Destinations (BACD)
- British Exhibition Contractors Association (BECA)
- Incentive Travel and Meetings Association (ITMA)
- Meetings Industry Association (MIA).

Further details of the services and activities of these associations are given in Chapter 3.

Trade media

The conference industry trade media are primarily magazines published on a monthly, bi-monthly or quarterly basis. They contain articles on new developments, topical issues, how to stage successful events, destination reports, personnel changes, summaries of new books and reports, a correspondence section, and so on. They fulfil a very important role in keeping the industry abreast of the constant changes and developments taking place. Through their circulation to buyers, they also provide an important advertising and PR medium for suppliers wishing to promote their facilities/services to potential clients. Most of the magazines are international in content, emphasising once again the global nature of the conference industry.

A list of the principal trade magazines is given in Appendix B.

National tourism organisations

Most countries in the world now have some form of national tourism organisation, publicly funded, established for promotional activities to the international tourism industry. Such bodies are primarily concerned with marketing, but some may also fulfil a lobbying and representational role. Within the conference sector of the tourism industry, a number of countries have established a national convention bureau specifically to market to this sector. There is no standard format for such national convention bureaus – indeed, it would be difficult to find two which operate in the same way with similar levels of funding and resources and providing the same kind of services.

Within the British Isles, the Scottish Tourist Board and the Northern Ireland Tourist Board have both established a national convention bureau, while the Wales Tourist Board currently has a dedicated Business Travel Unit. In England the Business Tourism Unit of the English Tourist Board operates jointly with the British Tourist Authority's Business Tourism Unit. Each of the above provides a range of information, advisory and practical support services to event organisers.

The British Tourist Authority's (BTA's) main role is to promote Britain's leisure tourism and business tourism facilities and services to overseas markets. Its dedicated Business Tourism team, both in London and in the BTA overseas offices, seeks specifically to attract conference and convention, trade fair and exhibition, and incentive business from overseas markets.

Further details of these National Tourism Organisations are given in Chapters 3 and 5.

Consultants

Consultants play an important role in undertaking projects on a fee-paying basis for clients who are normally operating on the supply side of the conference industry. Typically, consultancy covers:

- the potential market for a proposed new conference centre
- the specification for a new conference centre or for a major refurbishment to an existing venue
- advice on marketing strategies for a destination or venue
- a feasibility study to establish and run a new convention and visitor bureau.

Consultancy can, however, cover any aspect of the industry. Consultancy firms include specialist teams within the larger management consultancies (e.g. KPMG, Deloitte & Touche, Price Waterhouse, Pannell Kerr Forster) as well as a number of consultancies catering specifically for the tourism industry.

Educational institutions

The education and training of the conference industry's future workforce is vitally important in ensuring the continued growth and development of the industry. College and university institutions are now beginning to give attention to conference and business tourism in their course programmes and syllabuses. Other UK training programmes within the wider tourism industry, such as 'Welcome Host' and 'Investors in People', also contribute significantly to the improvement of skills and expertise for those already working in the industry.

Further details of education and training opportunities are given in Chapter 7.

Summary

- The buying side of the conference industry includes corporate organisations, associations and government/public sector agencies.
- Corporate organisations plan a wide variety of conferences, meetings and other events. Staff involved in the organisation of these activities have many different job titles, but relatively few are employed as full-time event organisers. ▷

For the most part, corporate events attract less than 100 delegates and have comparatively short lead times. They have a higher average per capita expenditure than association conferences, with costs being borne by the companies themselves.

● The term 'association' is used to describe a sector of the industry which encompasses professional and trade bodies, voluntary organisations, charities, political parties and other non-corporate entities. Association conferences are different in many respects from those held in the corporate sector, especially in their average size, duration, types of venues used and accommodation required.

● Government/public sector organisations have many similar buying characteristics to associations, although delegate expectations are rising and some comparisons with the corporate sector may be drawn, particularly in respect of the types of venues used.

● The supply side of the conference industry comprises venues, destinations and myriad other companies offering specialist services, from audio-visual equipment supply to contract catering, from interpreting to coach hire.

● The industry also features an important group of intermediary agencies which provide services ranging from conference management to venue finding, and from incentive travel planning to exhibition organising.

● This complex industry is reliant on a range of other institutions to enable it to operate professionally and develop in a structured way. Such institutions include trade associations, trade media, national tourism organisations, consultants and educational bodies.

Review and discussion questions

1. Assess the benefits and disadvantages, for a corporate organisation, of maintaining its own, in-house event department. Include an analysis of the pros and cons, for the company, of employing a business travel agency as an 'implant'.

2. Compile two incentive travel programmes to reward:
(a) a company's top sales executives
(b) the same company's most productive 'blue collar' employees.
Explain any differences in the programmes offered.

3. Identify and give reasons for the most appropriate types of conference/events business for the following venues:
(a) a 4-star city-centre hotel in the Midlands with 120 bedrooms and conference facilities seating up to 200 delegates.
(b) a multi-purpose Victorian building in a seaside resort with a seating capacity of 1500.
(c) a residential conference centre with six conference rooms (the largest seating 80), accommodation of 3-star standard, located on the edge of the Pennines in Yorkshire.

4. As an employee of a major trade association which holds an annual conference for approximately 1200 delegates, with an exhibition running alongside the conference, you have been asked to contract out the planning of the conference and exhibition. Describe the kinds of agencies you would consider and give reasons for your choices.

References

- British Association of Conference Destinations (1997) *British Conference Destinations Directory 1998,*
- *UK Conference Market Survey 1996,* carried out by The Right Solution and published by the Meetings Industry Association (1997), available at £95 from the MIA: 34 High St, Broadway, Worcestershire, WR12 7DT, tel: 01386 858572, fax: 01386 858986.
- *Incentive Travel Usage and its Impact on UK/Ireland* (1996) British Tourist Authority/ English Tourist Board, Northern Ireland Tourist Board, Scottish Tourist Board, Wales Tourist Board, Bord Failte Eireann.

Further Reading

- *Incentive Travel Fact Book* (1997) Society of Incentive Travel Executives.

Chapter 3

A Fragmented Industry?

Introduction

The conference industry has been described, or more accurately criticised, as being fragmented, because of its multiplicity of representative bodies and organisational structures. Even those working full-time within the industry are frequently confused by the bewildering array of abbreviations and acronyms in use. Within the British Isles alone, widely differing public and private sector structures for the 'management' of the industry are to be found, whether at national, regional or local level. At an international level, an ever-growing number of professional associations and industry forums, almost all established since 1950, seek to raise industry standards, increase recognition for the economic importance of conference tourism, and develop a clear vision for the evolution of the industry into the twenty-first century.

Objectives

This chapter attempts to identify the key players and explain their current roles. It looks at:

- public sector involvement in the conference industry in the British Isles
- the roles of national trade associations
- the activities of international organisations and associations
- an assessment of the conference industry's fragmentation.

Public Sector Involvement in the Conference Industry in the British Isles

Up until the late 1960s there was relatively little government involvement in either leisure or business tourism. A fact sheet published by the Scottish Tourist Board (1997) (entitled *Development, Objectives and Functions 1997–1998*) lists several problems and weaknesses in respect of the organisation of tourism at this time:

1. There was no comprehensive government policy on tourism: many actions affecting the industry were poorly coordinated, and were often conflicting.

2. The national tourist boards which then existed were non-statutory, and had little influence.

3. Tourist facilities were often of a poor standard.

At the same time, the dramatic growth in tourism to the United Kingdom in the post-war years, from 200 000 overseas visitors in 1946 to 5.8 million in 1969, highlighted the potential of tourism as a creator of wealth and jobs. As a result, in 1969, the government introduced the Development of Tourism Act. This legislation established a statutory British Tourist Authority, Scottish Tourist Board, English Tourist Board and Wales Tourist Board, each with responsibility for the promotion and development of tourism to and within Great Britain, and for the encouragement of the provision and improvement of tourist facilities and amenities. The Northern Ireland Tourist Board had been formed earlier under separate legislation in 1948.

At a pan-Britain level, there are two conference destination marketing organisations: the British Tourist Authority, a government agency, operating primarily in overseas markets, and the British Association of Conference Destinations, a trade association with local authority and convention bureau members, operating principally in the domestic marketplace.

Scotland and Northern Ireland also have their own national conference bureaus, operating under the umbrellas of their national tourist boards, while England and Wales have Business Tourism/Travel Departments, again subsumed within their national tourist boards.

The islands of Guernsey, Jersey and the Isle of Man have independent tourist boards, responsible to their own island governments. The island tourist boards have conference marketing functions although, in Jersey's case, responsibility for the Jersey Conference Bureau was contracted out to the principal private sector suppliers in 1996 (with the States of Jersey Tourism still contributing funds to the Bureau).

Department for Culture, Media and Sport (DCMS)

The Tourism Division of the Department for Culture, Media and Sport (DCMS), formerly the Department of National Heritage, has led responsibility within central government for policy on tourism, working through the English Tourist Board (ETB) and the British Tourist Authority (BTA) and with the close involvement of the industry itself.

DCMS's Tourism Division:

- advises Ministers on tourism and related matters (this includes both policy development and briefing and response to representations from the industry and consumers)

- guides and monitors the work of ETB and BTA to ensure they deliver DCMS objectives with value for money and financial propriety. The Chairman of BTA/ETB is appointed by the Secretary of State at DCMS

- monitors and, where necessary, intervenes on European and national issues affecting tourism

- sponsors the industry through strategic leadership and coordination

- raises the industry's profile in government and commissions research and disseminates information to help improve competitiveness.

Contact: Tourism Division, Department for Culture, Media and Sport, Third Floor, 2–4 Cockspur Street, London SW1Y 5DH (tel: 44–(0)171–211–6322; fax: 44–(0)171–211–6319).

British Tourist Authority (BTA)

The British Tourist Authority (BTA), a government agency (or 'non-Departmental public body') responsible to the Department for Culture, Media and Sport, is the official, non-profit-making body charged with the promotion in overseas markets of Britain as a leisure and business tourism destination. It also has a general responsibility for coordinating and monitoring the development of tourist facilities within Great Britain as a whole, as well as for advising the government on tourism matters. In 1997–98 BTA had a total operating budget of £51 million (£35 million of this being grant-in-aid from the government, to which the industry was expected to add a further £16 million). It maintains a network of 43 offices in 37 countries. That is more overseas offices than any other country.

BTA has a dedicated Business Tourism Department at its headquarters in London, with a staff complement of five: Head of Business Tourism, three Marketing Executives and one Secretary. There are also a number of specialist Business Tourism personnel in key BTA overseas offices around the world, and there is a separate coordinating department in London which oversees business tourism marketing activities in Europe. Overseas office staff report directly to their own office/regional managers, and not to the Head of Business Tourism in London, although of necessity there is close and regular collaboration between headquarters and the overseas office staff.

The Business Tourism Department has a dual role:

1. direct marketing on an international level, particularly to the international association conference sector, and to potential visitor groups to British trade fairs

2. servicing the needs of the BTA overseas offices, particularly in the incentive travel and corporate conference sectors.

The BTA estimates that, in 1996, business tourism accounted for 24 per cent of incoming visitors and 27 per cent of Britain's tourism revenue. While a significant part of this is individual corporate travel (as defined in Chapter 1) and is non-discretionary, a growing proportion consists of group travel for conferences, exhibitions and incentives, the discretionary sector.

The Department's activities include:

- research into the conference, incentive and exhibition sectors and maintenance of appropriate databases
- encouraging promotional activity by marketing consortiums and operating joint schemes with British suppliers. Such joint schemes involve the BTA in part-funding agreed overseas marketing activities, usually up to 20 per cent of the total project costs
- publishing promotional print and directories, as well as advisory materials and information for the British trade
- coordination of workshops in Britain to which overseas buyers and intermediaries are invited
- coordination of British participation in overseas missions, trade fairs and presentations (participants include other national marketing organisations within the United Kingdom, namely the Scottish Convention Bureau, Northern Ireland Conference Bureau, Wales Tourist Board Business Travel Unit)

- coordinating press trips, familiarisation trips and site inspections, as requested by overseas offices
- ensuring maximum publicity for business tourism marketing opportunities offered by BTA's overseas offices.

Contact: British Tourist Authority, Business Tourism Department, Thames Tower, Black's Road, London W6 9EL (tel: 44–(0)181–563–3253; fax: 44–(0)181–563–3257; e-mail: Pmoore@mail.org.uk; Internet: http://www.visitbritain.com).

English Tourist Board (ETB) Business Tourism Department and English Regional Tourist Boards

The English Tourist Board (ETB) received £9.9 million grant-in-aid from the government in 1997–98, to which the industry was expected to add a further £2.9 million. It performs a range of functions, both centrally and through the ten Regional Tourist Boards in England:

- it supports the work of BTA by assisting the industry to develop the domestic tourism product, so improving competitiveness
- it undertakes research to help the industry identify market trends and plan accordingly
- it seeks to raise standards through developing the accommodation grading and classification schemes for serviced accommodation and other sectors of the industry
- it provides business advice as well as information on training
- it helps the industry to market its product to UK residents.

The ETB Business Tourism Department operates jointly with the BTA Business Tourism Department. A minuscule budget (only a fraction of the budget awarded to the Scottish Convention Bureau and Wales Tourist Board Business Travel Unit) is allocated to promote English conference facilities and services in the domestic market. The limited budgetary resources are used to support the following activities:

- publication of 'Meetings and Incentive File' to promote the ETB Business Tourism Department as a source of help, advice and information
- monitoring conference research projects
- production of a directory entitled 'England – THE Venue' (published on a self-financing basis through advertising support)
- collaboration with the other national tourist boards to publish advisory information on quality assurance issues
- organisation of an England presence at Confex, held in London every Spring
- cooperation and liaison with industry bodies and trade associations.

Contact: English Tourist Board, Business Tourism Department, Thames Tower, Black's Road, London W6 9EL (tel: 44–(0)181–563–3253; fax: 44–(0)181–563–3257).

Approximately half of the ETB's total grant-in-aid goes to the ten English Regional Tourist Boards (RTBs). The RTBs are independent, autonomous bodies, mostly commercial companies limited by guarantee, which receive income from local authority and commercial membership subscriptions as well as from commercial activities. They work with the Government Offices for the Regions, local authorities and other local agencies to develop tourism strategies and to advise on the merits of tourism applications for funding from European and other sources. They run a number of national programmes and operate the accommodation schemes on the ETB's behalf.

There are wide variations across the country in respect of RTB involvement in the conference and business tourism sector. Some regions have very little direct activity while others undertake specific conference marketing initiatives and have a dedicated budget. Consultations took place in 1997 between the RTBs and the British Association of Conference Destinations (BACD), representing individual conference destinations, to find ways of reducing areas of duplication and maximising the use of limited public sector funds. Proposals for a clear framework for RTB involvement in the conference sector were submitted to the ETB under the 'Agenda 2000' consultation by BACD in May 1997. At the time of writing, a response to this document was expected towards the end of 1997 when the outcomes to the consultation process had been finalised and published.

Northern Ireland Conference Bureau (NICB)

The Northern Ireland Conference Bureau (NICB) was established in February 1994. The Bureau is part of the Northern Ireland Tourist Board (NITB), the statutory organisation responsible for encouraging and developing tourism in Northern Ireland. NITB, in turn, is responsible to the Department of Economic Development for Northern Ireland.

The Northern Ireland Conference Bureau, as part of the national tourist board, is wholly funded by government, although the industry in Northern Ireland pays to participate in marketing activities, generating additional operating income. The Bureau has a small team, consisting of a manager and administrative backup. However, as part of a larger organisation, the Bureau has representation through the NITB offices in the following countries: Republic of Ireland, England, Scotland, mainland Europe (principally France and Germany), USA, Canada, Australia and New Zealand.

NICB's main role is to work with the conference and hotel industry in Northern Ireland to maximise the number of national and international conferences that can be attracted. In this regard, the Bureau works to coordinate a positive market awareness of Northern Ireland, through exhibitions, public relations (PR), sales calls, workshops and direct marketing. In many cases the Northern Ireland presence at international exhibitions is as part of a British Pavilion or an all-Ireland stand, with the choice being made as a result of buyers' perceptions of the destination. The Bureau has a marketing spend in excess of £100 000 per annum.

The Bureau continues to work with conference organisers once they have made a formal decision to meet in Northern Ireland, ensuring that they have the necessary information and contacts to run a successful event. The Bureau advises organisers on the logistics of meeting in Northern Ireland and on the marketing of the destination to potential delegates.

Contact: Northern Ireland Conference Bureau, St Anne's Court, 59 North Street, Belfast BT1 1NB (tel: 44–(0)1232–315513; 44–(0)1232–315544; e-mail: conference.bureau. nitb@nics.gov.uk).

Scottish Tourist Board (STB) and Scottish Convention Bureau (SCB)

The Scottish Tourist Board's (STB's) remit is to attract leisure and business tourists to destinations in Scotland, to encourage the development of visitor facilities, and to coordinate tourism interests. The Board submits to the government (i.e. the Scottish Office) an annual Corporate Plan which details STB's targets and priorities. In 1996–97 the Board's gross budget was £22.5 million, comprising £18 million grant-in-aid from the government and around £4.5 million income from other (mainly private sector) sources. In 1984 the Tourism (Overseas Promotion) (Scotland) Act came into force which enabled STB to market Scotland overseas.

The National Strategic Plan, produced by STB in 1995, identified three main tasks: improving facilities for tourists; improving the promotion of Scotland as a tourism destination; and improving skill levels within the industry. In April 1996, 14 new Area Tourist Boards covering the whole of Scotland came into operation. Working closely with Local Enterprise Companies, local authorities and STB/SCB, the Area Tourist Boards have now produced local area tourism strategies for their areas, which in most cases have included convention and business tourism activities.

In 1991 STB established the Scottish Convention Bureau as its specialist business tourism division. Its aims are to promote Scotland as a destination for conferences, meetings and incentive travel, and to increase the economic benefit and development potential of this high yield sector. Prime importance is placed on increasing value, and on geographical and seasonal spread.

A programme of targeted sales, marketing and research activities is undertaken in conjunction with local convention bureaus, Scotland's business tourism suppliers and the British Tourist Authority. This includes coordination of a Scotland stand at prime trade exhibitions in the UK and overseas; organisation of sales missions; production of appropriate print items; direct mail; industry and business press work. The Bureau also operates a business tourism enquiry service, passing specific enquiries on to local area convention bureaus and tourist boards and coordinating their responses. The service handles over 1800 enquiries a year. The Bureau has eight staff (six full-time, two job-sharers): Director, Head of Sales and Marketing, Marketing Manager (job share), Sales Manager – Europe, Sales Manager – UK, two sales coordinators, and a net budget of £560 000.

Contact: Scottish Convention Bureau, Scottish Tourist Board, 23 Ravelston Terrace, Edinburgh EH4 3EU (tel: 44–(0)131–343–1608; fax: 44–(0)131–343–1844; e-mail: conventionbureau@stb.gov.uk; Internet: www.convention.scotland.net).

Wales Tourist Board (WTB) Business Travel Unit

The Wales Tourist Board, which is responsible to the Welsh Office, set up a Business Travel Unit in 1992 with the aim of raising the profile of Wales as a destination for conferences, meetings, incentives and events.

The creation of the Business Travel Unit was the outcome of a research study which revealed that business tourism was a seriously under-exploited market segment in Wales. Two members of staff were appointed. The production of a Business Travel Planner followed by direct mail and insert campaigns led to the establishment of a Business Travel Database, which now holds details of 4500 buyers interested in holding events in Wales. Research undertaken in 1995 showed that 17 per cent of recipients of the Planner had subsequently organised events in Wales, generating business worth £11 million.

In 1996, in recognition of the importance of the conference and incentive sector, the Unit received an additional £94 000 a year for three years from the European Regional Development Fund, giving a total annual budget of £250 000. The second Business Travel Planner was launched in 1996, followed by an incentive guide to Wales in 1997. A new Conference and Meetings Planner, replacing the Business Travel Planner, was launched at Confex '98. The Unit now has three staff: Business Travel Manager, Senior Business Travel Executive, and an administrative assistant.

The main activities of the Unit include:

- impartial servicing of enquiries to destinations and venues throughout Wales
- publication of a biannual newsletter
- coordination of a Wales stand, with partners, at major industry exhibitions
- active participation in marketing initiatives with members of the Wales Chapter of the British Association of Conference Destinations
- attendance at a series of overseas promotional events organised by BTA in key target markets
- PR and the organisation of familiarisation visits for potential buyers and for trade journalists
- support for bids to attract conferences to Wales.

Contact: Wales Tourist Board Business Travel Unit, Brunel House, 2 Fitzalan Road, Cardiff CF2 1UY (tel: 44–(0)1222–475202; fax: 44–(0)1222–475321; e-mail: emmab@tourism.wales.gov.uk).

Other government departments

Department of Trade and Industry (DTI)

The Department of Trade and Industry (DTI) has a key role in helping to improve the competitiveness of British industry. Through its Consumer Goods and Business Services Division it is able to part-fund specific projects in the events sector. It encourages initiatives to raise standards, develop benchmarking and, in conjunction with the Department for Education and Employment, to improve training. In 1997 the Division published a new study on *The Future of the British Exhibitions Industry* (DTI 1997), which made a number of recommendations for enhancing the industry and consolidating its future development, such as:

- benchmarking the more innovative and profitable exhibition centres to encourage the spread of best practice
- stimulating new exhibitions by targeting the sectors of the economy in which the UK is strong
- undertaking more international promotion for British exhibitions.

The Export Services Division (ESD) of the DTI provides funding assistance to encourage UK firms to exhibit at overseas trade fairs and to organise seminars overseas. Seminars are particularly relevant to the service industries. Participation in trade fairs takes the form of groups organised by sponsor bodies (such as trade associations) who coordinate the activity and pay the grants on the Department's behalf. As demand always exceeds supply, there is a competitive bidding process. This is often for events several years ahead. At the time of writing, the Export Forum (set up by the new Labour government) was about to recommend the shape of support from April 1999 following wide consultation with UK industry. ESD also provides funding (again via sponsors) for overseas buyers and journalists to visit UK exhibitions, venues and business premises.

Contact: Department of Trade and Industry, Business Services Section, 3rd Floor, 151 Buckingham Palace Road, London SW1W 9SS (tel: 44–(0)171–215–1781; fax: 44–(0)171–215–2975). Department of Trade and Industry, Export Services Directorate,

Kingsgate House, 66–74 Victoria Street, London SW1E 6SW (tel: 44–(0)171–215–2400; fax: 44–(0)171–215–2424).

Department for Education and Employment (DFEE)

The Department for Education and Employment (DFEE) is responsible for advising the government and for implementing government policies in the spheres of education, training and employment. Such responsibilities apply to all tiers of education (schools, colleges, universities) as well as to every economic sector, including tourism.

Educational provision in preparation for careers in the tourism industry is burgeoning, with a rapid growth in the numbers of full-time and part-time courses available, many commencing as early as Year 10 in secondary schools (i.e. 14–15 year-old students). To date most such courses include only limited reference to the conference and business tourism sector, although new courses are emerging targeted more specifically at conferences and events. (A summary of current educational opportunities is given in Chapter 7.)

DFEE also oversees the development of national training provision to ensure that the country's workforce has the qualifications and skills to optimise UK competitiveness in the international marketplace. The Department's responsibilities cover new entrants to the labour market, the unemployed and those in employment. At a local level training is delivered through Training and Enterprise Councils (TECs) (variations in terminology and structure exist in Scotland), which report to the Government Offices for the Regions. The government offices in turn report to several government departments, including DFEE and DTI.

The TECs are responsible for encouraging training and enterprise, and support schemes to stimulate business growth and profitability at a local level. Businesses operating in the tourism sector can seek TEC advice and funding support for employee training programmes. At the time of writing, significant changes in the role of the TECs were anticipated, with the introduction of the modern apprenticeship scheme and national traineeships, as a result of major government initiatives to equip the longer-term unemployed with the skills and confidence to re-enter the labour market.

At a national level Industry Training Organisations (ITOs) and Lead Bodies (such as the Hotel and Catering Training Company and the Travel Services Lead Body) have almost completed the establishment of national occupational standards and vocational qualifications for all commercial and industrial sectors (although not, as yet, for the events industry – see Chapter 7). Such standards and qualifications form the basis of the National Vocational Qualifications (NVQ) structure. Though still at an embryonic stage, National Training Organisations (NTOs) are now being formed which are taking over from the Industry Training Organisations and Lead Bodies. The NTOs will have a broader remit, providing not just representation but also leadership and strategic planning for their industry sectors, bringing together appropriate trade associations. At the time of writing, it was not clear whether a NTO specifically representing the tourism industry was to be set up. ITOs are in existence representing related fields such as hospitality and travel services.

Local authorities

Even though tourism is a non-statutory responsibility for them, local authorities have an important role to play in the development, marketing and servicing of the British conference product. Local authority planning and economic development departments control, to a greater or lesser extent, the development of the infrastructure (buildings, amenities, public services, transport systems, for example) within their areas. Local authorities have traditionally been the principal funders of major, purpose-built convention centres. They are also the conduit through which most applications are made for external funding (from the European Union or from the National Lottery, for example) for tourism infrastructure projects.

A paper, 'Guidance on Tourism', published by the then Department of National Heritage (DNH 1996), makes the following pertinent comment on the role of local authorities:

> *Tourism is a very fragmented industry. It is made up of businesses from many different sectors, with large numbers of small operators. It is not easy for the industry to take concerted action. In addition, tourism is a composite product, which no one business can control or deliver; from the tourist's point of view, the product he or she is buying is a **destination**, not a stay in a hotel or a visit to a number of attractions. Against this background, **the involvement of local authorities in providing strategic direction and helping pull together the efforts and disparate elements of the commercial sector can be particularly valuable**, especially in areas where tourism is important to the local economy.*

Local authorities are, for the most part, fully involved in the marketing and servicing of conference facilities in their areas, either by running 'conference desks' or through partnerships with the private sector in establishing 'convention and visitor bureaus' (see Chapter 5). However, the non-statutory nature of local authority responsibility for tourism development and marketing does lead to significant variations in the funds and resources allocated in different parts of the country, an issue which will be further explored in Chapter 8.

The Roles of National Trade Associations

Association for Conferences and Events (ACE)

The Association for Conferences and Events (ACE) was founded as the Association of Conference Executives in 1971, with membership being taken up by individuals. It changed its name to the Association for Conferences and Events in 1992, adopting a corporate membership structure, and now has some 600 member organisations, a mixture of buyers and suppliers.

ACE acts as a forum for member organisations, its objective being to provide reliable information to all members and assist them in their own particular spheres of interest within the meetings industry. ACE puts emphasis on: monitoring proposed UK legislation and draft Directives of the European Union; the development of competence qualifications and occupational standards (see Chapter 7); and the holding of seminars, workshops and training courses on various aspects of the events business where members can meet and network (also summarised in Chapter 7). ACE also publishes a monthly newsletter, organises familiarisation visits, and operates a confidential Helpline service.

Contact: The Association for Conferences and Events, ACE International, Riverside House, High Street, Huntingdon, Cambridgeshire PE18 6SG (tel: 44–(0)1480–457595; fax: 44–(0)1480–412863; e-mail: ace@martex.co.uk).

Association of British Professional Conference Organisers (ABPCO)

The Association of British Professional Conference Organisers (ABPCO) was established in 1982. Membership is selective and is limited to individuals who have a proven record of achievement nationally and internationally. Members are required to uphold an agreed Code of Practice.

The principal activities of ABPCO and its members include meetings, training, advice to conference venues and other suppliers, monitoring new legislation and technical developments, and seeking to ensure that business is practised to the highest ethical and professional standards. ABPCO has designed a new Higher National Certificate Course in Business for Conference and Event Management (see Chapter 7).

ABPCO has some 20 Full Members (all PCOs with intermediary agencies). A new category of 'Associate Membership' was introduced in July 1997, open to in-house conference managers, project managers, proprietors of conference businesses, and senior conference organisers.

Contact: Mr David Campbell, Chairman, Association of British Professional Conference Organisers, c/o Banks Sadler Ltd, 100 Chalk Farm Road, London NW1 8EP (tel: 44 (0)171–424–3331; fax: 44 (0)171–424–3329).

British Association of Conference Destinations (BACD)

The British Association of Conference Destinations (BACD) was founded in 1969 and represents some 110 destinations throughout the British Isles, from the north of Scotland to the Channel Islands. Its members are conference offices (of local authorities), convention bureaus and area tourist boards, through which it represents over 3000 conference venues. BACD also has formal links with the British Tourist Authority and the four national tourist boards, which have seats on its Management Committee. BACD activities include:

- an enquiry fulfilment service ('Venue Location Service'), providing a destination response to clients with a quality-assured standard of service
- the organisation of an annual exhibition, 'Confer', as well as participation in a number of other key industry trade shows
- publication of an annual directory (*British Conference Destinations Directory*)
- maintenance of several industry databases (buyers, venues, destinations, universities and colleges, trade press, trade associations)
- organisation of education and training programmes (annual conference, annual Summer School, one-day workshops)
- supporting conference industry research programmes and providing information and consultancy services
- running buyer familiarisation visits to BACD member destinations
- contributing to various collaborative initiatives with government agencies and other professional associations to increase recognition of, and support for, conference and business tourism as a major benefactor to the national economy.

Contact: British Association of Conference Destinations, 1st Floor Elizabeth House, 22 Suffolk Street, Queensway, Birmingham B1 1LS (tel: 44–(0)121–616–1400; fax: 44–(0)121–616–1364; e-mail: bacdassoc@aol.com).

Corporate Hospitality and Event Association (CHA)

In 1986, a number of corporate hospitality agents, concerned at the way the corporate hospitality sector was expanding with no governing body, met to discuss the idea of an association. No agreement was, in fact, reached until November 1988 when the Corporate Hospitality Association was launched. It changed its name to the Corporate Hospitality and Event Association in 1996, but is still known in abbreviated form as CHA.

The objectives of the Association are to:

- promote the expansion of the industry in a manner which will benefit both members and clients
- improve and maintain a high standard of corporate hospitality at all events and locations
- ensure that clients, when dealing with a member of the CHA, do so in the knowledge that they are dealing with a reputable and responsible company
- promote confidence in corporate hospitality generally, and act as a spokesman for the industry as a whole
- educate those employed in the industry to develop their individual skills.

Membership is open to a variety of organisations, including PR companies, corporate hospitality organisers, sponsorship and sales promotion companies, suppliers (marquee contractors, caterers, for example), venues and promoters. Four categories of membership are available. CHA now has over 110 members.

Membership benefits include information via meetings and a newsletter, networking, representation, educational seminars (on legislation and other topical issues), PR activity, and discounts on products/services.

Contact: Corporate Hospitality and Event Association, Arena House, 66–68 Pentonville Road, Islington, London N1 9HS (tel: 44–(0)171–278–0288; fax: 44–(0)171–837–5326).

Incentive Travel and Meetings Association (ITMA)

The Incentive Travel and Meetings Association (ITMA) was founded as the Incentive Travel Association for the United Kingdom in 1985, changing to ITMA in 1991. It is the representative body for those organisations specialising in the provision of motivational travel programmes and corporate events. ITMA's key objective are:

- to provide a register of the most highly respected companies, all of whom are able to offer their clients financial security
- to protect members' interests through representation to law-makers, the media and relevant commercial bodies
- to raise standards of professionalism by pooling members' collective expertise and protecting clients' interests.

It offers two categories of membership, which are available to companies and not to individuals: a) full membership – for professional conference and incentive travel organisers; b) associate membership – for suppliers of travel, hospitality and ancillary services (airlines, hotels, representation companies, tourist offices, destination management companies, cruise lines and air charter brokers). Full members are required to be bonded through an Air Travel Organiser's Licence (ATOL) as well as holding worldwide public liability and professional indemnity insurance. In 1997 ITMA had some 40 full members and 190 associate members.

Membership benefits and services include: information on new legislation and lobbying issues; educational seminars and training workshops; advice on a range of subjects such as taxation, insurance and legal obligations, including a free hotline for legal and accountancy queries; documentation and market research; networking with other members and marketing support.

Contact: Incentive Travel and Meetings Association Ltd, PO Box 195, Twickenham, Middlesex TW1 2PE (tel: 44–(0)181–892–0256; fax: 44–(0)181–891–3855).

Meetings Industry Association (MIA)

The Meetings Industry Association (MIA) was established in 1990. It now has 350 organisations in membership, drawn from the supply side of the British conference industry, and including professional conference organisers and conference placement agencies. The MIA aims to improve the quality of service and facilities offered by its members, encouraging adherence to the highest possible standards. It seeks to strengthen the position of its members' businesses in an increasingly competitive marketplace, raise the profile of the United Kingdom as an international conference destination, and improve the standing of the industry as a major part of the British economy. Specific member services and benefits include:

- marketing opportunities via publications, exhibition representation and media relations
- sales opportunities
- networking at MIA national and regional events (an Annual General Meeting, Autumn Convention, and breakfast seminars)
- training courses (see Chapter 7)
- research and information
- consultancy and arbitration services
- parliamentary representation via the government's Tourism Adviser, Roy Tutty.

Contact: Meetings Industry Association, 34 High Street, Broadway, Worcestershire WR12 7DT (tel: 44–(0)1386–858572; fax: 44–(0)1386–858986; e-mail: mia@meetings.org; Internet: http://www.webcom.com/-venues).

Society of Event Organisers (SEO)

Founded in 1996 by Peter Cotterell, a writer and trainer for the conference industry, the Society of Event Organisers (SEO) has over 200 corporate and association organisers in membership. The SEO has one aim only: to help its members organise successful events. Membership services provided by the SEO include seminars, training courses, networking opportunities, a monthly newsletter, familiarisation and inspection visits, a list of suppliers used and recommended by other members, and discounts on a range of products and services.

Contact: Society of Event Organisers, 29a Market Square, Biggleswade, Bedfordshire SG18 8AQ (tel: 44–(0)1767–316255; fax: 44–(0)1767–316430).

The exhibitions sector has its own trade associations. Among the key British associations are:

- Association of Exhibition Organisers (AEO), 26 Chapter Street, London SW1P 4ND (tel: 0171–932–0252; fax: 0171–932–0299)
- British Exhibition Contractors Association (BECA), 36 The Broadway, Wimbledon, London SW19 1RQ (tel: 0181–543–3888; 0181–543–4036)
- Exhibition Venues Association (EVA), Mallards, Five Ashes, Mayfield, East Sussex TN20 6NN (tel: 01435–872244; fax: 01435–872696)

The Activities of International Organisations and Associations

American Society of Association Executives (ASAE)

Although not directly a conference industry trade association, the American Society of Association Executives (ASAE) is, nevertheless, a very important body for the international convention industry because of the scale of convention activity undertaken by its members. ASAE was founded in 1920 as the American Trade Association Executives, with 67 charter members. Today it has over 23 500 members worldwide who manage approximately 10 000 trade associations, individual membership societies, professional organisations and not-for-profit associations which, between them, serve more than 287 million people and companies. Over 40 per cent of its members are chief executive officers.

ASAE's mission is to 'promote and support excellence and professionalism among association executives and to work diligently to increase the effectiveness, the image, and the impact of associations as they serve their members and society'. ASAE services to its membership include two annual conventions, publications, educational programmes (with a professional certification programme known as 'Certified Association Executive'), an information clearing house on association management, and representational activities.

Contact: American Society of Association Executives, 1575 I Street, NW, Washington, DC, 20005–1168 USA (tel: 1–202–626–2723; fax: 1 202 371–8825).

Asian Association of Convention and Visitor Bureaus (AACVB)

Established in 1983, the Asian Association of Convention and Visitor Bureaus (AACVB) is a regional association of ten leading national conference destinations in Asia. Its full members are: China, Hong Kong, Indonesia, Japan, Korea, Macau, Malaysia, the Philippines, Singapore and Thailand. It has six membership categories representing a diverse range of entities including national tourist organisations, city convention bureaus, convention centres, destination management companies, and industry publications.

AACVB aims to realise the full potential of Asia as a destination for meetings, incentives, conventions and exhibitions. Its activities include joint marketing and promotions in key target markets, education programmes, research and information exchange, international networking and affiliation.

Contact: AACVB Secretariat, c/o Macau Government Tourist Office, 2/F Tourism Activities and Conference Centre, Rua Luís Gonzaga Gomes, Macau (tel: 853–798–4156; fax: 853–703–213; e-mail: aacvb@macau.ctm.net).

Association Internationale des Palais de Congrès (AIPC)

The Association Internationale des Palais de Congrès (AIPC) (International Association of Congress Centres) was founded in 1958 as a professional association for senior convention/conference centre executives. It now has over 100 members worldwide, for whom it acts as a catalyst in networking and data exchange. AIPC provides its members with assistance and consultation on design, technical, marketing, personnel, environmental, public relations and other significant aspects of facility management. It has an ongoing research programme aimed at more efficient convention-centre operation.

For the meeting planner, AIPC provides a 'guarantee of outstanding meeting facilities, high quality technical equipment, modern and caring management and careful attention to detail'.

AIPC publishes a quarterly newsletter and also takes stands at leading industry exhibitions. It holds an annual conference which is staged in a different country each year (Moscow 1997, Orvieto 1998, Jakarta 1999). AIPC maintains close contact with other international conference industry associations, and also contributes to the wider development of the industry as a founder member of the Joint Meetings Industry Council.

Contact: Marcos Carvalho Pereira, Secretary General, AIPC, Centro de Congressos de Lisboa, Praça das Industrias, Apartado 3200, 1301 Lisboa Codex, Portugal. (tel: 351–1–360–14–86; fax: 351–1–360–14–63; e-mail: secretariat@aipc.org; Internet site: http//www.aipc.org).

Convention Liaison Council (CLC)

The Convention Liaison Council (CLC) comprises 25 organisations representing the convention, meeting and exhibition industry, and travel and tourism generally. It is a US organisation, although some of its members (such as MPI, IACVB) are international in nature. CLC's purpose is to provide a focal point for the industry to work collectively to exchange information, recommend solutions to industry problems, develop programmes to serve the industry and its publics, and create an awareness of the magnitude of the industry.

This is achieved principally by the following:

- providing an open forum for identifying trends and problem-solving
- administering a Certified Meeting Professional (CMP) programme
- publishing the CLC Manual/Glossary
- recognising industry leadership through the CLC Hall of Leaders
- acquainting the general public with the economic impact of the industry
- monitoring legislation and establishing positions on public issues.

Contact: Convention Liaison Council, 1575 I Street, NW, Suite 1190, Washington, DC, 20005, USA (tel: 1–202–626–2764; fax: 1–202–408–9652).

European Federation of Conference Towns (EFCT)

In 1964 a few far-seeing people met in Brussels to establish the European Federation of Conference Towns (EFCT). Their main ambition was for EFCT to be a focal point for the youthful European conference industry; although many things have changed, this remains a key objective. A second prime aim was to provide advice and assistance for conference organisers to identify suitable destinations and venues for their events.

EFCT now has over 80 member destinations in 34 countries. It has assumed a major role in seeking to persuade the European Union of the vital economic importance of conference and business tourism. Its Liaison Office in Brussels has built good working links with the staff of appropriate European Union Directorates, and is active in scrutinising new legislation and providing guidance on all aspects of the industry. In 1995 EFCT stimulated wider liaison on European matters via the creation of EMILG, the European Meetings Industry Liaison Group, in conjunction with the International Congress and Convention Association, the International Association of Professional Congress Organisers, and Meeting Professionals International.

EFCT is one of the founder members of the Joint Meetings Industry Council (JMIC), is active in the European Travel and Tourism Action Group (ETAG), and enjoys Consultative Status with ECOSOC – the United Nations Economic and Social Council.

Regular EFCT publications include an annual member Directory, an annual 'Report on Europe' (published each Spring) and a newsletter. EFCT holds a General Assembly each year, and an annual Summer School (see Chapter 7).

Contact: European Federation of Conference Towns, BP 182, B-1040 Brussels, Belgium (tel: 32–2–732–69–54; fax: 32–2–735–48–40; e-mail: EFCT@pophost.eunet.be; Internet: http://www.ua.ac.be/TourWeb/EFCT.html).

European Meetings Industry Liaison Group (EMILG)

The European Meetings Industry Liaison Group (EMILG) was established in 1995 as a forum through which key issues could be discussed and representations made to political institutions. The four founder members were IAPCO, ICCA, MPI and EFCT. In 1997 the Association Internationale des Interprètes de Conférence (AIIC) was accepted into membership.

Contact: Mrs Rita de Landtsheer, Secretary General, EMILG, Keiweg 12, B-1730 Asse, Belgium (tel: 32–2–452–9830; fax: 32–2–452–2150).

International Association of Convention and Visitor Bureaus (IACVB)

The International Association of Convention and Visitor Bureaus (IACVB), now with over 820 members in over 420 member bureaus in 31 countries, was founded in 1914 to 'promote sound professional practice in the solicitation and servicing of meetings, conventions and tourism'. As the international association representing destinations around the world, IACVB provides public relations for the industry, represents convention and visitor bureaus on legislative and regulatory issues, publishes a monthly news magazine and two annual directories (one for members and one which sells destinations to meeting professionals and tour operators), offers educational programmes and a professional designation for members (CDME – Certified Destination Management Executive), runs the on-line Convention Industry Network (CINET) with a broad spectrum of data on client meetings (over 19 000 association and corporate meeting profiles, most of which are of North American organisations), and sponsors three 'Destinations Showcase' trade show events where members exhibit their destinations to meeting professionals, in Washington, DC, Chicago and New York.

The IACVB Foundation was established in 1993 to meet the needs of the destination management community and its clients by facilitating research, scholarship and philanthropy and by providing recognition and visibility for the destination management profession.

Contact: International Association of Convention and Visitor Bureaus, 2000 L Street, NW, Suite 702, Washington, DC, 20036–4990 (tel: 1–202–296–7888; fax: 1–202–296–7889; Internet: http://www.iacvb.org).

International Association of Professional Congress Organisers (IAPCO)

The International Association of Professional Congress Organisers (IAPCO) is a professional association exclusively for organisers of international meetings and special events and has over 60 members in 20 countries around the world. Prospective members are required to provide evidence of their experience and competence. IAPCO aims to:

- further recognition of congress (conference) organising as a profession
- further and maintain a high professional standard in the organisation of meetings
- study theoretical and practical aspects of international congresses, research problems which confront professional organisers, and promote solutions
- offer a forum for PCOs and provide members with opportunities to exchange ideas and experiences
- maintain effective relations with other organisations concerned with international meetings
- assist PCOs in obtaining the skills and expertise required to organise congresses
- encourage meetings convenors (organisers) to seek the assistance of reputable PCOs.

IAPCO is well known for its congress management courses, particularly the annual 'Wolfsberg' Seminar in Switzerland (see Chapter 7). It also publishes a range of useful conference guidelines for PCOs, planners and suppliers, such as: *Planning a Conference Centre – the requirements of PCOs, Pre-requisites for a Conference Hotel, Guidelines for Co-operation between the International Association, the National Organising Committee and the PCO*, and *Guidelines for the International Scientific Programme Committee*. Its newsletter is published three times a year.

Contact: International Association of Professional Congress Organisers, 40 rue Washington, 1050 Brussels, Belgium (tel: 32–2–640–71–05; fax: 32–2–640–47–31); e-mail: iapco@pophost.eunet.be or iapco@agoranet.be; Internet: http://www.iapco.org).

International Congress and Convention Association (ICCA)

The International Congress and Convention Association (ICCA) was founded in 1963 and is the only international association that represents the interests of all the various professional meetings suppliers. Its membership (numbering around 500 in over 70 countries) is organised in nine chapters (by regions of the world) for networking, and structured into seven categories: a) congress travel agents b) airlines c) professional congress and/or exhibition organisers d) tourist and convention bureaus e) ancillary congress services f) hotels g) congress, convention and exhibition centres.

ICCA exists to help all types of suppliers to the meetings industry to develop their skills and understanding, to facilitate the exchange of information, to raise and encourage professional standards, and to provide quality networking opportunities.

ICCA membership benefits and services include:

- special events at international trade shows
- business workshops, where members can discuss business with potential clients
- *International Meetings News*, a quarterly magazine distributed to 6500 international associations and corporate meeting planners
- worldwide distribution of the annual Membership Directory, which includes detailed information on every member and their services
- access to privileged information via ICCA DATA (a selection of ICCA statistics is reproduced in Chapter 1)
- monthly published factsheets containing detailed information on international meetings
- access to the ICCA database for tailor-made listings
- international networking, and education and training programmes via ICCA's International Meetings Academy (see Chapter 7).

Contact: International Congress and Convention Association, Entrada 121, NL – 1096 EB Amsterdam, The Netherlands (tel: 31–20–690–1171; fax: 31–20–699–0781; e-mail: icca@icca.nl; Internet: http://congresscity.com/icca).

Joint Meetings Industry Council (JMIC)

The Joint Meetings Industry Council was founded in 1978 as a forum for the exchange of conference-related news and views, and to explore ways of cooperating in conference education, publications and research. It meets twice a year and now includes 13 professional associations as members: Asian Association of Convention and Visitor Bureaus, Association Internationale des Interprètes de Conférence, Association Internationale des Palais de Congrès, Confederación de Entidades Organizadoras de Congresos y Afines de América Latina, European Federation of Conference Towns, International Association of Convention and Visitor Bureaus, International Association of Municipal Sports and Multi-Purpose Centers, International Association of French-speaking Towns, International Association of Professional Congress Organisers, International Congress and Convention Association, Meeting Professionals International, Society of Incentive Travel Executives, Union of International Associations.

Contact: Marcos Carvalho Pereira, JMIC Secretariat, Centro de Congressos de Lisboa, Praça das Industrias, Apartado 3200, 1301 Lisboa Codex, Portugal (tel: 351–1–360–14–86; fax: 351–1–360–14–63; e-mail: secretariat@aipc.org).

Meeting Professionals International (MPI)

Meeting Professionals International was founded in 1972 and is now the world's largest association of meeting industry professionals with more than 14 000 members in 56 countries. Membership belongs to an individual, not to a company/organisation. Membership categories include: planners, suppliers, and students. Planners and suppliers are represented in equal proportions. MPI has a permanent Secretariat based in Dallas (USA) as well as a European Bureau based in Brussels. Members are organised in national chapters (and clubs). The UK chapter has approximately 150 members. Membership benefits and services include:

- *education*: an annual conference, the Certificate in Meeting Management programme (see Chapter 7), regular network evenings, other educational programmes
- *publications*: a monthly magazine, *MPI Global Membership Directory*, plus a European Membership Directory, Chapter newsletters
- information: MPI Foundation (research and development arm), Resource Centre (library), MPINet (global on-line communications network)
- professional recognition: Meeting Professional Awards
- special interest groups: there is an opportunity to join one of four special interest groups: association meeting management, corporate meeting management, PCO, sales and marketing.

Contact: Meeting Professionals International, 4455 LBJ Freeway, Suite 1200, Dallas, Texas 75244–5309 (tel: 1–972–702–3000; fax: 1–972–702–3070; Internet: http://www. mpinet.org). MPI European Bureau, Boulevard St-Michel 15, B-1040 Brussels, Belgium (tel: 32–2–743–15–44; fax: 32–2–743–15–50).

Professional Convention Management Association (PCMA)

Founded in 1957, the Professional Convention Management Association (PCMA) has as its mission to increase the effectiveness of meetings and conventions through education and promotion to its members, the industry, and the general public. Membership in PCMA was initially restricted to meeting managers in the medical and healthcare fields. In 1990 the Association opened its membership to chief executives and meeting professionals from not-for-profit associations in all sectors. It has also established a network of local chapters and now has 15 chapters in the USA and Canada. In addition to large conventions and exhibitions, PCMA members plan an estimated 250 000 smaller meetings each year.

In 1985 PCMA created an Education Foundation, designed to support college and self-study courses, professional training and book publishing. The Foundation recently published the third edition of *Professional Meeting Management*, widely recognised in North America as the 'bible' of the industry. PCMA publishes its own magazine, *Convene*, one of the leading industry magazines. In 1992 the Association launched the 'North American Meetings Databank', which provides detailed profiles of association and corporate meetings in the USA and Canada. In 1994 PCMA initiated the 'Space Verification Program', designed to help meeting managers and hotels validate meeting room specifications. PCMA is currently working with other industry partners to develop a computer network that will standardise meeting communications and documentation.

Contact: Professional Convention Management Association, 100 Vestavia Parkway, Suite 220, Birmingham, Alabama 35216, USA (tel: 1–205–823–7262; fax: 1–205–822–3891; Internet: www.pcma.org).

Society of Incentive Travel Executives (SITE)

The Society of Incentive Travel Executives (SITE) is an international professional association for executives involved in every discipline of incentive travel. Membership, which currently numbers over 2000 in 83 countries worldwide, is open to qualified individuals who 'subscribe to the highest standards of professionalism and ethical behaviour'.

SITE has over 20 national and regional chapters around the world, including a Great Britain chapter. Among the membership benefits and services offered are:

- an annual conference which brings together experts from around the world to examine business trends and the application of relevant business products
- SITE certifies members who meet stringent requirements as 'Certified Incentive Travel Executives', proof that they have achieved the highest level of expertise in the industry
- members subscribe to a 'Code of Ethics' that is recognised by both users and suppliers of incentive travel as a guarantee of trustworthy service
- SITE provides opportunities worldwide – seminars, networking, social functions – for members to increase their level of professionalism. Such opportunities include three annual Universities of Incentive Travel: in Europe, in the Americas, and in Asia
- SITE funds research into the nature and effectiveness of motivational methods
- the publication of a Resource Manual and a Directory of Members.

Contact: Society of Incentive Travel Executives, 21 West 38th Street, 10th Floor, New York, NY 10018–5584, USA (tel: 1–212–575–0910; fax: 1–212–575–1838; e-mail: sitel@ix.netcom.com; Internet: www.site-intl.org; SITE). Great Britain Chapter may be contacted via: Mr Harvey Martin, President, SITE Great Britain Chapter, Sterling Travel London, 41 Queen Street, Maidenhead, Berkshire SL6 1ND (tel: 44–(0)1628–783682).

Union of International Associations (UIA)

The Union of International Associations (UIA) was formed in 1907 as the Central Office of International Associations, becoming the UIA in 1910. It was created in an an endeavour to coordinate international organisation initiatives, with emphasis on documentation, including a very extensive library and museum function. Gradually the focus has shifted to promoting internationality, as well as to a role in representing the collective views of international bodies where possible, especially on technical issues.

The UIA undertakes and promotes study and research into international organisations. Of particular importance to the conference industry is the UIA's production of statistics on international congresses and conventions, statistics which have been collected annually since 1949. The meetings taken into consideration are those organised or sponsored by international organisations appearing in the UIA publications *Yearbook of International Organisations* and *International Congress Calendar*. Some of the UIA's conference statistics are reproduced in Chapter 1.

The UIA is represented on a number of international conference industry forums, including the Joint Industry Council and the European Meetings Industry Liaison Group.

Contact: Union of International Associations, Congress Department, Rue Washington 40, 1050 Brussels, Belgium (tel: 32–2–640–41–09; fax: 32–2–646–0525).

An Assessment of the Conference Industry's Fragmentation

It cannot be denied that the tourism industry as a whole is fragmented. It is composed of thousands of mainly small operators and businesses, providing accommodation, restaurants, attractions, coach and taxi services, and so forth. The conference sector shares this same infrastructure, but also encompasses conference venues and other suppliers specific to the industry. With the exception of chain hotels, conference venues are, for the most part, run as discrete business units, independent of any centralised management or structure.

The sense of fragmentation is reinforced by the apparent proliferation of trade associations and similar bodies representing segments of the conference industry. In comparison with many other professions and industries, architecture or the automotive industry for example, the conference industry can be said to lack a single, cohesive voice.

At another level, however, the industry enjoys a very real sense of unity across the world. It is characterised by an openness and sharing, by friendships and networking between colleagues, which are immensely attractive and create almost a sense of family. Martin Lewis pays eloquent testimony to this aspect of the industry in his career profile in Chapter 7, quoting another colleague who described the industry as a 'global village hall'.

There is undoubtedly scope to bring some greater harmonisation to the industry, and there would also be benefits arising from a rationalisation of the industry's representative bodies, but it is to be hoped that these can be achieved without damaging the international friendship and collaboration which is such an important, and winsome, feature of the conference sector today.

Summary

- Active public sector management of the tourism industry in the United Kingdom effectively dates from 1969 when the Development of Tourism Act was introduced. The Isle of Man and the Channel Islands were not covered by this legislation, but have established their own tourism management and conference marketing organisations.

- The Department for Culture, Media and Sport has the main responsibility, with central government, for tourism policy and oversees the work of the English Tourist Board and the British Tourist Authority. The tourist boards for Northern Ireland, Scotland and Wales are responsible to the Department of Economic Development for Northern Ireland, the Scottish Office and the Welsh Office respectively.

- Marketing of the British Isles as a conference and meetings destination is undertaken by a number of bodies, both by national tourist boards as statutory agencies and by trade associations. Significant variations in structures and resources are apparent between the constituent countries of the United Kingdom.

- Local authorities have a key role to play in the development and management of the tourism and conference 'product'. While most local authorities have now recognised the economic importance of business and conference tourism, the non-statutory nature of their responsibilities towards tourism in general means that the level of support and commitment to this 'product' varies enormously from area to area.

- There are many trade associations and similar bodies operating within the conference sector, both at national and international levels. Some have clearly defined roles and a niche membership which is not being served by other associations. Some, however, appear to duplicate the activities of other associations, suggesting that rationalisations and mergers may become necessary both to ensure their own survival and for the wider health of the industry.

Review and discussion questions

1. Compare the structures and functions of the British Tourist Authority and UK national tourist boards vis-à-vis the conference industry with those of overseas national tourism organisations described in Chapter 5. Summarise the strengths and weaknesses of each and use these to make recommendations for an 'ideal' national conference destination marketing structure for the UK.

2. To what extent is the description of the conference sector as 'fragmented' justified? Is there a greater degree of fragmentation within the conference and business tourism sector than in the leisure tourism sector?

References

● DNH (1996) *Guidance to Successor Local Authorities on Tourism*, Department of National Heritage.
● DTI (1997) *The Future of the British Exhibitions Industry*, Department of Trade and Industry, Industry Economics and Statistics Unit.
● Scottish Tourist Board (1997) *Development, Objectives and Funding 1997–1998*.

Chapter 4

A Multi-billion Pound Industry

Introduction

Conferences are a vital economic generator for both local and national economies. Investment in conference facilities and infrastructure can bring substantial returns through the expenditure of delegates, with both direct and indirect benefits for the destinations in which conferences are held. Despite the relative shortage of statistics on the industry, sufficient information and research findings do exist to enable estimates of its true value to be made with confidence.

Objectives

This chapter looks at:

- conferences within the wider tourism context
- factors affecting conference sector demand
- the inadequacy of the information base
- the size of the industry
- the value of the industry.

Conferences within the Wider Tourism Context

It has already been seen that conference tourism is a sub-sector of business tourism, itself a sector within the overall tourism industry comprising both business and leisure tourism. Figures published by the British Tourist Authority (1997) put the total value of tourism to the United Kingdom in 1996 at £39 544 million (see Figure 4.1), contributing 4 per cent of gross domestic product. The tourism industry in that year supported 1.7 million jobs directly and indirectly, around 7 per cent of total UK employment. Tourism-related employment increased by 21 per cent during the ten years to September 1995. All projections by economists confirm that the tourism industry is set to become the world's largest industry by the millennium or in the decade thereafter.

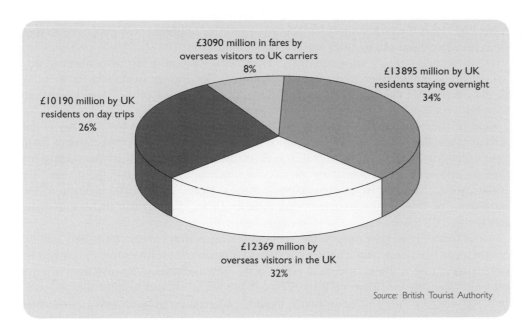

£3090 million in fares by
overseas visitors to UK carriers
8%

£13895 million by UK
residents staying overnight
34%

£10190 million by UK
residents on day trips
26%

£12369 million by
overseas visitors in the UK
32%

Source: British Tourist Authority

Figure 4.1
Value of tourism
to the UK, 1996
(total £39 544
million).

Within the United Kingdom, estimates suggest that almost one-third of the total value of tourism, around £12 billion, might be accounted for by business tourism (business/corporate travel and conferences/exhibitions/incentives). There is no doubt that, within this overall figure, conferences account for several billion pounds per annum. While precise figures are not yet available, Roy Tutty, Government Tourism Adviser, suggested in a speech to the Tourism Society (December 1996) that 'meetings and conferences were worth approximately £4 billion a year to UK tourism, 10 pence in every £1 of tourism earnings'. If it were possible to produce aggregated figures for the conference industry on a global scale, the totals would certainly reach hundreds of billions of pounds.

There are a number of research projects now under way which are beginning to build a more accurate and comprehensive picture of the size and value of the conference industry. This chapter will draw on these and on other sources, both domestic and overseas, to illustrate and emphasise that the conference industry is a major benefactor to both local and national economies, as a job creator and sustainer, as an income generator, and as a vehicle for attracting inward investment.

Factors Affecting Conference Sector Demand

In line with most other industries, demand for conferences is driven to a large extent by the buoyancy of the national, and increasingly global, economy. There was strong evidence, during the recession of the early 1990s, of business activity levels declining with conferences being cancelled or, more typically, being run on much lower budgets. Companies traded down, reducing delegate numbers, cutting out the residential aspect of conferences, spending less on catering, even using lower quality venues, for example 3-star hotels rather than 4-star.

However, one of the positive characteristics of the conference industry is its resilience, even in times of economic downturn. While there may be a trading down, many events still go ahead: public companies are required to hold an Annual General Meeting for their shareholders, senior managers need to engage in management retreats to explore ways of reviving their business, new products are launched, staff have to be trained and motivated, sales forces need to be brought together for briefings, and many other types of 'conference' take place, albeit with reduced budgets.

From the mid-1990s, conference demand has been increasing just as confidence and activity levels in the wider economy have improved. The 'buyers' market' of the first half of the decade has changed and the pendulum in certain parts of the United Kingdom (London especially) has swung in favour of suppliers.

One of the other factors expected to affect demand for conference facilities is the advent of satellite, video and teleconference technology. Evidence of the effects of these new technologies is at best anecdotal. It is clear that their usage is slowly increasing but there is little evidence to show they are causing significant reductions in the demand for conference facilities away from company premises. More venues have invested in the installation of video and teleconferencing facilities in an effort to win these new niche markets.

Social factors must have some effect on people's interest in conferencing, although no research has been undertaken to quantify these. Predictions that, for example, many more people would be working from or at home as the new millennium approaches have not proved to be correct. However, if the 'office-in-the-home' should become a more common feature of everyday life in the future, its end result might well be an increased demand for conferences as people respond to their gregarious instincts by coming together in regular meetings.

Changes within the country's industrial and commercial structures have also impacted on the demand for conference facilities. Reductions in trade union membership since 1980 have led to trade unions merging which, in turn, has meant fewer trade union conferences (particularly affecting seaside conference destinations) but, paradoxically, with larger numbers of delegates than previously. Some resorts, the traditional hosts of many trade union conferences, have found that their conference venues are no longer big enough to accommodate their former clients.

Fluctuations in conference demand are more noticeable in the corporate sector than in the association sector, often because of factors such as lead times. Corporate events, with relatively short lead times, can quickly respond to changing economic situations. Association conferences, with much longer lead times, find it less easy to adapt to alterations of this kind.

The Inadequacy of the Information Base

Before looking at some of the available figures on conference tourism, it might be useful to understand why the information and intelligence base for the industry is incomplete.

The Economist Intelligence Unit, in a report entitled *The European Conference and Meetings Market* (Rockett and Smillie, 1994), lists four main reasons why not enough is known about business and conference tourism in quantifiable terms (with the author's comments on these shown in italics):

- fragmentation of industry sectors (in terms of both geography and markets). Each sector has its own trade association, and often more than one. International associations and organisations have varying degrees of representation in their member countries. *In part this seems to be a reflection of the tourism industry as a whole; in part it may also be due to the immaturity of the conference industry, with some rationalisation of the industry's representative bodies likely to take place, if only because the market cannot sustain such a diversity of organisations. There is also a genuine desire among the industry's leading associations to forge collaborative partnerships with like-minded bodies in order to achieve a more cohesive voice for the industry.*

● lack of consensus on terminology and definitions. Segmentation of the market makes it difficult to produce a clear definition of each sector.

● certain segments of business and commercial tourism are difficult to measure. *This is particularly true of 'business travel', but similar problems can arise with incentive travel and conferences.*

● information about certain activities is sensitive and closely guarded. *This can apply to buyers and suppliers alike, with hotels enjoying special notoriety for their reluctance to release information on their bookings lest they give a competitive edge to neighbouring properties.*

One or two practical examples may make clear why statistics and intelligence are far from comprehensive:

Many of the individuals and organisations which contribute to the conference industry do so as part of a wider role. For example, a training manager will use the services/facilities of the conference industry to run a training course or seminar away from company premises, but may only do this once or twice a year. It would be inaccurate, therefore, to categorise him as a full-time conference/event organiser even though he is a buyer at certain times of the year. Public relations consultancies will often be involved in organising conferences, product launches or corporate hospitality events on behalf of their clients, but they remain first and foremost public relations consultancies and may also escape classification as 'conference organisers'.

Likewise, an hotel will hire out its function rooms to conference organisers, but may equally hire them out to someone staging weddings or other social events. In most cases the hotel will not differentiate in its record-keeping between the different types of client or function, making it impossible to build up an accurate picture of the amount of conference business compared with other categories of business. This 'problem' can be replicated several thousand times in respect of many of the other venues across the country.

There are no comprehensive listings or databases of events held or events planned to take place in the future, whether at a local or national level. It seems unlikely that such records will ever be compiled because of the sensitivities and fears of competition referred to above. It would also be a huge undertaking to build and maintain such a database, particularly as it would only have very limited commercial applications. The best that can be hoped for are the ad hoc pieces of research which provide snapshots of business levels and their values, as exemplified in this chapter, but when brought together make up a stunning collage of one of the leading industry sectors nationally and internationally.

The Size of the Industry

National

The following facts and figures provide some measurement of the size of the British conference industry:

● There are an estimated 10 000 conference organisers or 'buyers' in the UK. Many of these combine conference organising with other responsibilities, but they organise a sufficient number of events per annum to justify their details being held on marketing databases such as that maintained by the British Association of Conference

Destinations. Full-time conference organisers, whose sole responsibility is the management of conferences and other events, probably number less than 1000. Organisers representing corporate organisations outnumber those from associations by a ratio of at least 2:1.

● Around 120 destinations are being actively marketed to the conference sector. Such destinations include cities, towns, counties, parts of counties, and islands. Some of the larger destinations represent over 100 venues (London is the largest with around 450 venues), whereas smaller destinations (Lincoln or Morecambe, for example) may only represent 10 to 20 venues.

● There are over 4000 venues of all kinds being promoted for conferences and business tourism events.

● There is an unknown number of other suppliers to the industry. Some of these provide a very localised service (e.g. an audio-visual company or floral contractor working in just one town or city), whereas others operate on a regional or national or even international level (e.g. coach companies, airlines, interpreters and translators). It is once again the case that only a small proportion of suppliers are dedicated to the conference industry; the majority are also servicing other industry sectors.

International

The following facts help to provide some dimensions for the conference industry at an international level:

● There are at least 65 countries now active in marketing their facilities and services to the conference and conventions industry. The Union of International Associations (UIA) has records of international conferences being staged in 187 countries in 1996.

● The International Association of Convention and Visitor Bureaus (IACVB) has members in over 420 bureaus in 31 countries.

● Meeting Professionals International (MPI) has over 14 700 members in 58 countries. MPI members comprise a 50/50 ratio of buyers and suppliers.

● The International Congress and Convention Association (ICCA) has around 500 members in more than 70 countries.

A study of the German conference market, undertaken in 1994–95 by the German convention Bureau (1996), revealed a market in which 50 million participants were involved in 610 000 events on 1.4 million event days. Case Study 4.1 provides a more detailed analysis of the German conference market.

Case Study 4.1   The German Meetings Market, 1994–95

The German Convention Bureau commissioned a study of the German conference market at the beginning of 1995. The study was carried out by the research institute Infratest Burke and the principal findings were published under the title of 'The German Meetings Market 1994–95' (and summarised in *Tagungs Wirtschaft* magazine). These findings covered the size and value of the industry, as well as other characteristics. The study was based on events with a minimum of ten participants. ▷

The findings showed:

- The German conference market was worth DM43 billion in 1994, with some 50 million delegates participating in 610 000 events on 1.4 million event days. Of this turnover, DM8 billion was spent in hotels and DM2 billion in conference halls. Additional expenditure of DM25 billion was in support sectors such as retailing, restaurants and taxis. The DM43 billion meant that the conference industry accounted for more than 1 per cent of Germany's gross national product.

- Conference venues totalled 6800, of which 6300 were hotels. Other venues included 350 conference centres and approximately 160 universities. The meeting venues provided over 20 000 rooms with a combined capacity of almost 2 million people. Four out of every five of the 6800 venues seated a maximum of 200 people theatre-style in their largest room. 12 per cent of venues could accommodate between 200–500 delegates in their largest room, and about 8 per cent had capacities in excess of 500.

- Conferences and meetings lasted an average of 2.3 days, with two-thirds of the events lasting two days or less. Conference business provided the German hotel industry with 55 million room nights.

- Of the 610 000 events surveyed, 27 per cent involved 10–15 delegates, 36 per cent between 16 and 30 delegates, and a further 13 per cent between 31 and 50 delegates. Only one in five conferences involved 51–400 attendees, while events with 400+ delegates accounted for just 4 per cent of the total. The study did show, however, that the 23 per cent of events with more than 50 delegates generated no less than 62 per cent of total conference revenues.

- Cars were the most important means of transport to conferences. Three-quarters of delegates arrived in their own cars, 13 per cent travelled by rail, 5 per cent by coach and 6 per cent by plane.

- The 'typical' delegate was male (76 per cent), younger than 50 (81 per cent being aged between 20 and 49), with a higher level of education (57 per cent with college certificates or university degrees), and in a salaried position. Only 9 per cent of delegates attended with partners or family.

The Value of the Industry

Measurements of economic impact

Assessments of the value of the conference industry to the United Kingdom economy are at best only estimates, based on information drawn from national and local surveys. Such assessments of the value, or economic impact, of conferences must also take account of a number of factors, outlined by Cooper et al. (1993), which apply to the tourism industry as a whole:

Tourists spend their money on a wide variety of goods and services. They purchase accommodation, food and beverage, communications, entertainment services, goods from retail outlets and tour/travel services, to name just a few. This money may be seen as an injection of demand into the host economy: that is, demand which would otherwise not be present. However, the value of tourist expenditure represents only a partial picture of the economic impact. The full assessment of economic impact must take into account other aspects, including the following:

- *indirect and induced effects*
- *leakages of expenditure out of the local economy*
- *displacement and opportunity costs.*

Cooper and colleagues refer to the 'cascading' effect of tourist expenditure, with the benefits of tourist spending being felt in hotels, restaurants, taxi firms and shops, and then permeating through the rest of the economy. From this total direct impact, however, must be subtracted the cost of 'imports necessary to supply those front-line goods and services . . . for example, hotels purchase the services of builders, accountants, banks, food and beverage suppliers, and many others'. These suppliers will, in turn, purchase goods and services from other suppliers, generating further rounds of economic activity, known as the indirect effect.

> *The indirect effect will not involve all of the monies spent by tourists during the direct effect, since some of that money will leak out of circulation through imports, savings and taxation. Finally, during the direct and indirect rounds of expenditure, income will accrue to local residents in the form of wages, salaries, distributed profit, rent and interest. This addition to the local income will, in part, be re-spent in the local economy on goods and services, and this will generate yet further rounds of economic activity. It is only when all three levels of impact (direct* plus *indirect* plus *induced) are estimated that the full positive economic impact of tourism expenditure is fully assessed.*

Cooper and colleagues also make reference to certain 'negative economic impacts' of tourist expenditure. These include opportunity costs and displacement effects. Opportunity costs refer to the use of resources such as labour and capital for the benefit of one industry rather than another. Decisions to invest limited capital resources in tourism infrastructure, for example, will have negative impacts on other industries which failed to attract that investment.

> *Where tourism development substitutes one form of expenditure and economic activity for another, this is known as the displacement effect. Displacement can take place when tourism development is undertaken at the expense of another industry, and is generally referred to as the opportunity cost of the development. However, it is more commonly referred to when a new tourism project is seen to take away custom from an existing facility. For instance, if a destination finds that its all-inclusive hotels are running at high occupancy levels and returning a reasonable yield on investment, the construction of an additional all-inclusive hotel may simply reduce the occupancy levels of the existing establishments, and the destination may find that its overall tourism activity has not increased by as much as the new business from the development. This is displacement.*

The use of multipliers

Measurement of the economic impact of tourist spending is effected by using multiplier analysis. Various types of multiplier exist, and it is important to use the correct multipliers for specific functions. The main ones are well described by Cooper and colleagues, as are the methodological approaches based on these. In summary, the principal multipliers are as follows.

A transactions (or sales) multiplier
This measures the amount of additional business revenue created in an economy as a result of an increase in tourist expenditure.

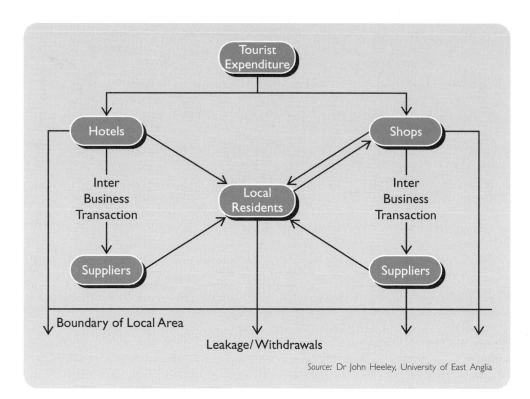

Figure 4.2 The tourism multiplier concept.

Source: Dr John Heeley, University of East Anglia

An output multiplier

This measures the amount of additional output generated in an economy as a result of an increase in tourist expenditure. The principal distinction between this multiplier and the transactions multiplier is that the output multiplier is concerned with changes in the actual levels of production and not with the volume and value of sales.

An income multiplier

This measures the additional income (wages and salaries, rent, interest and distributed profits) created in the economy as a result of an increase in tourist expenditure.

An employment multiplier

This is a measurement of *either* the total amount of employment generated by an additional unit of tourist expenditure *or* the ratio of the total employment generated by this same expenditure to the direct employment alone.

A government revenue multiplier

This measures the impact on government revenue, from all sources, associated with an increase of tourist expenditure.

Figure 4.2 illustrates the application of the multiplier concept to tourist expenditure.

Research findings

The following research findings have resulted from the application of economic impact studies and multiplier analysis to the conference and business tourism sector. In their totality they underline the importance of this tourism sector at the high quality, high yield end of the tourism spectrum.

Table 4.1
Business and
conference
visitors, 1975–96

	Total visitors	Business visitors		Conference visitors*	
	'000	'000	% of total	'000	% of total
1975	9 490	1 778	18.7	143	1.5
1977	12 281	2 142	17.4	169	1.4
1979	12 486	2 395	19.2	n.a.	–
1980	12 421	2 565	20.7	162	1.3
1981	11 452	2 453	21.4	n.a.	–
1982	11 636	2 393	20.6	142	1.2
1983	12 464	2 556	20.5	n.a.	–
1984	13 644	2 863	21.0	204	1.5
1985	14 449	3 014	20.9	n.a.	–
1986	13 897	3 286	23.6	213	1.5
1987	15 566	3 564	22.9	n.a.	–
1988	15 799	4 096	25.9	261	1.7
1989	17 338	4 363	25.2	n.a.	–
1990	18 013	4 461	24.8	298	1.7
1991	17 125	4 219	24.6	n.a.	–
1992	18 535	4 462	24.1	417	2.2
1993	19 863	4 706	23.7	471	2.4
1994	20 794	4 986	24.0	482	2.3
1995	23 537	5 763	24.5	569	2.4
1996	25 293	6 133	24.2	720	2.8

Note: * Excluding residents of the Irish Republic
Source: International Passenger Survey: Overseas Conference Visitors to the UK, 1996

International Passenger Survey (IPS)

The International Passenger Survey (IPS) is a one in ten sampling of all overseas visitors undertaken as they depart from the United Kingdom, sponsored by the Office for National Statistics. The figures (see Table 4.1) show that the number of conference visitors, as a proportion of total visitors, has increased steadily since 1975, growing from 1.5 per cent (143 000 people) in that year to 2.8 per cent (720 000 people) in 1996. In the same 21-year period business visitors have increased proportionately from 18.7 per cent to 24.2 per cent of the total.

The reasons for the growth in conference visitor traffic from overseas are undoubtedly linked to the global growth in this industry sector. The United Kingdom's position as one of the leading conference nations has meant that it has been well placed to take advantage of the buoyancy of the market, although it remains to be seen whether it can stem the steady haemorrhaging of business to growing competition from around the world and once again begin to grow its market share.

As important as visitor numbers is visitor expenditure. IPS figures for 1996 show that, while total visitor expenditure increased by 5 per cent and business visitor expenditure by 1 per cent, the spending of conference visitors grew by 31 per cent to a total of £373 million (see Table 4.2). After incentive visitors, conference visitors are the highest spending of all categories of visitors to the United Kingdom, spending an average of £656 per visit in 1995 compared with an average of £485 per visit for all types of visitor. Figures 4.3 and 4.4 highlight the value of conference visitors in terms of their average spending

	Total visitors		Business visitors		Conference visitors*	
	1995	1996	1995	1996	1995	1996
Visits (000)	23 537	25 293	5 763	6 133	569	720
Nights (m)	220.3	221.0	29.0	28.1	2.7	3.1
Expenditure (£m)	11 763	12 369	3 216	3 244	361	472
Average length of stay (nights)	9.4	8.7	5.0	4.6	4.8	4.3
Average expenditure per day (£)	52.9	55.5	111.1	115.4	132.6	151.1
Average expenditure per visit (£)	495	485	558	529	634	656

Note: * Excluding residents of the Irish Republic

Source: International Passenger Survey: Overseas Conference Visitors to the UK, 1996

Table 4.2
Business and conference visits, nights and spending, 1995 and 1996

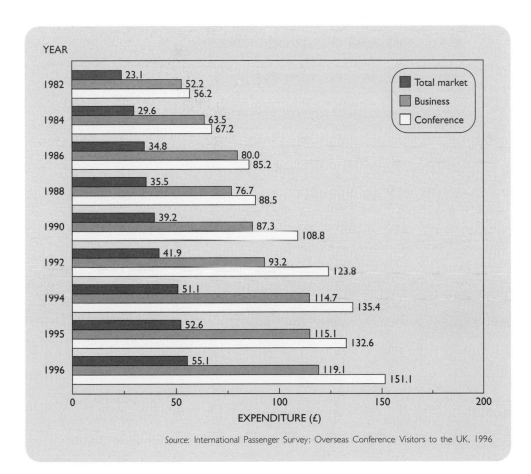

Source: International Passenger Survey: Overseas Conference Visitors to the UK, 1996

Figure 4.3
Average spending per day – conference visitors compared.

per day and per visit, and underline the position that they have always occupied, alongside incentive travellers, as the most lucrative of visitor categories.

Conference visitor expenditure includes payments made by the visitor and by his employer, both in advance and during the course of a visit. It is not restricted to attendance fees and other necessary outgoings in relation to the conference itself. It includes

Figure 4.4
Average spending
per visit –
conference
visitors
compared.

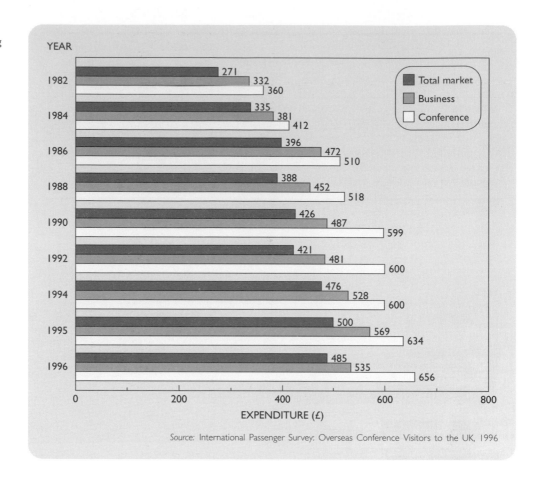

Source: International Passenger Survey: Overseas Conference Visitors to the UK, 1996

Figure 4.5 Quarterly distribution 1996 – conference visitors compared.

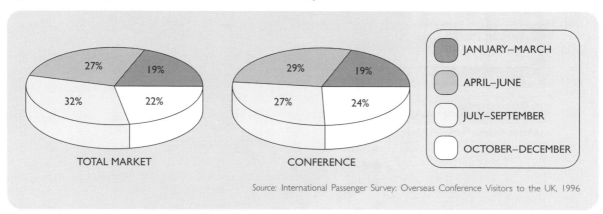

Source: International Passenger Survey: Overseas Conference Visitors to the UK, 1996

spending on all other aspects of the trip, except fares paid to carriers for travel to and from the United Kingdom.

Reference has already been made to the all-year-round nature of conference tourism, a fact which is well portrayed in Figure 4.5, illustrating the quarter of departure from the

	Visits		Expenditure		
	000	**%**	**£m**	**%**	**Sample size**
USA	107	15	107.1	23	374
Canada	9	1	4.6	1	32
Total North America	116	16	111.7	24	406
Germany	90	12	36.9	8	184
France	84	12	34.5	7	183
Netherlands	47	7	17.2	4	143
Sweden	46	6	24.5	5	147
Belgium/Luxembourg	40	5	14.0	3	68
Italy	36	5	20.1	4	68
Spain	24	3	10.7	2	50
Denmark	17	2	10.5	2	53
Finland	11	2	7.4	2	26
Austria	9	1	4.0	1	16
Greece	8	1	5.4	1	18
Portugal	8	1	4.0	1	20
Total EU	412	57	185.3	39	956
Switzerland	28	4	22.8	5	48
Norway	22	3	11.6	2	58
Other Rest of Western Europe	11	1	11.2	2	31
Total Rest of Western Europe	60	8	45.6	10	137
Eastern Europe	32	4	28.7	6	57
South East Asia	15	2	18.3	4	47
Japan	12	2	12.5	3	39
Central & South America	12	2	13.4	3	40
Australia/New Zealand	12	2	10.9	2	49
Middle East	13	2	11.6	2	41
South Africa	5	1	3.1	1	25
Other Rest of World	37	5	34.2	7	121
Total Rest of World	132	18	129.7	27	394
Total	720	100	472.3	100	1893

Table 4.3 Area of residence of conference visitors, 1996

Source: International Passenger Survey: Overseas Conference Visitors to the UK, 1996

United Kingdom of conference visitors. Table 4.3 shows the source of conference visitors by region of the world and their respective value in terms of spending.

The benefits of overseas conference visitor traffic are not spread evenly around the country. Table 4.4 (overleaf) emphasises London's pre-eminent position, attracting around three-fifths of visitors and expenditure although, as has been seen already, competition from other United Kingdom cities is increasing and beginning to make inroads into London's market share. There are, however, ripple-down benefits (see section on Sydney later in this chapter) accruing to other regions of the country as conference delegates participate in tours from London either before the conference starts or after it finishes, or indeed as part of a social programme during the event itself.

Table 4.4

Regions stayed in by conference visitors, 1996

	Staying Visits		Nights		Expenditure	
	000	%	000	%	£m	%
England:	623	86	2800	99	436	117
London	404	56	1510	54	295	79
Rest of England:	303	42	1280	46	141	38
Heart of England TB	83	12	300	11	39	10
Southern TB	67	9	220	8	28	8
South East TB	55	8	170	6	24	6
East of England TB	52	7	190	7	20	5
North West TB	31	4	130	5	12	3
Yorks & Humberside TB	24	3	100	3	8	2
West Country TB	21	3	70	2	6	2
Northumbria TB	11	2	100	3	4	1
Cumbria TB	3	*	10	*	1	*
Channel Islands**	1	*	*	*	*	*
Isle of Man**	*	*	*	*	*	*
Unspecified	1	*	*	*	*	*
Scotland	53	7	260	9	25	7
Wales	13	2	40	1	4	1
Northern Ireland	5	1	20	1	2	1
Travelling, etc.	2	*	*	*	*	*
Nil nights in UK	53	7	–	–	4	1
Other UK	*	*	*	*	*	*
Total	720	–	2820	100	373	100

Notes: Nights figures are rounded to the nearest 10 000.

* Less than 500 staying visits/5000 nights/0.5 million pounds/0.5%

** Excludes direct departures.

Source: International Passenger Survey: Overseas Conference Visitors to the UK, 1996

British Conference Market Trends Survey

The British Conference Market Trends Survey is sponsored by the British Tourist Authority, British Association of Conference Destinations, British Universities Accommodation Consortium, Conventions Great Britain, International Congress and Conventions Association (UK Chapter), Meetings Industry Association, and the Scottish Tourist Board. Its purpose is to monitor trends and activity levels in the British conference industry through the collation and analysis of monthly reports from venues of all types in all regions of the country. It monitors events involving a minimum of 15 delegates.

The Survey commenced in January 1994 and several years' figures have now been aggregated enabling year-on-year comparisons to be made. The Survey's weakness is its relatively small sample size, with only just over 100 venues reporting consistently over the initial three-year period. These venues are, however, significant players in the conference market and are representative of the different categories of conference venue.

The Survey figures for 1996 showed continued growth in the corporate conference sector, compared with a reduction in the numbers of association and government sector events. The growth in corporate meetings is, no doubt, a reflection of the greater confidence and activity levels of businesses in general. The fall in the numbers of association

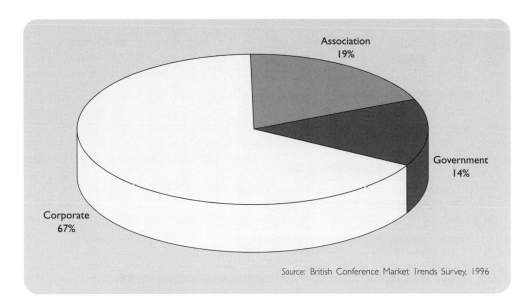

Association
19%

Government
14%

Corporate
67%

Source: British Conference Market Trends Survey, 1996

Figure 4.6
Breakdown of
conferences by
conference type,
1996.

and government meetings is less easy to explain, although this may be due in part to their longer lead time (especially for the larger association events) which would have meant that initial plans for a proportion of 1996 conferences would have been made in the period 1992–4 when the effects of economic recession were still being experienced. A decline in trade union membership since the 1980s had led to a number of mergers between trade unions which, in turn, has translated into fewer, but larger, union conferences. It may also be that some professional association conferences which previously had just a national dimension are now becoming more international, or at least pan-European, and are consequently being staged in different countries each year.

Figure 4.6 shows the breakdown of conferences reported by conference type. It also confirms the 2:1 ratio of corporate buyers to association organisers, including government buyers, referred to earlier in this chapter.

In 1996 over 80 per cent of conferences reported by venues in the survey involved 100 delegates or less, with over 65 per cent consisting of 50 delegates or less (see Figure 4.7, overleaf). These findings mirror those of the survey into the German conference market (Case Study 4.1), and give the lie to the commonly held impression of conferences as events attracting hundreds and even thousands of delegates. The reality is that large, high-profile events (political or trade union conferences, for example) are merely the tip of a very big iceberg, with the bulk of the industry 'hidden' in small events for well under 100 delegates.

The Survey also underlined the year-round nature of conference business (see Figure 4.8, overleaf), with the only significant reductions in business occurring during the peak holiday seasons of July/August and December. The duration of conferences was also measured by the Survey, distinguishing between residential and non-residential events (see Figures 4.9 and 4.10, page 91).

IACVB Foundation 'Convention Income Survey'

The International Association of Convention and Visitor Bureaus (IACVB) Foundation carries out 'Convention Income Surveys' on a regular basis. Eight full economic impact studies have been completed since 1948, the last being in the period June 1992 to June 1993 (the next is due to be completed by July 1998). Seventy-three IACVB member

Figure 4.7
Number of
conferences by
delegate
attendance,
1994–96.

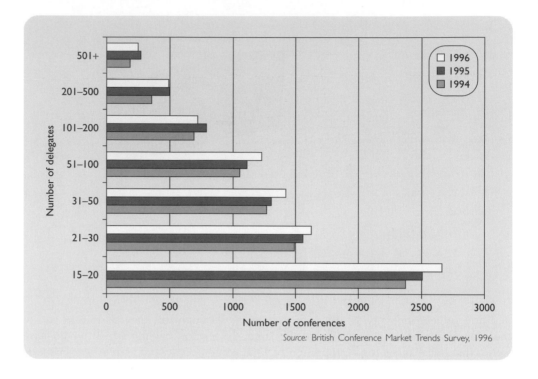

Source: British Conference Market Trends Survey, 1996

Figure 4.8
Conferences
reported by
month, 1996.

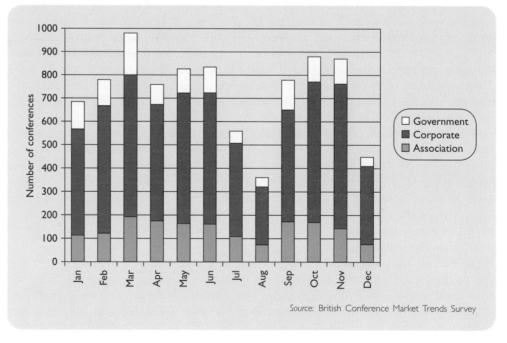

Source: British Conference Market Trends Survey

bureaus (67 US and 6 non-US) participated in the 1992–3 study, each surveying up to 30 conventions, meetings and expositions held in its city.

In between the full surveys, annual updates are produced with figures based on the US *Travel Price Index*. The 1995 update, published in March 1996, showed that the average attendee at an international, national or regional convention spent US$862.79 during

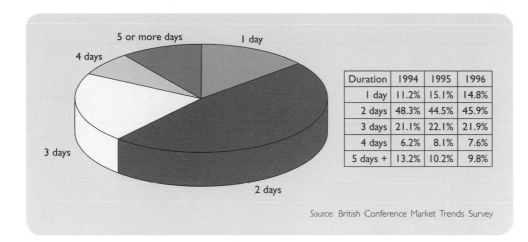

Figure 4.9
Conference
duration – 1996
residential
conferences.

Duration	1994	1995	1996
1 day	11.2%	15.1%	14.8%
2 days	48.3%	44.5%	45.9%
3 days	21.1%	22.1%	21.9%
4 days	6.2%	8.1%	7.6%
5 days +	13.2%	10.2%	9.8%

Source: British Conference Market Trends Survey

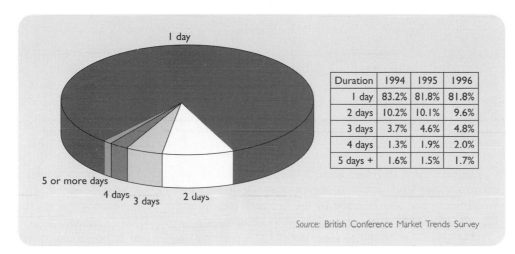

Figure 4.10
Conference
duration – 1996
non-residential
conferences.

Duration	1994	1995	1996
1 day	83.2%	81.8%	81.8%
2 days	10.2%	10.1%	9.6%
3 days	3.7%	4.6%	4.8%
4 days	1.3%	1.9%	2.0%
5 days +	1.6%	1.5%	1.7%

Source: British Conference Market Trends Survey

a four-day stay. This includes hotel rooms, restaurants, retail stores, taxis, car rentals and other expenses.

The update also revealed that the associations themselves spent an average of US$59.86 per attendee in local services. Many of the large association conventions have an exhibition running alongside, and the update figures showed that each exhibitor spent an average US$2638.97, further adding to the economic impact of these large conventions.

Economic impact study in the USA – Convention Liaison Council

In 1994 the Convention Liaison Council (CLC) commissioned management consultants Deloitte & Touche LLP to undertake a study of the economic impact of conventions, exhibitions, meetings and incentives in the USA. The study revealed an industry worth US$82.8 billion in direct spending, making it the twenty-second largest contributor to the gross national product. It generated more than one-third of the hotel industry's estimated US$66 billion annual revenue, accounted for 22 per cent of airline industry operating income and provided more than US$12.3 billion in sales and income taxes.

The research findings were based on detailed responses from more than 500 hotels, convention centres and other meeting facilities. Comparisons with an earlier Economic Impact Study carried out by CLC in 1991 show that the industry's total direct spending grew by US$7.2 billion or 9.5 per cent over the three-year period, well ahead of the rate

Table 4.5 Total itemised expenditure per delegate

Item	Expenditure per delegate 1996 ($)	Expenditure per delegate 1995 ($)	Variance (%)	Daily expenditure per delegate 1996 ($)	Daily expenditure per delegate 1995 ($)	Variance (%)
Registration fees	763	560	36	112	81	39
Shopping	551	394	40	81	57	42
Hotel accommodation	1142	1019	12	168	148	13
Convention social functions	238	233	2	35	34	3
Local ground transport	113	108	5	17	16	4
Restaurants	347	316	10	51	46	11
Domestic air	488	657	−26	72	95	−24
Theatre/concerts/ cinema	151	151	0	22	22	1
Telephone/fax	76	62	23	11	9	24
Recreational facilities	185	164	13	27	24	13
Tours	289	230	26	43	33	29
Other expenses	380	308	23	56	45	24
Total	4723	4202	12	695	609	14

Source: 1996 Sydney Convention Delegate Study (Sydney Convention and Visitors Bureau)

of inflation. These increases were largely attributed to substantial gains in attendance, occupancy and load factors in the post-recession year (1994) that was measured. The overall figure was also boosted by the first-time measurement of university venues, religious facilities and other non-traditional meeting sites.

The largest share of the meeting dollar (32.5 per cent) was spent in hotels and other meeting venues. Air transport accounted for 23.3 per cent, after which the biggest categories of delegate, exhibitor and sponsor spending were restaurants (12.1 per cent), ground transport (8.7 per cent), retailing (6.7 per cent) and business services (6.6 per cent).

Destination surveys
Many individual destinations undertake, from time to time, their own research surveys into the economic impact of convention business. The following findings, based on several very distinct destinations, add further pieces to the jigsaw and help to build a more complete picture of how much conference visitors spend and where they spend it.

Sydney　In Australia, the Sydney Convention and Visitors Bureau conducted its second 'Convention Delegate Study' in 1996, surveying 3808 delegates at international conventions in the city.

The findings showed that international delegates spent an average A$4723 (approximately A$2.20 to £1 in September 1997) each during their stay in Sydney, not including pre-paid air fares and package tours. The average time spent in the city was calculated at 6.8 nights, giving an average daily spend of A$695. By way of comparison, the average international tourist spent only A$1987 per visit, or A$85 per day. Table 4.5 and Figure 4.11 give a more detailed breakdown of delegate expenditure.

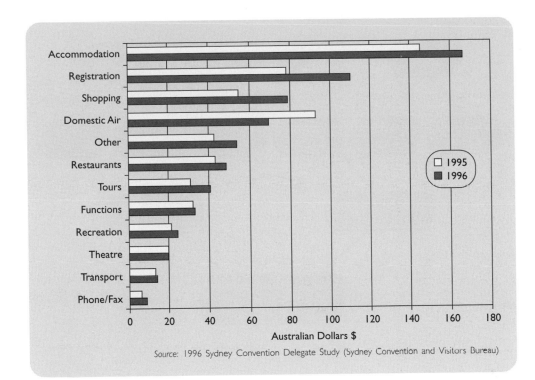

Figure 4.11
Itemised expenditure per delegate – daily.

Source: 1996 Sydney Convention Delegate Study (Sydney Convention and Visitors Bureau)

Sydney's experience is that conference and incentive tourism are the highest yielding and fastest growing segments of the tourism industry. The value of such business was estimated at A$3 billion for Australia and A$1 billion for Sydney in 1996, figures which are expected to have trebled by the year 2000.

There is also a 'ripple-down' or 'cascading' effect from conference business, with other regions of the country benefiting as delegates extend their stay (or arrive several days before the convention) in order to travel and see some of the sights and attractions of other cities and destinations. The Sydney research found that international delegates were spending an average of 10.7 nights in total in Australia, three nights of which were devoted to pre- or post-convention touring. Seventy-two per cent of delegates were found to be visiting Australia for the first time: prior to the convention, only one in three had considered visiting the country, whereas after the convention two-thirds wanted to return on holiday within the next five years.

Birmingham   NEC Ltd, the company responsible for managing Birmingham's National Exhibition Centre, International Convention Centre (including Symphony Hall), and the National Indoor Arena commissioned management consultants KMPG to conduct a study of the economic impact of these venues on the City of Birmingham and the West Midlands region. The study was carried out during the period September 1992 to August 1993 and was based on a survey of some 2500 visitors, exhibitors, delegates and spectators at 38 events at the venues, selected as representative of the wide range of different types of events held. Such events include rock and classical concerts, dog shows, musicals, and sporting events which clearly do not impinge on the conference industry. Nevertheless, the venues do obtain much of their business from the conference and business tourism sectors and, indeed, were purpose-designed for such, and it does seem to be appropriate to include the survey findings in a book on the conference industry.

Figure 4.12
Total direct
expenditure in
Birmingham and
the rest of the
West Midlands
(ROWM) 1/1/92
to 31/8/93.

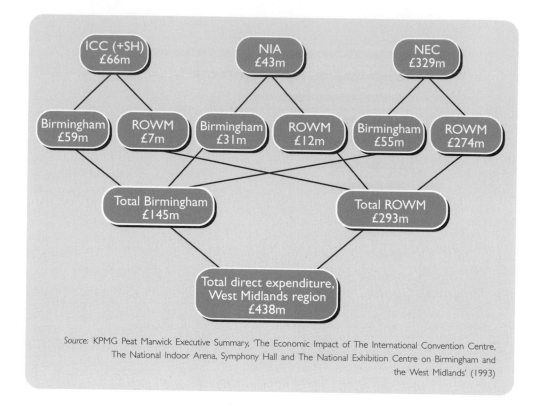

Source: KPMG Peat Marwick Executive Summary, 'The Economic Impact of The International Convention Centre, The National Indoor Arena, Symphony Hall and The National Exhibition Centre on Birmingham and the West Midlands' (1993)

The study found a total direct expenditure of £438 million in the 12-month period (62 per cent personal spending by the venues' visitors, 38 per cent business expenditure by organisers, promoters and exhibitors). This is expenditure which was truly additional in that it would not have been generated without the new venues and their events. A breakdown of this expenditure is shown in more detail in Figure 4.12.

The study assessed 'retained income' in Birmingham and the West Midlands by researching the relevant spending multipliers which take into account leakages and indirect and induced expenditure. In addition, it researched and incorporated the annual retained income, a total of £10.3 million, attributable to those businesses specifically located in the region or city because of the venues. The total retained income for the West Midlands region was £180 million, with Birmingham itself accounting for £58 million, significantly in excess of the net running costs of the venues (including capital repayment costs) of £22 million borne by Birmingham City Council.

The use of employment multipliers showed a total full-time equivalent (FTE) employment in the West Midlands region of 16 800 jobs, with 5800 of these specifically in Birmingham, a cost per job created of £3800 in Birmingham and £1300 in the West Midlands in that year. Table 4.6 shows the FTE employment for which the venues were responsible in 1992/93.

Figure 4.13 summarises the substantial economic impact and other benefits to the City of Birmingham and the whole of the West Midlands region, even during a period of major recession and at a time when the International Convention Centre (opened 1991) and the National Indoor Arena (also opened 1991) were still very much in their infancy.

In 1997 Birmingham's International Convention Centre hosted the annual congress of the World Small Animal Veterinary Association (WSAVA), an event which attracted

	ICC (plus SH)	NIA	NEC	Total
FTE employment in Birmingham	1 100	700	4 000	5 800
FTE employment ROWM	1 600	1 200	8 200	11 000
Total FTE employment	2 700	1 900	12 200	16 800

Source: KPMG Peat Marwick Executive Summary, 'The Economic Impact of The International Convention Centre: National Indoor Arena, Symphony Hall and National Exhibition Centre on Birmingham and the West Midlands' (1993)

Table 4.6 FTE employment in Birmingham and the rest of the West Midlands, 1/9/92 to 31/8/93

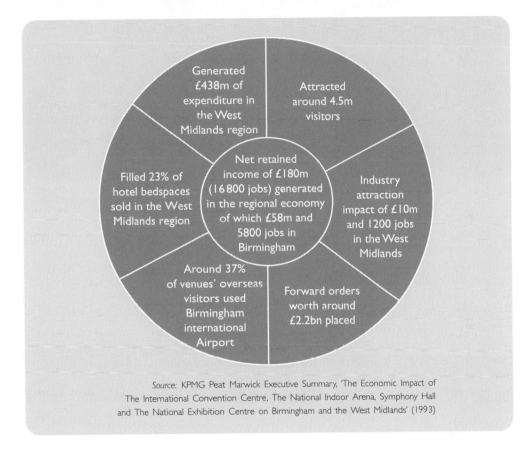

Source: KPMG Peat Marwick Executive Summary, 'The Economic Impact of The International Convention Centre, The National Indoor Arena, Symphony Hall and The National Exhibition Centre on Birmingham and the West Midlands' (1993)

Figure 4.13 Summary of the annual economic impact of the venues, 1/9/92 to 31/8/93.

over 6700 delegates from 49 countries (over 1100 of them were from overseas). Some 13 000 bednights were booked during the event both in city centre hotels and at hotels throughout the region. Total delegate expenditure was estimated at £2 million, covering accommodation, travel, eating out, entertainment and shopping (based on an average expenditure of £130 per day, very similar to the IPS figures quoted in Table 4.2). In reality, the full economic impact was even higher than this, as the expenditure estimate was only based upon congress delegates. Many delegates were accompanied by partners and some by their families, but this spending was not included in the figures.

Bournemouth Bournemouth hosted the Conservative Party conference in 1996 and calculates that the event (a four-day conference with an eight-day build-up period) generated over £10 million for the resort. It attracted over 12 000 people, including delegates,

Figure 4.14
Bournemouth
International
Centre.

Source: Bournemouth International Centre

exhibitors (participating in an exhibition which was run in parallel with the conference), media and police. The main venue for the conference, Bournemouth International Centre, received £120 000 in catering revenue alone, with over 30 000 teas and coffees, 1500 oysters and 400 bottles of champagne being consumed, not to mention thousands of Danish pastries, muffins and sandwiches.

Bournemouth estimates that conference tourism is worth between £45–£55 million annually to the town. In 1996 the economic benefit of conferences at the Bournemouth International Centre (see Figure 4.14) and the Pavilion (two local authority-run venues) was calculated at £26 million, with conference business within the town's hotels generating a similar figure. It is calculated that the total tourism industry (an estimated 5.5 million visitors to the town annually, of whom 1.3 million are staying visitors and 4.2 million day trippers) injects £479 million per annum into the local economy and directly supports 15 000 jobs.

Llandudno The North Wales seaside resort of Llandudno has, for many years, been successful in attracting association conferences. In 1993, the local authority undertook a survey of delegates to ascertain where delegates were spending money outside the conference venue and outside the hotel or guest house in which they were staying. The findings are summarised in Figure 4.15.

The surprise finding was the amount spent by delegates in petrol stations, 10p in every £1 spent. It was discovered that delegates were filling up their cars with petrol in Llandudno before embarking on their journey home, a 'spend' which had not been appreciated beforehand. In that year the local authority estimated the value of conferences at £6 million, representing a return of over £48 for every £1 invested in marketing Llandudno as a conference destination.

Now Llandudno hosts over 30 major conferences a year, generating an income of some £9.2 million, an average of £300 000 per conference.

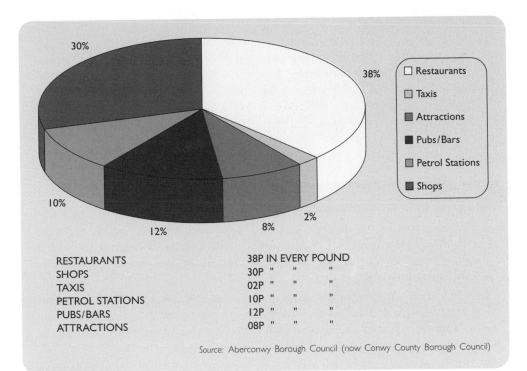

Figure 4.15
Llandudno survey:
spend by
delegates outside
hotels, 1993.

RESTAURANTS	38P IN EVERY POUND
SHOPS	30P " " "
TAXIS	02P " " "
PETROL STATIONS	10P " " "
PUBS/BARS	12P " " "
ATTRACTIONS	08P " " "

Source: Aberconwy Borough Council (now Conwy County Borough Council)

Summary

- Conferences are a segment of business tourism, which is itself a sector of the wider tourism industry. Estimates suggest that, within developed economies such as the United Kingdom, business tourism may account for around one-third of the total value of tourism (approximately £12 billion in 1996). The conference segment of business tourism is worth hundreds of billions of pounds per annum on a global scale.

- Comprehensive statistics for the conference industry do not yet exist. There are many reasons for this, including the somewhat fragmented nature of the conference sector, the lack of consensus on terminology, and the sensitivity of certain commercial information.

- Measurements of the size of the conference industry are possible, even though these are based on partial rather than fully comprehensive surveys. They point to an industry which is active and growing in almost all parts of the United Kingdom, and one which is increasingly represented in more and more countries worldwide.

- Calculations of the economic impact of conference business must take into account a number of negative economic impacts, such as opportunity costs and displacement costs, as well as the cascade of positive benefits, in order to arrive at an accurate assessment of net beneficial effects.

- Measurement of the economic impact of tourist spending is achieved by the use of multipliers. Multipliers can be used to measure revenue, production levels, income and employment.

Summary continued

● National surveys and local studies confirm that conference tourism occupies one of the top places at the high yield end of the tourism spectrum. It provides substantial economic benefits for those countries who have embraced it vigorously and invested in the necessary infrastructure to attract and retain conference business. It sustains jobs which are all-year-round and brings income through delegate expenditure, with benefits for many sections of local communities.

Review and discussion questions

1. Consider and list the different kinds of events and functions which might be held in a conference hotel. Explain why it would be in the interests of such a venue to keep accurate records of its different client groups and to be able to distinguish between them.

2. If you were responsible for marketing an entire destination, what arguments would you put forward to the hotels you are representing to encourage them to disclose to you information on their client groups and bookings? What might be the benefits to them of so doing?

3. List the main arguments for and against the establishment of a comprehensive national database of conferences and similar events.

4. Look at the analysis of overseas conference delegates shown in Table 4.4. Suggest reasons for London's pre-eminent position. What actions could other British destinations take to attract a greater market share?

5. As a restaurant owner whose restaurant is situated close to a major convention centre, suggest the practical steps you might take to ensure that you gain maximum benefit from having this facility on your doorstep.

References

● *British Conference Market Trends Survey 1996* (1997) British Tourist Authority, British Association of Conference Destinations, British Universities Accommodation Consortium, Conventions Great Britain, International Congress and Convention Association (UK Chapter), Meetings Industry Association, Scottish Tourist Board.

● Cooper, Chris, Fletcher, John, Gilbert, David and Wanhill, Stephen (1993) *Tourism: Principles and Practice*, Addison Wesley Longman.

● *The Economic Impact of the International Convention Centre, the National Indoor Arena, Symphony Hall and the National Exhibition Centre on Birmingham and the West Midlands (Executive Summary)* (1993) NEC Group Ltd.

● *The German Meetings Market 1994/95* (1996) Infratest Burke, German Convention Bureau.

● Heeley, J. (1980) *Tourism and Local Government, with Special Reference to the County of Norfolk, Vol. 1*, University of East Anglia, p. 72.

● *International Passenger Survey: Overseas Conference Visitors to the UK 1996* (1997) Office for National Statistics and BTA/ETB Statistical Research.

● *National Facts of Tourism* (1997) British Tourist Authority.
● Rockett, G. and Smillie, Gill (1994) *The European Conference and Meetings Market*, The Economist Intelligence Unit (reprinted from Travel & Tourism Analyst, Issue 4).
● *1996 Sydney Convention Delegate Survey* (1997) Sydney Convention and Visitors Bureau.

Chapter 5

A Destination Industry

Introduction

Location has always been one of the key factors in decisions over the choice of conference venues. Its importance has led to the creation of marketing organisations whose prime focus is that of location or 'destination' promotion, operating at national, regional or city level. Following a summary of general marketing principles and their application to the conference industry, this chapter will look at the role of destination marketing organisations. It will also examine some of the other ways in which individual venues, or groups of venues, bring their product to the marketplace through branding and the establishment of consortiums.

Objectives

Specific sections in this chapter include:

- a definition of destination
- marketing principles
- relationship marketing
- destination marketing organisations
- conference venue marketing
- branding
- yield management
- overseas marketing.

A Definition of Destination

'Location, location and location' is a commonly heard expression within the conference industry. When it comes to choosing a conference venue, the most important initial consideration for event organisers is its location. This factor often assumes greater importance than factors such as price, type of venue, quality of facilities and proximity to tourist attractions. Research by the Meetings Industry Association (see Chapter 2) confirms that, among corporate buyers, the convenience of a venue's location is more than twice as important as competitive pricing. Buyers purchase location first and foremost.

Location can mean a number of different things: a town, a city, a county, a region, an island, a rural area, a city centre, even a country in the context of huge international conventions. In some cases an organiser will express location in terms of 'proximity to an international airport', 'within a 20-mile radius of a certain town', 'somewhere between two named motorways'.

Where the reference is to a discrete area, the term most frequently and aptly used to describe this area is 'a destination'. Gartrell (1994) defines destinations as follows:

> From the perspective of the consumer, destinations are perceived as those geographic areas that have attributes, features, attractions, and services that appeal to the prospective user. How the consumer defines a geographic area varies greatly and may or may not include specific geographic boundaries.

The key phrase here is 'areas . . . that appeal to the prospective user'. The marketing of conference venues and destinations must be driven by what makes sense to the consumer, in this case the conference organiser and the delegates he is seeking to attract. It cannot be undertaken successfully by the artificial 'destinations' which are sometimes created to satisfy bureaucratic or political whims, a criticism which may justifiably be levelled at some of the current regional tourism structures within Britain.

Marketing Principles

Before looking at conference venue and destination marketing activities, it will be useful to summarise some of the general principles of marketing and how they apply to the conference and tourism industry.

Customer focus

There are many definitions of marketing. One of the more straightforward ones is that adopted by the (British) Chartered Institute of Marketing, which defines marketing as: 'The management process responsible for indentifying, anticipating and satisfying customers' requirements efficiently and profitably'.

This focus on customers' needs is the key to all successful marketing activity. There are alternative philosophies which are well described by Cooper et al. (1993) and reproduced in Figure 5.1 (overleaf).

> Examples 1 and 2 [in Figure 5.1] can be ineffective due to problems encountered in having the wrong product for the market, and therefore having to devote more resources to promotion and selling in order to achieve sales. In these examples it is normal to find companies which believe their products are acceptable, and all that is required for sales to occur is the identification of prime markets and methods of selling.

The emphasis is on the product, and in tourist promotional literature it is often characterised by photographs of empty bedrooms or conference rooms, of buildings and views of the destination. It is selling 'features' rather than the 'benefits' the consumer is seeking, and fails to show pictures of tourists and delegates enjoying themselves and receiving good service.

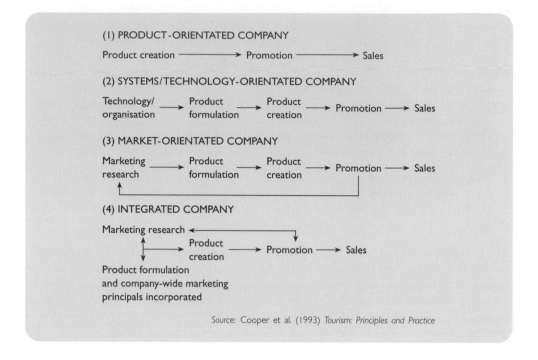

Source: Cooper et al. (1993) *Tourism: Principles and Practice*

On the other hand, examples 3 and 4 in Figure 5.1

offer the ideal approach to organising business in today's tourism marketplace. They are driven by research which creates an understanding of the consumer, the business and the marketplace ... The tourism industry is spending vast sums of money on developing new attractions, improving products, building hotels and investing in technology. The only way for the risk level to be kept to a minimum is through adoption of a marketing philosophy which provides products related to the needs of consumers.

The establishment of a customer orientation which permeates every department of a conference venue or conference marketing organisation is essential to its success. This provides the basic building blocks upon which marketing strategies can be constructed. It will ensure that the physical product is suited to market needs: the multi-purpose hotel function room, for example, is less and less able to meet the increasingly sophisticated needs of today's conference planners. It will also ensure that the people servicing a venue have a proper understanding of the specific needs of the conference organiser and his delegates, and that they are equipped with the personal and technical skills to meet such needs in ways which will encourage the customer to return again and again.

Marketing plan

The practical steps involved in preparing to approach the marketplace include development of a marketing plan or strategy. The plan will need to set out what an organisation is trying to achieve, in other words its corporate mission and goals, and include an analysis of where it is at the present time, sometimes referred to as an internal and external audit. The plan must also assess the general business situation and make projections for the organisation's likely performance. It should set out clear objectives, create an appro-

priate marketing mix strategy and determine effective monitoring systems and performance measures. The process is likely to include a PEST analysis, looking at the political,
economic, social and technological changes which may affect the organisation and the
market, and a SWOT analysis, assessing the major strengths, weaknesses, opportunities
and threats facing the company. (Appendix C shows a SWOT analysis of the UK conference industry.)

Figure 5.2 (pages 104–5) shows an extract taken from the Edinburgh Convention
Bureau Business Plan 1997–2001, showing how the plan is structured and setting out the
principal objectives and targets to be met.

Marketing mix strategy

Through a process of market research, target markets of current and potential customers
must be identified, whether in broad terms (for example, corporate conferences for up
to 100 delegates or professional association conferences for 500 to 1000) or in more
specific niche and segment terms (for example, very high-spend pharmaceutical conferences for 20 to 40 delegates, or residential educational sector conferences for 50 to 100).
Once this has been done, an appropriate marketing mix strategy can be developed.

The marketing mix is frequently defined as comprising the four Ps: product, price, promotion and place (distribution). Other marketing gurus would extend these traditional
four points to eight, to include packaging, planning, the prospect, and post-sale.

In the marketing of a conference destination or venue, these terms signify:

1. *Product* is the destination/venue and its facilities and resources. To conference
   organisers and meeting planners, it means a destination/venue which can handle
   the convention, meeting or exhibition requirements. It covers such issues as service, quality, branding, and those unique features which differentiate it from competitors (USPs or unique selling propositions).

2. *Price* may cover a variety of issues including conference centre/venue hire charges
   and delegate rates, hotel or guest house accommodation costs and transport costs.
   Pricing policies must take account of many factors including projected future
   demand and any seasonal fluctuations expected; the need to maximise yield (see
   later in this chapter); the perishable nature of the product (it is something that
   cannot be stored for future use, like a conference room that is unused on a particular day and brings in no revenue and that potential revenue is lost forever);
   the psychological impact on clients of raising or lowering prices; the activities of
   competitors; and the wider economic situation.

3. *Packaging* relates to the way in which the product and price are offered in the
   market. Special delegate packages may be offered in conjunction with local tourist attractions or between conference venues and hotels: for example the Riviera
   Centre, Torquay's purpose-built conference centre, has developed a 24-hour delegate package in conjunction with local hotels, a package only normally available
   from residential venues. Most venues, both residential and non-residential, promote
   their own delegate packages (the Chatsworth Hotel in Eastbourne offers 12-hour,
   24-hour and 36-hour delegate packages complete with a service guarantee, see
   Figure 5.3, on page 106) and the Meetings Industry Association puts forward
   'Minimum Components of Residential/Non-Residential Conference Packages' as
   part of its Meetings Magna Carta (see also Appendix E). Some convention centres will offer their accommodation rent-free to certain types of not-for-profit
   organisations.

Figure 5.2
Edinburgh
Convention
Bureau Business
Plan, 1997/98
(Index and
Objectives and
Targets only).

4. *Place (or distribution)* focuses on the activities used by a destination or venue to make its product available and accessible to prospective clients. Such distribution channels may include trade shows, destination or venue guides and brochures, CD-Roms or videos, and Internet sites.

5. *Planning* is the strategic process of analysing markets, assessing the competition, identifying programmes, and selecting appropriate marketing strategies.

6. *Promotion* communicates information about the destination/venue and its products to prospective clients. There is a need to inform and persuade current customers to remain loyal, potential future customers to experience the product, but also journalists and other key people (leading figures in the local community and politicians, for example) who may in some way influence business activity levels. Advertising, public relations, direct marketing, selling and familiarisation visits are some of the promotional activities undertaken.

7. *Prospect* (or client/customer) is the sole reason for, and the object of, all the destination or venue's marketing endeavours. The Body Shop retail company expressed the importance of the customer in its mission statement as follows:

Figure 5.2
(cont.)

I. OBJECTIVES AND TARGETS

The role of Edinburgh Convention Bureau as the business tourism division of Edinburgh and Lothians Tourist Board is to generate, for Edinburgh and the Lothians, the maximum income from conference and incentive travel, particularly in the 1st quarter.

The aims of the Convention Bureau are to:

● increase the economic impact of tourism generated through marketing and sales initiatives
● generate enquiries, bids and confirmed conferences
● enhance Edinburgh's reputation as an international conference destination
● provide a high quality of service
● generate trade and national press coverage
● raise Edinburgh's position in the ICCA International Association league table from 15th position to within the top 5 by 2001

In order of priority our Goals for 1997 are as follows:

● Expand the number of long range bookings of International Association Conferences from 1999 onwards
● Maximise short lead corporate business revenue
● Increase economic benefit from confirmed conferences

The targets for the period 1997–2001 for the Convention Bureau are as follows:-

PERFORMANCE INDICATOR	TARGETS			
	1997/98	1998/99	1999/2000	2000/01
Number of General Enquiries	500	600	700	800
Number of Specific Enquiries	700	800	1200	1500
Number of Confirmed Conferences	500	700	900	1200
Economic Benefit of Confirmed Conferences	£35m	£40m	£45m	£60m
Advertising Equivalent Press Coverage	£135 000	£150 000	£175 000	£200 000
Convention Bureau Membership Income	£85 000	£90 000	£95 000	£100 000
Quality Targets	Telephone Calls	Letters		
Response Times	1 Day	Day		

Source: Edinburgh Convention Bureau

A customer is the most important visitor on our premises. She is not dependent on us. We are dependent on her. She is not an interruption to our work. She is the purpose of it. She is not an outsider in our business. She is part of it. We are not doing her a favour by serving her. She is doing us a favour by giving us the opportunity to do so.

It is this same customer orientation which is crucial to the success of all venues and destinations seeking to attract conference delegates.

8. *Post-sale* processes address the continuing need to provide service to and for prospects and to ensure that the sense of expectation generated at the sales meeting is not just met but exceeded in the run-up to an event and, indeed, in the provision of service during and after it. Client retention is not always possible

Figure 5.3
Delegate
packages –
Chatsworth
Hotel,
Eastbourne.

12-HOUR DELEGATE PACKAGE INCLUDES:

- conference room hire
- complimentary syndicate room
- overhead/35mm projector and screen
- video monitor
- flip charts and pads
- conference stationery and pens
- coffee and bacon rolls/cheese croissants on arrival
- morning coffee and doughnuts
- three course hot and cold buffet or sit down lunch with mineral water and orange juice
- afternoon tea and shortbread
- mineral water, cordials and mints.

24-HOUR DELEGATE PACKAGE INCLUDES:

- accommodation in double room for single occupancy
- full English breakfast
- hire of conference room and equipment
- refreshments and buffet lunch
- three course dinner with four choices on each course.

36-HOUR DELEGATE PACKAGE INCLUDES:

- the 24-hour package plus the 12-hour package.

Each of the above packages is delivered with the hotel's 'Service Guarantee'.

Source: Chatsworth Hotel

within the conference industry because of the buying patterns of certain organisations, especially within the association sector, but keeping satisfied clients is a much more cost-effective way of maintaining and building market share than having constantly to find and attract new clients. Recommendations of venues and destinations by colleagues is frequently found to be a key way in which these are sourced, as a satisfied customer becomes an unpaid ambassador (or distribution channel) whose value should never be under-estimated.

Other marketers suggest further Ps be added to the marketing mix, such as *people* – those who are between the product and the prospect, delivering the product/services to the client including convention bureau staff, venue personnel, destination management companies, professional conference organisers, restaurateurs, shop and visitor attraction staff.

There is clearly some overlap between these different marketing mix tools, but in total they provide the essential ingredients for bringing a conference venue or destination to the marketplace in a way that is professionally planned and likely to enjoy the greatest success.

Relationship Marketing

One of the key features of conference venue and destination marketing is the forging of relationships between suppliers and buyers, the building of trust between those offering facilities and services and those looking to make use of them to stage events. Gartrell (1991) suggests that 'though a convention bureau is a sales organisation, its premise of operation is the development of a relationship with planners that cultivates understanding and trust. Though such a relationship may not initially appear mutually supportive, the reality is that the bureau and planner have common goals and in essence need one another.'

The meetings planner or conference organiser needs, for example, to carry out familiarisation or inspection visits to a destination and its venues, to assess its appropriateness for specific events. The convention and visitor bureau is the ideal vehicle through which such visits can be organised because the bureau can provide a comprehensive overview, pull together all the necessary information, arrange a schedule of visits to venues and attractions and usually escort them as well, and then advise on the availability and accessibility of all the other components of a given conference package. PCOs and DMCs may also be involved in this process in a similar way. For the individual conference organiser to plan such a visit using his own resources, possibly from hundreds or thousands of miles away, would require a huge investment in time and resources.

Trust and understanding are also of critical importance between the venue which is to stage the conference and the conference organiser. A chain of relationships is formed, initially between the venue sales manager and the conference organiser and then between the conference and banqueting manager/coordinator and the organiser. All need to have confidence in each other: the conference organiser needs to trust the venue staff to deliver what has been promised within agreed budgets, and the venue staff need to feel comfortable that their client will keep his side of the deal (for example, in numbers of delegates, in the conference programme, and in any specially planned arrangements). When such strong and trusting relationships exist, there is a much greater prospect of successful events and of future repeat business. When relationships are less strong, often because of high staff turnover in the venue or because of insufficient planning time allocated by the conference organiser, problems are much more likely to occur.

In the author's experience, one of the real attractions of the conference industry is the many opportunities it affords for the development of relationships between buyers and suppliers, between buyers and buyers, and between suppliers and suppliers. It is very much a people industry and, while there may be fierce competition for business, this takes the form of friendly rivalry rather than cut-throat aggression. Formal and informal networks are established, and it is quite common for one destination to pass on information about a client or an event to the destination which will play host to them next. Similarly, buyers will exchange their experiences of venues and destinations and peer recommendation is one of the most important ways in which future venues are sourced.

It is easier to use relationship marketing within the conference sector than, for example, the leisure tourism sector because the number of clients and potential clients is much more restricted. This is not mass leisure tourism. It is, as mentioned earlier in this chapter, about identifying specific markets and building a rapport with individual decision-makers within these defined markets. Relationship marketing provides a complementary approach to conventional marketing strategy by focusing upon the search for mutually beneficial partnerships with customers.

A crucial tool in relationship marketing is the development of customer profiles in a client database, which is normally computerised but could also take the form of a card index system. Such databases are built from a core record giving full contact details (client name, job title, company name and address, telephone and fax numbers as a minimum), but will then go on to establish a profile of the client's buying requirements (kinds of conferences organised, types of venues used, sizes of events, locations considered).

Relationship (or database) marketing facilitates direct contact with customers in ways which should generate real response. The more sensitive and creative the use of the data, the better the reaction (or 'response'). Frequently, direct marketing is linked with some form of incentive to encourage recipients to respond. Relationship marketing is about one-to-one contact with an organisation's clientèle, involving strategies for customer retention and a more targeted approach to the creation of customer value.

Destination Marketing Organisations

Destination or 'place' marketing is undertaken at both a local level (city or county, for example) and a national level (by a national tourism organisation). This section looks at a number of models of destination marketing organisations at both levels.

Local destination marketing

Convention and visitor bureaus

A number of references have already been made to the role of convention and visitor bureaus in the formation of the conference industry (Chapter 1) and in the provision of services to that industry (Chapter 2).

In structure, conference or convention bureaus (variations on the name are to be found) are usually formed and financed as partnerships between public and private sector bodies. In Britain this can include local authorities, chambers of commerce, training and enterprise councils, hotels, venues and other private sector suppliers. They are set up as not-for-profit organisations, controlled by a management board, and represent a specific destination, frequently a city. In most cases the bureau is established at arm's length from the local authority or authorities which it represents, but in others (Hull Conference Bureau, Telford and Shropshire Conferences, for example) the bureau remains an integral part of the local authority structure.

Funding is derived from public sector contributions (usually the largest single source), private sector membership fees (members including venues of all kinds, accommodation providers, professional conference organisers (PCOs)/destination management companies (DMCs), transport operators, audio-visual companies and other kinds of suppliers), sponsorship, joint commercial activities with members and, in some cases, commission which is charged to venue members on business placed. Some bureaus prefer to have a high membership fee which covers a full package of benefits and services to their members (with no or few hidden or extra charges). Other bureaus opt for a much lower membership fee which provides a core of benefits but they then invite their members to buy into additional activities and services on a partnership basis. Both models have their strengths and weaknesses:

- *High Membership Fee* – for the bureau, the high membership fee, which can amount to as much as £5000 per annum for large hotels, enables longer term planning to be undertaken with greater confidence, provided of course that the bureau can also achieve a high retention level among its membership. The bureau knows that it should receive a certain membership income in ensuing years and can plan its activities and expenditure accordingly. The high membership fee model also means that the bureau does not have to go back to its members on a regular basis to seek their financial support for particular activities during the year, which can be time-consuming for the bureau and a cause of irritation to its members. The weakness, or perhaps more accurately the challenge, of this funding model is the need to guarantee significant returns to the membership for their high investment in the bureau.

● *Lower Membership Fee* – this would typically be a membership fee of several hundred pounds (£500–£1000 is the normal range). For the bureau this can make it easier to 'sell' bureau membership to potential members because the initial outlay for them is much smaller. For bureau members there is greater flexibility in buying into those activities of the bureau (a stand at a trade exhibition or an entry in a piece of promotional print, for example) which are of most interest to them and which match their budgets. They do not have to buy into a full package of benefits, some of which they may not require. On the downside, there are significantly higher administrative costs with this model. It can also be argued with some justification that those members paying a lower membership fee are likely to be less committed to the bureau than those who have paid a high fee and need to see the bureau succeed to justify their investment.

There is no right or wrong model. Each destination and the suppliers within it must agree what is appropriate for themselves and then develop and fine-tune the model in the light of experience. Bureaus are dynamic entities which must continue to evolve in the light of local circumstances, changes in market trends, the demands of clients and a multitude of other factors.

In the British Isles there are around 40 conference bureaus. Bureau is a generic term which, as has been seen, disguises a variety of models in terms of their staffing, funding and operations, although all share the same fundamental mission which, in the words of Gartrell (1994), is to 'solicit and service conventions and other related group business and to engage in visitor promotions which generate overnight stays for a destination, thereby enhancing and developing the economic fabric of the community'.

British conference bureaus have an average of two or three staff (typically a general manager, a sales executive, and an administrative assistant with computing skills), but the range is from just one member of staff up to 9–10. The staffing structure for the Greater Glasgow and Clyde Valley Tourist Board, encompassing one of the best-resourced British bureaus, is shown in Figure 5.4 (overleaf). It is interesting to compare this with one of the larger convention and visitor bureaus (or CVBs) from North America: an organisational chart for Tourism Vancouver – The Greater Vancouver Convention and Visitors Bureau is shown in Figure 5.5 (on page 111). If Tourist Information Centre staff are excluded, it will be seen that Vancouver has almost twice the number of staff as Glasgow.

Bureaus in North America operate on a different scale, largely because there is a longer tradition of CVBs (even relatively small towns have a CVB). In the USA bureaus are also funded differently, principally through a system of *hotel transient occupancy tax* (or bed tax) which means that hotel guests pay a tax which goes to the local city or town council, and can be added to the resources available to market the destination. Research undertaken by IACVB found that this bed tax contributed approximately two-thirds of US CVB budgets (many of which run into hundreds of thousands or even millions of dollars). US CVBs also play a prominent role at the centre of community life, being involved in a wide spectrum of community development issues which may impact on the future prosperity of the visitor industry. The world's first visitor and convention bureau, Detroit, or Metropolitan Detroit Convention and Visitor Bureau to give its full name, had more than 600 businesses of various sizes and interests in membership in 1996, part of a tourism industry which attracted 15.1 million visitors spending US$3.9 billion during that year.

Figure 5.4 Greater Glasgow and Clyde Valley Tourist Board; organisational and staffing structure.

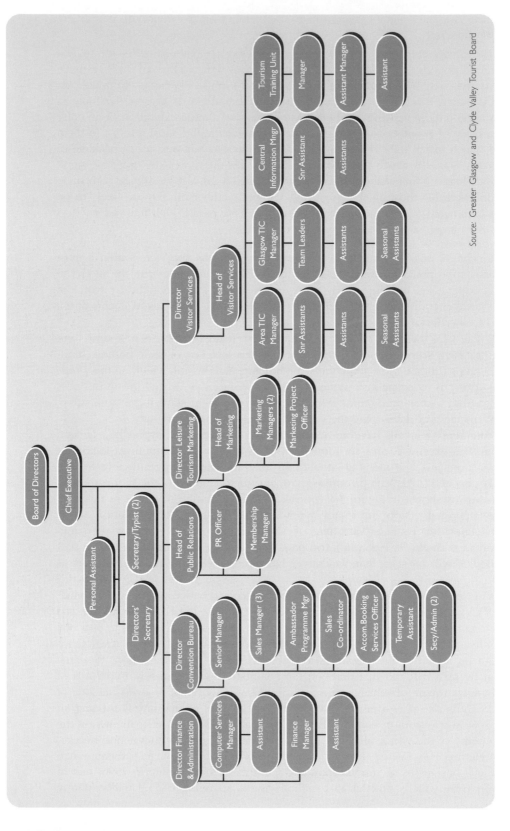

Source: Greater Glasgow and Clyde Valley Tourist Board

Figure 5.5 Organisation chart: Tourism Vancouver – the Greater Vancouver Convention and Visitors Bureau.

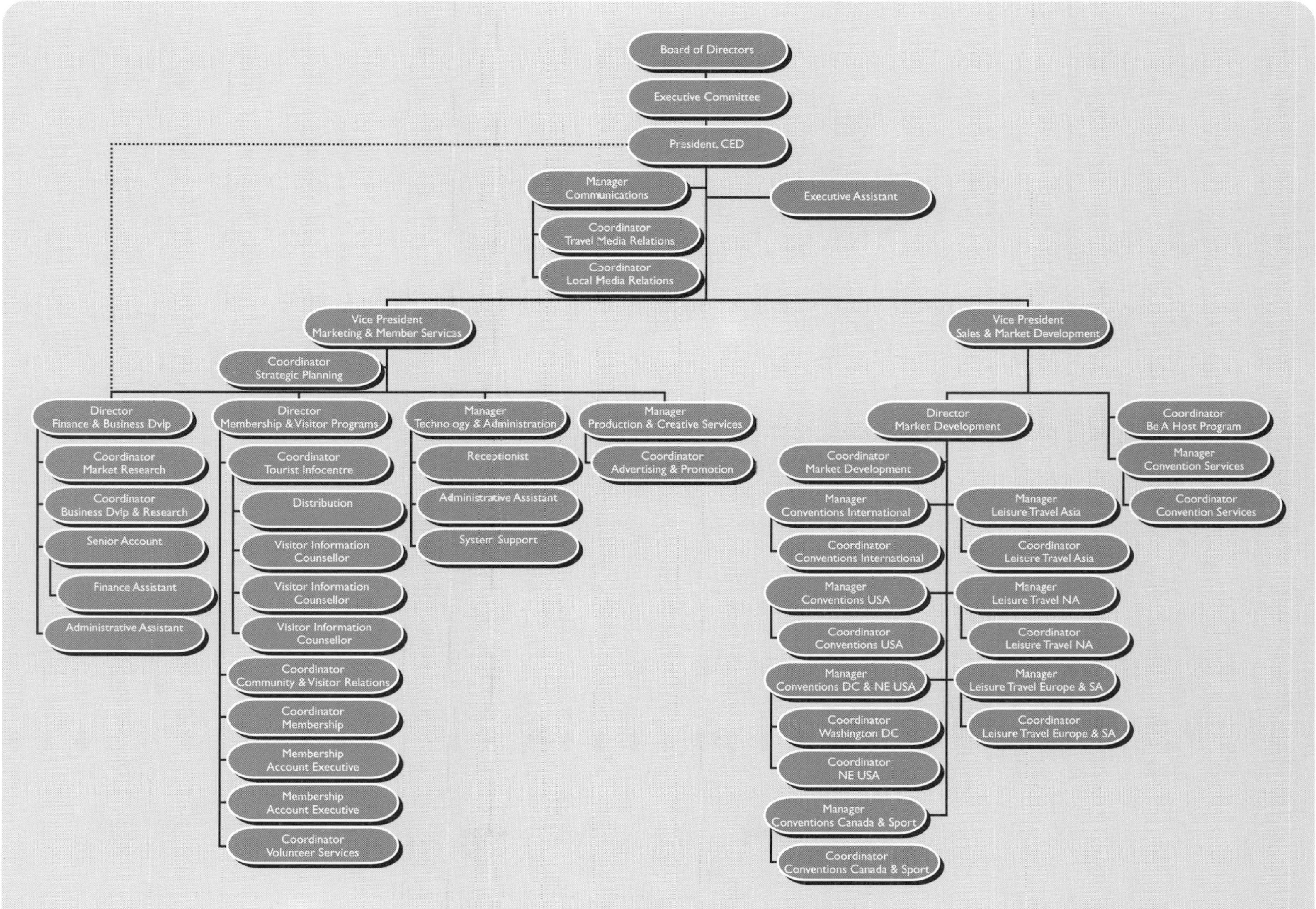

Source: The Greater Vancouver Convention and Visitors Bureau

The challenge for British convention and visitor bureaus is to achieve a similar status within their communities as their US and Canadian counterparts, though this in turn may demand a higher level of funding and resources than currently available – a true 'Catch–22' situation.

Research carried out in 1994 by the International Congress and Convention Association into 55 CVBs worldwide found that the average city convention bureau in Europe had six staff, compared with an average of 22 in non-European bureaus, which also had budgets on average 75 per cent higher. In many cases the reason for these differences is that non-European bureaus are responsible for leisure and business tourism, whereas European bureaus focus more specifically on the conventions market. In Europe, 82 per cent of city convention bureaus were part of the local city tourist organisation, whereas outside Europe this applied to only 11.7 per cent.

Convention and visitor bureaus provide a range of services, many free of charge, to conference organisers and meeting planners. They aim to offer a 'one-stop' enquiry point for their destination, with impartial advice and assistance. Such services are likely to include some or all of the following:

Pre-booking the event:

- literature and information
- venue location and selection advice
- availability checks
- rate negotiation
- provisional booking service
- familiarisation/inspection visits
- preparation of bid documents
- assistance with presentations to a selection committee/board
- negotiation of subventions and sponsorship.

Preparing for the event:

- block accommodation booking service for delegates
- coordination of the full range of support services including transport, registration, translation, office support. In some cases these will be provided in conjunction with a professional conference organiser (PCO) or destination management company (DMC)
- provision of 'Welcome Desks' for delegates at major points of entry
- promotional and PR support to maximise delegate numbers and increase awareness of the event in the host destination
- supply of delegate information packs and undertaking delegate mailings and confirmations
- planning partner programmes, social programmes, and pre- and post-conference tours.

During the event:

- welcome hosts
- PR support
- helpline support
- guided tours and contributions to social and partner programmes

- coordination of destination resources, including transport and entertainment
- civic welcome and recognition
- provision of tourist information
- handling travel enquiries and ticket sales
- registration.

After the event:

- post-event evaluation and follow-up research
- collective billing, budget finalisation and reconciliation
- consultancy support to the destination which will next host the conference.

Many of a bureau's marketing activities are implicit or explicit in the list of services it offers to conference organisers. A typical portfolio of activities for a British convention bureau will include some or all of the following, dependent upon staff and financial resources:

- *direct marketing* – particularly direct mail, but also telesales and, occasionally, with a sales person 'on the road'
- *print and audio-visual production* – compiling conference destination guides and other promotional print, as well as videos, CD-Roms and Internet sites
- *exhibition attendance* – taking stands at trade shows such as Confex, Confer, Meetings and Incentive Travel Show, EIBTM
- *overseas trade missions* – participation in overseas roadshows and workshops, often organised by the British Tourist Authority
- *familiarisation visits* – organising visits for groups of buyers and press representatives
- *receptions* – coordinating receptions, lunches, occasionally small workshops to which key clients, existing and potential, are invited
- *advertising* – in local and national press
- *public relations* – circulating information and releases to the media and often to influential community organisations
- *ambassador programmes* – identifying, recruiting, training and supporting key individuals in the local community (often university academics, hospital staff, leading industrialists, members of the business community, trade unionists) as 'ambassadors' for the destination, assisting them to bid for and attract the annual conference of the professional institution or trade union to which they belong. Other variations on ambassador programmes, like that operating in London, aim to recognise and publicly acknowledge particular initiatives undertaken by companies and organisations designed to attract more conference business to the destination, while Portsmouth's 'city ambassador' programme seeks to attract events by working through former citizens who have moved to live in other parts of the country or, indeed, other parts of the world.

Telford and Shropshire Conferences is a medium-sized conference bureau established in 1992. It has three full-time staff and a marketing budget of just under £50 000 for a two-year period, over £30 000 of which is contributed by the private sector in membership fees. Salary costs and office overheads are paid by Wrekin Council, which is the other major funding partner. Case Study 5.1 shows the range of services and benefits to be provided for its members during the two-year period 1996–98. The membership information shown in Case Study 5.1 was compiled in January 1996 and describes 'over £1 million worth of additional conference business placed within the county'. Significantly higher levels of business were placed over the ensuing 18-month period, with one particular exhibition generating around £3 million of economic benefit for Telford and the surrounding area.

Case Study 5.1   Telford and Shropshire Conferences, 1996–98

Membership Information

The principal activities of Telford and Shropshire Conferences are outlined below and together they provide a comprehensive and beneficial service for all members.

Launched four years ago, Telford and Shropshire Conferences is a consortium of over 40 venues, attractions and services within Shropshire who have invested in a county-wide promotional campaign aimed at increasing the volume and value of business tourism to Shropshire.

As a direct result of its most recent campaigns over £1 million worth of additional conference business has been placed within the county. This figure does not include delegate spend or any multiplier effect.

Membership of Telford and Shropshire Conferences for the next two year period commencing 1st April 1996 is now open. Your investment and membership commitment to Telford and Shropshire Conferences involves a comprehensive marketing campaign.

Telford and Shropshire Conferences has the following clear marketing objectives:-
1. To enhance Telford and Shropshire as a conference destination to Local, Regional and National Markets.
2. Increase the volume and value of conference business to Telford and Shropshire generally and particularly through the Conference Bureau.
3. Sell the tourism attractions and service providers within the area as a background for conferences and exhibitions.

In the last two years we have achieved a number of successes particularly in our hosted buyer initiatives in hosting over 60 quality conference buyers over three Familiarisation Tours and stimulating a great deal of interest from over 150 more who attended a series of business lunches in London, Birmingham and Manchester. This success in turn has created 373 direct enquiries through our venue location finding service, 240 of which were live enquiries, achieving a 20% conversion rate. Our client list includes British Telecom, P & H McLane Ltd, Rentokil, GEC Alsthom and The Royal College of Nursing.

Each of the major activities undertaken by Telford and Shropshire Conferences hold principal benefits to members either individually or collectively. Carefully selected areas of activity which closely meet the potential conference buyers' or conference agencies' requirements and methods of decision taking are identified. The area's strengths are strongly promoted: the accessibility, no traffic jams, the diversity of the county, technology, modern business parks, birthplace of industry, tranquillity and the quality and range of venues, services and attractions available.

All areas of work identified by the Telford and Shropshire Conferences Consortium have a clear role which is not and could not be undertaken by individual members.

These major marketing activities are steered by a Marketing Group. The Marketing Group are Conference Members who represent a cross section of the entire membership and any member of Telford and Shropshire Conferences can join the group meetings held on a bi-monthly basis. ▷

Principal Benefit to Members

1. The Conference Brochure

The principal marketing tool of Telford and Shropshire Conference. A quality brochure (with a two year shelf life) which incorporates features on all members. Many improvements will be seen in the next version including a stronger welcome and introduction to the venue location finding service. A more comprehensive introduction to the destination, enhancement to the content and order of the check and summary listings and clearer and individual attraction and service features will also be provided

To promote Telford and Shropshire as a conference destination and to promote members individually. And to promote and complement the Venue Location Finding Service.

2. Venue Location Finding Service through a Central Conference Desk

To provide a comprehensive 'one stop shop' for the conference buyer, assisting them to find the ideal venue for their event. Collating information on availability and rates from **all** suitable venues and presentation of a written proposal within an agreed time scale. (24 hour basis) Increasing the awareness of the service benefits to existing and potential clients.
Further development of The Code of Practice which ensures an efficient and effective response system is maintained and well known to all members.
This serves three purposes:-

a) Lifting the profile of Telford and Shropshire Conferences within the industry.
b) Provides the client with a professionally managed response system with agreed timescales.
c) Provides an efficient 'feedback' system to each member on contacts and business to date.

Increased awareness of venues, attractions and services and the benefits of Shropshire to existing and potential clients, generating more new and repeat business enquiries for members.

3. Direct Mail Campaigns

Locally, Regionally and Nationally. Original and creative campaigns aimed at conference buyers, introducing new and reminding existing clients of Shropshire.

The introduction on a large scale basis of Telford and Shropshire to a national audience backed up by The Conference Brochure which educates buyers to individual venues, attractions and services offered in Shropshire. ▷

Telford and Shropshire Conferences, 1996–98 continued

Principal Benefit to Members

4. Business Lunches

The hosting of a series of business lunches aimed at conference buyers and agents to be held in major conurbations – London, Birmingham and Manchester – with the aim of promoting Telford and Shropshire as the ideal event destination. In London and the South East further development of the business lunch will be undertaken with workshop and presentation sessions for members on an individual or themed basis.

Offers members the opportunity to meet regional and national buyers in business or workshop environment.

5. Breakfast Seminars/ Business Lunches aimed at the Local Market

The hosting of a series of events aimed at local conference buyers and agents from Shropshire, North Wales, South Cheshire, South Staffordshire and the West/West Midlands.

Offers members the opportunity to meet quality buyers at a series of events held in Shropshire venues, which members may not have the resources to co-ordinate on an individual basis, encouraging local buyers to buy locally particularly for single day events.

6. Familiarisation Tours and Individual Inspection Visits

Hosting of conference buyers and agents locally, regionally and nationally over a one, two or three day period.
Particularly encouraging local buyers to attend a one day inspection.

To bring quality buyers to visit members' venues or attractions without the burden of full administrative work followed up with access to the database to identify buyers who meet the members' preferred criteria.

7. Development and Publishing of Telford and Shropshire Newsletter

Produced twice a year aimed at all market sectors containing features and profiles on venue types, facilities and services.

A complement to and update of the main conference brochure which provides members with the opportunity of a direct source of contact with quality conference buyers.

8. Attendance at Key Trade Exhibitions

Confex held annually in February at Earls Court, London.

Package One – Represented on destination stand and access to database contacts (cost included in Membership Fee)
Package Two – Exhibit at Show (additional cost to Membership Fee)

▷

Principal Benefit to Members

To co-ordinate the Telford and Shropshire Conferences co-operative stand and related activities.

To provide a cost effective opportunity to exhibit for members who may otherwise be unable to do so.

Confer held annually at Kensington Town Hall, London usually in October and organised by The British Association of Conference Destinations.
To attend as a conference destination promoting Telford and Shropshire. Organised by The British Association of Conference Destinations.

To provide a cost effective opportunity for members to exhibit or have brochure representation who may otherwise be unable to do so. Also to provide all members with quality database contacts and profile information for follow up.

9. Press/PR Publicity

To co-ordinate on a regular basis press releases to gain maximum media coverage in local and regional press and national trade magazines. To co-ordinate Familiarisation Tours for representatives of the trade press.

Opportunity to gain coverage and publicity in a variety of media.

10. Database

To provide members with the opportunity to access the conference database on a 'managed basis' identifying target market areas compatible with member product. Access would be at minimal cost in label format.

Opportunity to access and direct mail quality buyers as a follow up service to the destination marketing already undertaken.

11. Local Ambassador Links

Establish and support increased networking opportunities, encouraging more active participation in Telford and Shropshire Conferences by local associations, agencies, businesses and local people/celebrities connected directly or indirectly with our product for mutual benefit. These groups could include Telford Development Agency, Chambers of Commerce, Business Link and other such bodies.

Opportunity for working partnerships, promotional activities and increase awareness of venues, attractions and services via a local ambassador link.

12. Overseas Activity

To establish a forum of interested members to discuss opportunities and to agree a co-ordinated campaign for overseas marketing.

Provide access to markets which may otherwise be difficult to reach.

Telford and Shropshire Conferences, 1996–98 continued

Principal Benefit to Members

13. Association Membership of British Association of Conference Destinations (B.A.C.D.)

Membership through Telford and Shropshire Conferences maximising on the destinations promotion provided through a national association.

Access to enquiries received via BACD either directly through their venue location finding service, through their database or via their trade show 'Confer'.

14. The Internet

Develop co-ordinated access of Telford and Shropshire Conferences to The Internet.

Provides access collectively through a market which may otherwise be difficult to reach.

15. Telesales

To undertake using the present database telesales to re-establish leads and identify potential business.

To gain a live business lead or enquiry without undertaking the time consuming task of a telesales promotional campaign on an individual basis.

16. Member Support Activity

a) Provision of a Bed Booking Service for the Business Tourism Sector
Liaise with The Telford International Centre to establish a Bed Booking Service as an extension of the Conference Desk provided on a county-wide scale for delegates attending large conferences and exhibitions.

b) Research
Monitor through research projects the effectiveness of the marketing schemes undertaken by Telford and Shropshire Conferences and collate relevant statistics on conference business in Shropshire.

c) Communication Development
Assessing the needs of member support activities and communication through The Marketing Group.

The provision of a back up service for members on a wide range of activities to support members individually.

d) Additional Revenue Raising

Explore mechanisms for additional revenue raising activities outside of the membership through sponsorship.

e) Co-operative Advertising Opportunities

Where felt advantageous to jointly finance advertising activities. The membership to be kept updated of opportunities arising.

For further information please contact:

Sue Venables
Telford and Shropshire Conferences
Civic Offices, Telford
Shropshire. TF3 4LD

Tel: 01952 203029
Fax: 01952 203042

Source: Telford and Shropshire Conferences

Conference offices and conference desks

Conference offices (or conference desks) are normally established as part of a local authority's tourism marketing activity, where there is no convention bureau in operation. The staff, typically a conference officer with one assistant, are directly employed by the local authority and will usually be located in a department involved with economic development or leisure services. In some cases they can tap into other staff resources (computer and administrative services, marketing, inward investment) available within the broader local authority structure.

Conference offices undertake many of the same marketing activities as convention bureaus, and offer similar services to conference and event organisers. The main differences between a conference office and convention bureau relate to structure and funding. A conference office does not have a formal membership, but it may coordinate the activities of a conference or tourism association within the destination, bringing together the main conference players to collaborate in joint marketing activities, for which financial or in-kind contributions are required. The conference office staff do not report to a management board but to managers and councillors within a local authority department, although where a conference association has been established there is also a need to report back on the success of the marketing programmes. The budget for the conference office is determined by the appropriate council committee, but is often supplemented by private sector contributions. Not infrequently, the conference officer may also have direct responsibility for the promotion of one or more civic buildings as conference venues.

Case Study 5.2 provides a description of the objectives, structures and activities of the Newcastle Conference Office.

Case Study 5.2 Newcastle Conference Office

The Tourism and Conference Office is part of the Economic Development Unit of Newcastle City Council. The Council itself is committed to the regeneration of the economy of Newcastle, with the creation of new jobs, diversification of the economy and enhanced prosperity for its businesses and residents as main priorities.

The conference function was initially set up in 1978 with one member of staff and was expanded in 1986 with the appointment of a Tourism Officer. In 1997 the Tourism and Conference Office had a staff of four, two working on leisure tourism and two dedicated to conference marketing.

The annual budget for conference activities was £40 000 in 1997, divided evenly between conference destination marketing and the provision of civic hospitality to conferences being held in the City. During 1996–97, the Office received European funding for additional marketing activities, including marketing overseas. Further funding is provided by local suppliers, with support in kind (meals, accommodation, transport, etc., for visitors) and financial contributions to specific marketing projects, notably the conference guide to the City ('Venue Newcastle').

Marketing activities include attendance at major exhibitions (UK only), direct mail, advertising and feature support, familiarisation visits for individuals and groups, and the production of conference literature and information. The Newcastle Conference Office provides a single point of contact for conference organisers and offers 'friendly, helpful advice' on suitable venues throughout Newcastle. All services provided by the Office are completely free of any fees, charges or commissions to both organisers and venues alike.

The Conference Office deals with approximately 1000 enquiries a year, an increase of 350 per cent on the early 1990s. Confirmed bookings amount to some 15 per cent of the total number of enquiries taken within 12 months, with a further 10 per cent being converted within 24 months. The figure does not include bookings made directly with venues, a practice actively encouraged by the Conference Office. During 1996–97 a detailed conference enquiry handling system was developed which provides comprehensive marketing information as well as management reports to monitor business activity levels and performance. The Office seeks to provide a reply to all enquiries within 24 hours, giving personalised information and quotations.

Within the local conference industry, the Conference Office is established as a central resource for information, advice, guidance and general support. New managers and senior staff joining venues in the City regularly turn to the Conference Office as one of their first ports of call, both for practical assistance and for a general overview of the market locally.

Priorities for the Conference Office (as at July 1997) included:

- further computerisation of enquiry systems to increase efficiency
- market research
- an increased number of familiarisation visits
- the generation of more repeat business
- development of an Accommodation Reservation Service
- overseas marketing in Norway.

National destination marketing

The role of national conference destination marketing is undertaken by a variety of bodies which differ from country to country. In some cases these bodies equate to a national convention bureau – and frequently contain the words 'convention bureau' in their name

– and have many features in common with the city convention bureaus described earlier in this chapter. In other cases they are fully public sector organisations funded and administered within the central government structure.

The examples which follow, summarising some of the leading national conference destination marketing organisations, highlight the variations which exist but also point to a number of common characteristics.

United Kingdom

Within the United Kingdom, there are two national conference marketing organisations: the British Tourist Authority, operating primarily in overseas markets, and the British Association of Conference Destinations, operating principally in the domestic marketplace. Scotland, Wales and Northern Ireland also have their own national conference bureaus (in the case of Wales this is a Business Travel Department), subsumed within their National Tourist Boards, while the islands of Guernsey, Jersey and the Isle of Man also have independent conference marketing organisations. The marketing of England to the conference sector is now a joint operation with the British Tourist Authority Business Tourism Department. Further details of these organisations are given in Chapter 3.

Germany: German Convention Bureau (GCB)

The German Convention Bureau (GCB) is the marketing, not-for-profit organisation for the solicitation of international meetings for Germany's congress and convention industry. Founded in 1973, the GCB was established to provide impartial advice and suggestions to meeting planners concerning facilities, sites, accommodation, and programmes in Germany.

The GCB, based in Frankfurt with nine staff and with an overseas office in New York, is a single umbrella organisation representing the leading companies in the German meetings industry. Its 200 or so affiliate members include the principal congress cities, convention centres and hotels, professional conference/congress organisers (PCOs) and other convention service providers, Lufthansa German Airlines, German Railways and the German National Tourist Board.

The GCB arranges conference services in Germany for clients around the world. It also works in close cooperation with German representatives of international associations and organisations and with meeting planners of associations, agencies and companies from abroad. Services include the preparation of tailor-made bids and proposals, free of charge, for all types of meetings and conferences, with details of suggested venues, PCOs, pre- and post-convention tours, menus and banquets, speakers and government department support. Through its links with Lufthansa, it can offer discounted fares to those attending exhibitions and major conferences in Germany, as well as special congress tickets for use on German Railways. It has also negotiated discounted rates with its car rental affiliates for conference and exhibition visitors.

The GCB publishes its complimentary 'Convention Planner's Guide to Germany' (the 1998–99 edition runs to 194 pages), which can be ordered via its Internet home page. The home page also provides a general survey of convention services and news from the meetings industry. The GCB also organises an annual domestic trade exhibition ('Meetings Made in Germany'), which is held in Bonn.

Contact: German Convention Bureau, Münchener Strasse 48, D-60329 Frankfurt/Main, Germany (tel: 49–69–2429300; fax: 49–69–24293026; e-mail: info@gcb.de; Internet: http://www.gcb.de/).

Finland: Helsinki-Finland Congress Bureau

Helsinki-Finland Congress Bureau was founded in 1974 as a not-for-profit marketing organisation promoting Finland as a conference destination. The activities of the Bureau are financed by the Ministry of Trade and Industry, 19 major congress cities and 12 major congress centres. In addition, other members of the Bureau include hotels, travel agencies, transport businesses and conference service companies, giving a total of 90 members (as at July 1997). It is separate from, but works with, the Finnish national tourist organisation, which has nine offices throughout Europe.

The Bureau has seven staff: a managing director, a marketing manager, two project managers, a communications manager and two secretaries. Its Board of Directors consists of 14 members: six representatives from different member cities and eight from the conference industry. The City of Helsinki has a permanent seat, and is the second major sponsor of the Bureau. Helsinki hosts annually more than 50 per cent of all international congresses organised in Finland.

The Bureau, whose principal target groups are international associations,

- helps with planning
- gives information on conference facilities and services in Finland
- assists organisers to find suitable venues, accommodation, and transport
- makes preliminary reservations
- provides promotional material, such as films, videos, slides and brochures
- invites organisers to undertake inspection visits
- provides general information on conferences and exhibitions in Finland, as well as monitoring international events in a systematic way
- carries out studies and surveys and prepares statistics and forecasts.

The Bureau's regular publications include: *Congress News* (in Finnish and English), *International Conferences and Exhibitions in Finland*, a meeting planner's guide (in Finnish and English), and *Sensational Finland* (a brochure published in English, German and French).

Contact: Helsinki-Finland Congress Bureau, Fabianinkatu 4 B 11, FIN-00130 Helsinki, Finland (tel: 358–9–6689–540; fax: 358–9–6689–5410; e-mail; hfcb@hfcb.fi).

Japan

Convention and incentive travel promotion is the responsibility of the Japan Convention Bureau (JCB), a specialist department of the Japan National Tourist Organisation (JNTO). The JCB was first established in 1965, as a joint initiative with local public entities and other interested parties, and was merged with JNTO the following year.

In 1994 the Japanese Diet (parliament) approved a special law called the 'International Convention Promotion Law'. JNTO has subsequently restructured its Japan Convention Bureau to establish a cooperative relationship with 42 government-designated 'International Convention Cities' which are keen to attract more international meetings and events.

The reorganised Japan Convention Bureau comprises two departments in JNTO's head office in Tokyo: International Marketing Department, and Promotion and Support Department, the latter being responsible for domestic marketing within Japan. Operating alongside these two departments are two overseas marketing offices, one in New York and the other in London. Each is staffed by three convention specialists. Additionally, a convention manager has been appointed from the directorial/managerial staff of JNTO's 14 overseas offices to create a worldwide marketing network to promote Japan as an international convention destination.

In 1995, Japan Congress and Convention Bureau (JCCB) was established with the aim of promoting Japan as a location for international conventions and developing the convention industries in Japan. JCCB is composed of convention cities, convention bureaus, convention-related industries, the Ministry of Transport and JNTO. JNTO provides the Secretariat office and JCB the staff for JCCB's operation. In 1996, three new destinations were added to the list of government-designated 'International Convention Cities', bringing the total number to 45. This list does not include Tokyo, even though Tokyo is one of Japan's leading international meeting destinations, partly because the city does not possess a convention bureau or specialist business tourism department (although there are proposals to establish a convention bureau during 1998) but chiefly because the main aim of the Bureau's convention promotional activities is to achieve the decentralisation of international meeting traffic.

Japan Convention Bureau is not a membership organisation but its activities are partly funded by annual contributions from the 45 International Convention Cities. These are set contributions, at two levels, depending on the size of the cities concerned.

Marketing activities include market research and the publication of statistics, participation in convention industry trade shows, organising sales missions to the USA and Europe, coordinating an annual study tour (familiarisation visit), advertising, producing a detailed guide 'Convention Destination Japan', as well as newsletters and events calendars.

Contact: Japan Convention Bureau, 2–10–1, Yurakucho, Chiyoda-ku, Tokyo 100, Japan (tel: 03–3216–2905; fax: 03–3216–1978; e-mail: convention@jnto.go.jp). London office: Japan Convention Bureau, Heathcoat House, 20 Savile Row, London W1X 1AE (tel: 0171–439–3458; fax: 0171–734–4290; e-mail: jntolon@dircon.co.uk).

Spain

In a similar way to the United Kingdom, Spain has two organisations promoting the country to the conference market: Spain Tourism Board ('Turespaña') and Spain Convention Bureau.

Spain Tourism Board ('Turespaña')

Turespaña is a central government-run body under the auspices of the Ministry of Economics and Finance. It does not, therefore, have a membership structure and its staff are mostly civil servants.

Meetings and Incentive Travel is one of the sectors or products on which Turespaña concentrates its resources (the others being Sun and Beach, Sports and Nature, and Cities), although it has only had this involvement since 1995. Promotional activity is undertaken in conjunction with the 27 Spanish Tourist Offices overseas (18 in Europe, eight in America, and one in Japan), which assist with the provision of local market research and intelligence. Each overseas office has a business travel specialist dedicated to meetings and incentive travel.

Meetings and Incentive Travel sector promotional activities include organising the participation of the Spanish public and private sectors in international exhibitions, organising business workshops, and coordinating familiarisation visits in partnership with local authorities, convention bureaus or regional governments. Publications include 'Spain Land of Congresses', a comprehensive guide giving full details of the main conference facilities and support services offered by individual cities.

Contact: Turespaña, José Lázaro Galdiano 6, 28036 Madrid, Spain (tel: 34–1–343–35–00; fax: 34–1–343–34–46).

Spain Convention Bureau

The Spain Convention Bureau (SCB) is a non-profit organisation established by 28 convention towns and cities in Spain and integrated into the Spanish Federation of Municipalities and Provinces. It has two staff (a director and a secretary) and is financed by the members, who provide sufficient budget to maintain the office and cover administrative expenses. It occasionally undertakes special projects financed by Turespaña and the European Union.

The objectives of the Bureau are:

- to promote Spain and its towns in the national and international conference and incentive markets
- to encourage the sharing of information, statistics and expertise between members
- to promote courses and seminars to increase the knowledge and professionalism of its members
- to study the national and international conference markets in order to improve the marketing policies and practices of each member destination.

The main activities of the Bureau are:

- to participate in exhibitions and workshops jointly with Turespaña
- to provide information about the infrastructure, venues and facilities of its members
- to provide and exchange statistics about the conference and incentive markets in Spain
- to produce a conference calendar for Spain.

Contact: Spain Convention Bureau, Calle Nuncio 8, E-28005 Madrid, Spain (tel: 34–1–365–94–01; fax: 34–1–365–54–82).

Austria

Austria has two organisations involved in conference marketing, the Austrian National Tourist Office and the Austrian Convention Bureau.

Austrian National Tourist Office Despite the relatively small share of incentive and conference travel in the total tourism figures (2–5 per cent of overnight stays can be attributed to this sector), the Austrian National Tourist Office (ANTO) places special emphasis on a consistent and well-targeted promotion to the sector because the conference and incentive visitor is found to spend four times as much as the average tourist.

The ANTO is a non-profit organisation whose members comprise the Federal Ministry of Economic Affairs, the nine federal provinces and the Austrian Federal Economic Chamber. The President of the Austrian National Tourist Office is the Minister of Economic Affairs of the day. Sixty per cent of the budget is funded by the Federal Government, 20 per cent by the provinces and 20 per cent by the Austrian Federal Economic Chamber.

ANTO has convention specialists in its overseas offices in New York, Frankfurt, London and the Benelux countries. At its head office in Vienna, further resources were given to conference and incentive marketing in 1997 via the creation of a coordinating division for conventions, incentives and congresses within the Sales Promotion Department.

Contact: Austrian National Tourist Office, Margaretenstrasse 1, A-1040 Wien, Austria (tel: 43–1–588–66–269; fax: 43–1–588–66–41).

Austrian Convention Bureau The Austrian Convention Bureau (ACB) has some 50 members, including convention and exhibition centres, convention destinations and regional tourist organisations, convention hotels, convention agencies/PCOs, airlines, and ancillary suppliers. Members pay a standard annual membership fee and then pay extra to buy into specific marketing activities of their choice.

For conference organisers ACB offers a number of free services, including information and advice on convention venues, support in organising events, familiarisation visits, assistance with contacts and support services.

ACB maintains a database of meeting planners and organisers in Austria, and also operates a press service to inform its members and the wider public about news and developments in the Austrian convention industry. The Bureau is beginning to adopt a more active lobbying role on behalf of the industry. It also holds regular meetings among members for educational and networking purposes.

Contact: Austrian Convention Bureau, Neubaugürtel 38/8, A-1070 Vienna, Austria (tel: 43–1–522–88–85; fax: 43–1–522–88–89).

Hong Kong

Conference destination marketing for Hong Kong is undertaken by the Hong Kong Convention and Incentive Travel Bureau (HKCITB). There is no specific membership of the Bureau as the Bureau itself is an integral part of the Hong Kong Tourist Association (HKTA), a quasi-government body for promoting tourism and convention business. The HKTA membership includes major conference venues, hotels, tour operators, PCOs/DMCs, and retailers. There is no separately published budget information for the Bureau but, in the financial year 1995–96, HKTA spent approximately £18.5 million on promotions, advertising, literature production, research and development.

HKCITB is headquartered in Hong Kong but also has three dedicated overseas offices in Chicago, Sydney and London. The work of the Bureau is divided into two sections, one to cover incentive travel and corporate meetings, the other to research for association events and exhibitions. HKTA has a further 16 offices worldwide which can assist in the planning and promotion of events to be held in Hong Kong.

HKCITB offers impartial advice and practical assistance to conference organisers at every stage of planning their events, including:

1. identification of suitable venues and selection of accommodation
2. coordination of inspections of conference facilities by decision makers
3. sourcing reliable service suppliers such as airlines, PCOs, exhibition contractors
4. suggestions for social, sightseeing or accompanying persons' programmes
5. ideas and contacts for gifts and convention materials suppliers
6. promotions to delegates, and participation in planning committees
7. advising on customs and immigration procedures.

HKCITB publishes a range of support literature, including a convention planner's guide, *Coming Conferences and Exhibitions in Hong Kong (1997–2006)* and a promotional material catalogue.

Contact: Hong Kong Convention and Incentive Travel Bureau, Hong Kong Tourist Association, 9–11/F, Citicorp Centre, 18 Whitfield Road, North Point, Hong Kong (tel: 852–2807–6543; fax: 852–2806–0303; Website: http://www.hkta.org). London office: Hong Kong Convention and Incentive Travel Bureau, Hong Kong Tourist Association, 125 Pall Mall, 3rd Floor, London SW1Y 5EA (tel: 0171–930–4775; fax: 0171–930–4777; e-mail: hktalon@hkta.org).

Conference Venue Marketing

It is very difficult for an individual conference venue to market itself effectively by operating on its own. Venues seeking to establish a market presence must contend with factors such as the scale of the competition (several thousand other venues in Britain alone), the substantial costs of marketing (both in human and financial resources), and the predisposition of buyers to buy location first.

It is for these reasons that most venues work in partnership with the destination in which they are located to generate awareness, and enquiries from potential clients. The venues build links with the appropriate destination marketing organisation, be this a convention and visitor bureau or conference office, an area or regional tourist board, and/or a national tourism organisation. Many venues are also members of marketing consortiums (groupings of similar properties interested in the same types of clients) which give them a higher market profile and through which they engage in collaborative marketing activities. Examples of the major consortiums operating in the conference industry include:

● *hotel groups* such as Granada/Forte, Jarvis, Hilton, Moat House, Thistle, Stakis, Holiday Inn and Swallow. These are not strictly consortiums as they are groups of hotels under common management systems. Most, if not all, have central reservations and marketing departments which undertake national and international marketing campaigns and which control the promotional activities of the individual properties to a greater or lesser degree. Even so, the majority of hotels within these chains are also allowed some discretion and budget to engage in their own marketing campaigns, for which the broad strategy and promotional materials are determined by head office. Over recent years, all of the large chains have developed their own branded conference product (see 'branding' later in this chapter).

● *British Universities Accommodation Consortium (BUAC)* and *Connect Venues* are consortiums of academic venues, the former with over 60 venues in membership and the latter representing more than a hundred universities and colleges. BUAC and Connect produce directories of their member venues, organise their own trade shows as well as taking stands at other exhibitions, provide a one-stop enquiry service, and undertake other marketing activities on behalf of, or in conjunction with, their members.

● *Best Western, Consort Hotels Group* and *Minotel* are marketing consortiums for privately owned hotel properties.

Best Western is the world's largest global hotel brand, with over 3600 independent hotels in membership worldwide (and over 220 in the United Kingdom). It is a non-profit making organisation whose sole purpose is to enhance the success and profitability of members. It has reservations centres across the world with fully automated links to global distribution systems. Its recruitment brochure claims that 'Best Western brand markets to, and attracts, a bigger universe of customers than any single property on its own could ever hope to reach'. In Britain the consortium focuses on quality 4-star and 3-star hotels. For the conference and meetings market, 'Best Western First Place' is the consortium's venue sourcing service with a national conference sales network. Conference business placed through this service grew by almost 200 per cent over the period 1993–96. Best Western also offers marketing opportunities for its members, such as a presence at trade shows like Confex.

Contact: Best Western Hotels, Vine House, 143 London Road, Kingston upon Thames, Surrey KT2 6NA (tel: 0181–541–0050; fax: 0181–547–2653).

Consort Hotels Group was established in 1981 and now has almost 180 members throughout Britain. Though UK-based, the consortium has recently purchased a 25 per cent share holding in SA Neotel France, bringing 57 Neotel properties under the Consort banner. Marketing links are also in place with similar consortiums in Ireland, Germany and Sweden for which bookings can be made. Consort operates a central reservations system with fully automated links to the Global Distribution Systems, complementing a centralised sales and marketing service. Consort also administers a dedicated conference booking service, 'Meetings-to-Order', a service which will always seek to offer a venue even if a Consort hotel is not available. Consort hotels range from 12 to 200 rooms and from city centre to countryside locations. All hotels are inspected by the Automobile Association on behalf of the consortium, with the minimum requirement for membership being two, three or four star, 64 per cent.

Contact: Consort Hotels Group, Consort House, Amy Johnson Way, Clifton Moor, York YO3 4XT (tel: 44 (0)1904–695400; fax: 44 (0)1904–695401; Meetings-to-Order tel: 0345–697637).

Minotel is a consortium of 700 privately owned hotels in 30 countries throughout Europe. Almost 200 of the hotels are in Britain. Not all of the hotels offer conference facilities but those that do can be accessed via a one-stop booking service.

Contact: Minotel Central Reservations, 37 Springfield Road, Blackpool, Lancashire FY1 1PZ (tel: 44 (0)1253–292000; fax: 44 (0)1253–291191).

Conventions Great Britain is a unique consortium of the UK's major conference and exhibition centres together with the British Tourist Authority. The group was formed to promote the UK as the best choice for large-scale international conferences. Partners of the consortium fulfil criteria which demonstrate that they provide meeting facilities for a minimum of 1000 delegates, with additional facilities, exhibition space and infrastructure sufficient to meet the needs of the international conference and exhibition organiser. Current partners are: Bournemouth International Centre, Brighton Centre, NEC Group (Birmingham), Edinburgh International Conference Centre, Harrogate International Centre, Queen Elizabeth II Conference Centre, Scottish Exhibition and Conference Centre, St David's Hall (Cardiff) and the British Tourist Authority.

Contact: Peter Weston, CGB Secretariat, c/o PMW International Ltd, Dresden House, 51 High Street, Evesham, Worcestershire WR11 4DA (tel: 44(0)1386–422408; fax: 44 (0)1386–422465).

Other consortiums exist (*Conference Centres of Excellence* is an example, with over 20 dedicated residential conference centres, all independently owned and located country-wide), but the common thread which links all together is enhanced access to markets which, operating in isolation, they would find difficult and extremely expensive to penetrate. Such consortiums also generate buying power which, again, would not be available to them on their own.

Branding

Forte Hotels (now owned by Granada) pioneered a branded conference product in the early 1990s when it launched 'Venue Guarantee' as a standard package available at conference hotels across the Forte Group. Since then most, if not all, the major hotel chains have introduced their own conference brand, examples being: 'Meeting 2000' (Hilton National), 'Conferenceplan' (Thistle Hotels), 'Assured Meetings' (Stakis Hotels), and 'Modern Meeting' (Moat House Hotels).

There are certain variations in each branded product: the emphasis, for example, with 'Modern Meeting' is on high-specification, purpose-designed conference and meeting rooms whereas 'Meeting 2000' promotes a more broadly-based though dedicated conference facility and level of service. Overall, however, there is more common ground than distinctive features in these products, which are usually accompanied by a money-back guarantee if a hotel fails to deliver on any aspect of its quality-assured service. An example of such a guarantee is the Moat House Hotels' 'Seal of Assurance' shown in Figure 5.6.

Figure 5.6 Moat House Hotels Seal of Assurance (conference guarantee).

SEAL of
ASSURANCE
CONFERENCE GUARANTEE

We are determined to provide you, our conference customers, with the highest of standards. It is our goal to give you the best available service from start to finish.

Not only will we make this promise . . . we are also prepared to guarantee it with 'The Moat House Seal of Assurance'.

THE MOAT HOUSE SEAL OF ASSURANCE

Your Enquiry
1. Your enquiry, right from the start, will be looked after by professional dedicated Conference Managers.
2. Within two working days of contacting the hotel, you will receive a brochure, price details and proposal letter (where appropriate).
3. Our terms and conditions of business will always be included with our brochure and proposal letter.
4. You will always receive an invitation to visit the hotel, to view the facilities and discuss your requirements, at the first point of your enquiry.
5. We will always suggest conference rooms and package prices which are genuinely suitable for your particular event.

Pricing
1. You will not find any hidden extras. All prices – for packages and additional services – will be clearly presented, in plain English so they can be clearly understood.

Your Booking
1. We will confirm the full details of your booking, in writing, within three working days of a verbal booking being made.
2. At least three working days before your conference, we will contact you and check final details, changes and any amendments you may wish to make.
3. We will not depart from your confirmed details and timings unless this is agreed with you in advance.
4. Your billing arrangements and account details will be agreed when you confirm your booking. We will only make any changes, or supplementary charges, on receipt of signed authorisation from your nominated signatories.

The Service
1. A senior member of the staff will look after the smooth running of your event every day. They will meet you when you arrive and check with you that all details and timings are as you want.
2. Your meals and refreshments will be served promptly at the times you have requested.
3. Your main conference room and syndicate rooms will be serviced and refreshed during all meal breaks.
4. Telephone messages, faxes and E.Mails will be given immediate attention and delivered promptly according to your chosen system.
5. We will provide clear instructions on fire and safety procedures before your conference starts. If there are any planned fire drills or alarm tests during the conference, we will tell you about these in advance.

The Facilities
1. Your conference rooms will be correctly set up, in line with your specified requirements, at the agreed time before your conference is due to start. If you need to change anything at the last minute, we will do everything possible to do this for you.
2. Audio visual equipment will be fully tested and in good working order. If you would like, we will provide a demonstration of how the equipment works before your conference starts.
3. We will ensure that all heating, lighting and air conditioning (where available) is working properly for you. We will also explain all the controls to you before your conference starts.
4. The name of the event or your company, will be displayed on the hotel's notice board clearly, showing which conference rooms you will be in. Unless, of course, you would prefer total privacy and have requested otherwise.

The Bill
1. Your bill will be sent out no later than five working days after the conference is over. It will clearly reflect your written quotation plus any extra charges which you have authorised.
2. Extra charges will be clearly itemised and will only be charged if you, or your nominated signatories approved them.
3. If you have any queries, we will address these for you within five working days.

Your Money Back Guarantee – 'The Moat House Seal of Assurance'
1. If we fail to deliver any service covered by this conference guarantee, we will remove the charges relating to those elements of your bill.

Figure 5.6 (cont.)

TERMS & CONDITIONS FOR
CONFERENCE AND ASSOCIATED EVENTS

Definitions

'The hotel' and 'we' means the property(ies) for which a contract is agreed. The property is owned/managed by the company(ies) whose name(s) will appear on the contract which you will be asked to sign. Their registered office will also be stated on the contract document.

'The client' and 'your' means the organising body/company and organiser responsible for commissioning of and payment for the event, and will be stated as such on the contract document. Unless we agree otherwise in writing, the contract will be personal to you and you may not assign it.

'The contract' means the agreement between the hotel and the client for a specific booking or series of bookings. These terms & conditions will form part of the contract together with any other items stated in the contract. The contract will be governed by English Law.

Charges and Payment

1. The hotel requires at least 14 days notice prior to arrival date to arrange any credit facilities, and reserves the right to refuse credit. Credit accounts must not exceed their credit limit at any time.
2. Payment is due for credit accounts 14 days after date of invoice. Payment must be in pounds sterling (UKl) payable as directed in the contract.
3. In the event of payment becoming overdue, interest at 2.5% per annum above the current National Westminster base rate will be added to your account.
4. Should a deposit or pre-payment be required for any event, this will be specified on the contract.

Confirmation by the client

5. All bookings will be considered as provisional until the contract is signed by both the client and the hotel. Once the contract is signed by both parties, all such facilities, services, food and beverages reserved on your behalf will be subject to the terms and conditions of the contract.
6. The contract must be returned by the client and received by the hotel within 5 working days of the date of issue or, if such time is not available, prior to the date of arrival, within a maximum of 48 hours. If the contract is not received by the hotel within this period, the hotel reserves the right to release the provisional booking and re-let the facilities.
7. Numbers must be advised to the hotel at the time of verbal confirmation and will be identified on the contract. Final timings, menus and any special requests must be confirmed to the hotel at least 10 days prior to arrival.

Amendments by the client

8. Amendments to guest numbers and/or arrangements must be confirmed to the hotel in writing.
9. Reductions in the duration or contracted value of the booking shall be subject to the hotel's cancellation policy.
10. No charges will be made for any reductions in numbers of less than 10% from those stated on the contract, providing they are received in writing by the hotel at least 14 days prior to arrival.
11. Should a reduction in numbers of 10% or more be made at any time prior to the event, the hotel will first endeavour to re-sell any facilities and services released, to a similar value. In the event that the released facilities and services cannot be re-sold, then any reductions of 10% or more shall be subjected to the hotel's cancellation policy.
12. Final numbers within the terms stated in clauses 10 and 11 must be notified to the hotel at least 48 hours prior to the arrival. These will be the minimum number for which the client will be charged.

Cancellation by the client

13. In the unfortunate circumstances that you have to cancel or postpone your confirmed booking at any time prior to the event, the hotel will make every effort to re-sell the facilities on your behalf. The hotel's cancellation policy is 90% on contracted accommodation and room hire revenue and 65% on contracted food and beverage revenue, being our loss of profit.
14. Any cancellation, postponements or partial cancellation should be advised to the management of the hotel, in the first instance verbally. You will be advised at that stage, of a cancellation reference number. We also request that cancellations are put in writing by the client.
15. Definitive cancellation charges due can only be confirmed to you after the intended date of your event, when we shall reduce the charge by the profit on any alternative business we have been able to secure on your behalf.

Amendments or Cancellation by the hotel

16a Should the hotel for reasons beyond its control, need to make any amendments to your booking, we reserve the right to offer an alternative choice of facilities.
  b Should the client make significant changes to the programme or the expected number of guests, this may result in amendments in the applicable rates and/or facilities offered by the hotel.
17 The hotel may cancel the booking at any time:
  a If the booking might, in the opinion of the hotel, prejudice the reputation of the hotel.
  b If the client is more than 30 days in arrears of previous payments to a company in the Queens Moat Houses Group.
  c If the hotel becomes aware of any alteration in the client's financial situation.

Arrival/Departure

18. The bedroom accommodation is available from 3.00pm on the day of arrival, and must be vacated by 11.00am on the day of departure, unless specific alternative arrangements have been agreed.
19. Meeting rooms will be made available for the time shown on your contract and you will be expected to vacate by the end of that period. If requested, the hotel will do its best to accommodate you with any extension but this may not always be possible. Where the hotel is able to accommodate you with an extension then additional reasonable charges may be made.

General

20. The hotel reserves the right to approve any externally arranged entertainment, services or activities you have arranged and we cannot accept any liability for any resultant cost.
21. Should any of the delegates be unable to correct any aspect of poor behaviour or activities unacceptable to the hotel, the hotel reserves the right to terminate your stay. Should this occur, no monies will be refunded to you. The manager's decision is final.
22. The costs of repairing any damage caused to the property, contents or grounds by any of your guests must be reimbursed to the hotel by the client.
23. No wines, spirits or foods brought into the hotel may be consumed.
24. The hotel will not be liable for any failure to provide or delay in providing facilities, services, food or beverages as a result of events or matters outside its control.
25. The hotel's name/logo may be used in publicity, once a proof of the promotional material has been agreed with the hotel.
26. The client is responsible for ensuring that any band or musician employed by them complies with statutory requirements and the requirements of the management.
27. The hotel must comply with certain licensing and statutory regulations and requires the client to fulfil their obligations in this respect.
28. We are concerned for your health and safety and that of our hotel. You are required to obtain prior written approval if you wish to fix items to the walls, floors or ceilings.
29. Prices quoted include VAT unless otherwise specified. This shall be at the rate prevailing when the contract was prepared and is subject to alteration should the rate change.
30. Insurance can be arranged to protect you and your event against cancellation or abandonment with a minimum sum insured based on the anticipated income to the hotel. Insurance can also cover non-appearance of speakers or delegates, property damage at or to the venue or its contents, third party, bodily injury and third party damage. The hotel does not accept liability for these.

MOAT HOUSE

Source: Moat House Hotels (the Moat House logo is the registered trademark of Queens Moat Houses plc.)

The objective behind branding is to convey to the client that he can expect ethical practices and quality service and facilities at the same high standards, no matter whether the hotel is in Aberdeen or Exeter, Jakarta or Buenos Aires. It is to reassure customers that, having staged a successful conference at one hotel within the group, they can expect a similar outcome by using other hotels in the group. Branding is about building customer loyalty and increasing business retention because customers will have the confidence to keep their conferences and meetings within that particular group. Their own success is assured by the branded service and product which those hotels guarantee.

This approach has many strengths and, as all major chains have adopted branding, it seems to justify in financial returns the substantial investments required in venue and staff development. For customers it also has many attractions, yet it has one drawback: the very sameness of product can serve as a disincentive to its use. Conference organisers are constantly looking for somewhere new, somewhere a little different to make their event live long in the memory of their delegates. If delegates find that their surroundings and the type of service received are more or less identical at each conference, regardless of where it is being held, delegate perceptions of the event may not always be as favourable as the organiser would have wished.

In the author's experience, it is always important for an organiser to inspect a conference venue before booking because it is the quality of staff and their service standards which is always one of the most decisive factors in venue selection and re-selection. No matter how strong the branding, and how good the staff training, the cloning of conference sales managers and banqueting coordinators has not yet been achieved (fortunately!). Individual personality and friendliness are crucial and must be experienced at first hand.

Yield Management

The 1990s have also seen the adoption of the theory and practice of yield management by conference venues, hotels especially. The application of yield management is seen towards the end of the marketing process, at the time when a customer (conference organiser) is negotiating a booking with his chosen or short-listed venue.

Yield management aims to 'maximise revenue by adjusting prices to suit market demand' (Huyton and Peters, 1997). It 'emphasises high rates on high demand days and high occupancy when demand is low. The focus of yield management is to maximise revenue every day, not for seasons or periods. It places the needs of the customer secondary to those of the hotel.'

Huyton and Peters suggest that

> for many years prospective hotel guests have become used to bargaining for their room rates or at least expecting that a room, at the rate they normally pay, will be available. Hotels have been seen by their customers as simply providers of rooms and beds. The idea that they are organised establishments, whose sole purpose is to make money for the owners, appears not to be a part of hotel guests' thinking. For as many years as this attitude has been expressed by customers, the hotel industry has permitted it by acceding to guests' needs, wants and whims. The idea seems to have been that we should be grateful for who we can get to come and stay. Yield management has turned this aspect of hotel operation on its head. What the system now tells the customer is that there are certain rooms set aside at certain price categories and, once they are full, you will have to pay more.

Yield management principles apply not just to the sale of bedrooms. Hartley and Rand (1997) explain that:

For a venue having conference, function and/or exhibition space, yield management systems, designed to increase the overall profitability of the venue, must include consideration of many factors beyond room inventory and room pricing. While the yield-related information needed to handle a bedroom booking can be assessed relatively quickly, conference function and exhibition space can be sold and used in many different ways and for many different purposes – combinations which will produce significantly varying profit potential. Ultimately, yield will be determined by how you sell the total facilities available.

Hartley and Rand outline a 'Conference Capacity Strategy' which a venue's sales team should develop in order to maximise yield from conference business. The strategy looks at business mix, market strength and competitive edge, profitability, lead times and refused business. They expound the factors and techniques involved in allocating capacity to particular enquiries, and give practical tips on how to secure the business. They contend that: 'Price, and the way the pricing issue is managed by the venue, are components of the "package" that the venue constructs at this stage of the enquiry. The overall relevance and quality of the package will be determining factors in winning or losing the business.' They strongly discourage the frequently used terminology of '8-hour', '24-hour' or 'day delegate rates', preferring to use 'residential' and 'non-residential rates' as more appropriate terminology (see also Appendix E). They put forward what they describe as a: 'Radical but still potentially flexible approach: the "up to" tariff where the maximum rate is quoted as the published rate but it is still apparent that a reduced tariff may be available, dependent on the overall attractiveness of the booking to the venue.'

Figure 5.7 (taken from Hartley and Rand, 1997) illustrates the measurement of conference capacity yield in a venue over a period of one week, showing the potential and realised figures.

	Target (potential) (week)	Actual realised (week)
Accommodation		
Number of bedrooms (allocated to conference sector)	400 rooms	325 rooms
Accommodation rate	£70	£65
Conference space (capacity of 850* sq. mtrs) *inc. private dining facilities		
Revenue per sq. m	£93	£75

Conference sector bedroom yield

$$\frac{\text{Rooms sold}}{\text{Rooms available for sale}} \times \frac{\text{Average rate of rooms sold}}{\text{Average rate potential}} = \frac{325}{400} \times \frac{65}{70} = \frac{21\,125}{28\,000} = 75\%$$

Conference space – revenue earned

$$\frac{\text{Revenue per sq. m realized} \times 850}{\text{Potential revenue per sq. m} \times 850} = \frac{£75 \times 850}{£93 \times 850} = \frac{63\,750}{79\,050} = 81\%$$

Conference sector capacity yield

$$\frac{\text{Accommodation revenue realised} + \text{Conference space revenue realised}}{\text{Accommodation revenue potential} + \text{Conference space revenue potential}} \times 100$$

$$\frac{21\,125 + 63\,750}{28\,000 + 79\,050} \times 100 = \frac{84\,875}{107\,050} \times 100 = 79\%$$

(*Source*: Yeoman, I. and Ingold, A. (1997) *Yield Management – Strategies for the Service Industries*)

Figure 5.7
Measurement of conference capacity yield in a venue over one week.

Yield management systems are a relatively new science within the conference sector but they are here to stay. Any organiser's negotiating technique needs to take account of the yield management systems which will increasingly influence the responses given in discussions with conference venue sales managers.

Overseas Marketing

The promotion of destinations to overseas markets is a huge subject which cannot be covered adequately in this book. The international marketplace is becoming increasingly competitive and those organisations wishing to give themselves a realistic chance of success must take a long-term perspective, develop collaborative partnerships with other organisations (airlines, national tourist boards, and other marketing consortiums), identify substantial financial and human resources, and follow through a detailed marketing plan similar to that outlined earlier in this chapter.

Friel (1997) notes that: 'It is instructive to observe that the former Soviet states of Eastern Europe chose tourism as the engine of economic recovery but the focus of their market positioning was not Russia but Moscow and St Petersburg; not the Czech Republic but Prague; not Hungary but Budapest.' He contends that it will be the city or 'urban region' which will be the future unit of analysis and the vehicle through which overseas markets will continue to be approached.

Bids to stage international association conventions are presented by cities, though positioned within a national framework – Glasgow, for example, is positioned within the context of Scotland, and Helsinki is marketed under the umbrella of Finland. It is not a viable option for individual venues to market themselves overseas in isolation. It is even more important than in the domestic marketplace for venues, which are looking to attract overseas business, to work in partnership with their destination or to be marketed as part of an international chain or consortium.

No active steps into overseas markets should be taken without widespread consultation with experienced practitioners and the preparation of a detailed and costed marketing plan.

Summary

- The importance of location in decisions over the selection of conference venues has led to the creation of destination marketing organisations whose role is to promote the venues, facilities and attractions of a given area in order to generate increased conference business.

- A focus on the needs of customers should drive all marketing activity, which has to be planned through the specific application of marketing principles and strategy to the conference and business tourism sector.

- Destination marketing is undertaken by convention bureaus and conference offices/desks which involve the public and private sectors in collaborative partnerships. The structures, funding and activities of such organisations vary from destination to destination, although two basic models are apparent.

- The activities of city or local area convention bureaus are complemented in many countries by national tourism organisations.

- Some conference venues join marketing consortiums, which comprise venues with similar characteristics, in order to develop a stronger profile in the marketplace.
- Many hotel chains have invested substantial resources in the development of a branded conference product as a means of reassuring and retaining their customers. At the same time, sophisticated yield management systems have been introduced to maximise revenue from conference bookings.

Review and discussion questions

1. Undertake a 'SWOT' analysis of two conference destinations (one British, one overseas), summarising the strengths, weaknesses, opportunities and threats of each. Use the analysis to propose the most suitable target markets for both destinations.

2. Research the work of two convention and visitor bureaus (one British, one overseas). Compare and contrast their structures, funding and marketing activities, commenting on the strengths and weaknesses of each.

3. Compose a Marketing Plan for a 4-star conference hotel in central London, opened in 1994. The hotel has six conference rooms, the largest seating up to 200 delegates, and two other rooms seating up to 100 each. It has 160 bedrooms and well-equipped leisure facilities. The hotel is privately owned. Three staff are involved in sales and marketing activities, and have a marketing budget of £10 000.

4. Undertake an in-depth appraisal of one of the venue marketing consortiums listed in this chapter. The appraisal should, ideally, include comments from venue members of the consortium on the value and benefits of membership.

5. Compare the branded conference products offered by two of the large hotel chains, noting both differences and similarities. To which kinds of conference organisers might these products appeal, and why?

References

- Cooper, Chris, Fletcher, John, Gilbert, David and Wanhill, Stephen (1993) *Tourism: Principles and Practice*, Longman.
- Friel, Eddie (1997) 'Compete and Conquer', a presentation to the BACD annual convention.
- Gartrell, Richard B. (1991) 'Strategic partnerships for convention planning: the role of convention and visitor bureaus in convention management', *International Journal of Hospitality Management*, Vol. 10, No. 2.
- Gartrell, Richard B. (1994) *Destination Marketing for Convention and Visitor Bureaus*, 2nd edn, International Association of Convention and Visitor Bureaus, Kendall/Hunt Publishing Company.
- Hartley, Jerry and Rand, Peter (1997) 'Conference sector capacity management', in Ian Yeoman and Anthony Ingold (eds) *Yield Management: Strategies for the Service Industries*, Cassell.
- Huyton, Jeremy R. and Peters, Sarah D. (1997) 'Application of yield management to the hotel industry', in Ian Yeoman and Anthony Ingold (eds) *Yield Management: Strategies for the Service Industries*, Cassell.

Further Reading

- *Steps to Success in the Meetings Industry* (1995) Meetings Industry Association (designed for staff working in conference venues and for conference placement agents).
- Quain, William (1993) *How to Write a Hotel Marketing Plan*, Professional Convention Management Association.

Chapter 6

An Event Industry

Introduction

The conference industry is based upon events of different kinds (including conventions, meetings, seminars, product launches, management retreats) and of different sizes and durations, requiring sophisticated planning and administration to ensure their success. Events are organised by people with varying degrees of knowledge and experience, many finding themselves responsible for organising conferences without any previous formal training. This chapter provides a framework for those who take up the challenge, and summarises the main processes involved in planning and staging an event.

Objectives

This chapter looks at:

- a general introduction to conference organising
- pre-conference planning and research
- budgeting and financial management
- sourcing a venue
- negotiating with venues
- travel arrangements
- programme planning
- conference management and production
- event evaluation.

A General Introduction to Conference Organising

The organisation of a conference requires a similar strategic approach to that needed for planning and managing most other events. Clear objectives should be set from the beginning, a budget has to be established, a venue must be sourced and delegates' travel arrangements made, a programme has to be prepared and the conference managed for its duration. Then, after it is over, final administrative details have to be completed and some evaluation of the conference should take place. While there are different factors to take into account when organising a conference for 500 delegates rather than one for 50, the essential components are the same.

Similar steps are required for the organisation of other events, such as sporting events, concerts, celebrations and rallies, whether these are of national or international significance like the 'FA Cup Final' at Wembley or the Olympic Games, or of more localised importance, such as an antiques fair or agricultural show.

Organising conferences is a high-pressure activity, not recommended for those of a nervous disposition. Yet, well handled, it can be tremendously exciting and rewarding. It goes without saying that excellent organisational skills are a must, as are attention to detail and a willingness to work long and often irregular hours, especially in the immediate build-up period and during the event itself.

Conferences need to be planned with the precision of a military operation. Indeed, it is not surprising that a number of those now working successfully as conference organisers have come from a military background. Cotterell (1994) suggests that: 'A conference for 200 people for two or three days is likely to take up to 250 hours or around six normal working weeks, even without counting the two or three 18-hour days which will be needed just prior to the event.'

But, in addition to hard work and attention to detail, conferences need a creativity and flair to be brought to them which will make them memorable occasions. They should live long in the memories of delegates, not only because of the benefits accruing from what has been shared and learned during the formal programme, but also for the opportunities they provide for informal networking and socialising.

In some cases, systems will already be in place when it is, for example, an annual event which runs along similar lines year after year. In other cases, it will be an entirely new event for which no previous organisational history or tradition exists. Both scenarios have their advantages and disadvantages.

The regularly held conference may operate smoothly with just some fine tuning and updating to established systems and procedures. It might, however, be failing to achieve its real potential as a conference, having become staid and predictable, and it may be that a completely fresh approach would be beneficial. The challenge for a new organiser would be to revolutionise the organisation of the conference without alienating too many of the staff or members (if, indeed, it is a membership organisation) associated with the previous systems.

Where there is no previous event history, an organiser has the benefit of beginning with a clean sheet of paper. There are no set ways of doing things, no established contacts, no 'venues that we always use'. There is a freedom to bring something of his own identity to the event, to build up his own network of information and suppliers, and to ensure that the event management systems are put in place to his own design. But such freedom brings with it a responsibility which can appear daunting if the organiser has been thrust into the role of running a conference with minimal training and experience. This, regrettably, is still the position in which far too many conference organisers find themselves.

This chapter attempts, therefore, to sketch out a framework for the successful organising of conferences. A number of books have been written already on this subject and the chapter will make reference to some of these in summarising the principles and steps needed to ensure that a conference is run effectively. The chapter is written from the perspective of the conference organiser, rather than from that of a conference venue coordinator (whose role is also to ensure that events are run efficiently and profitably).

Pre-conference Planning and Research

The initial phase, of planning and research, is the one which lays the foundations for success. It is a crucial part of any event, and mistakes or oversights made at this stage can be difficult to remedy later on. It needs, therefore, to be approached thoroughly and systematically.

At the outset, the broad objectives for the conference must be set. These will vary from event to event. The main objective for a meeting with a company's sales force may be to present new products, introduce a new incentive scheme, update them on sales performance and motivate them to reach higher targets, or inform them about a re-structuring of sales territories. The annual conference of British rose-growing societies (non-existent, as far as is known!) may have as its main aim to exchange information on new varieties of roses or to demonstrate the effectiveness of the latest pesticides, as well as maximising attendance and generating a profit.

These broad objectives will need to be supplemented with detailed answers to questions about the 'who, what, when, where, why and how' (Maitland, 1996) of the conference.

Who?

Pre-event planning needs to consider who the delegates will be, how many should be invited, and how many are expected to attend (essential for budgeting purposes). Is it appropriate for delegates' partners to be invited? Are there likely to be any special guests, including media representatives? Will there be any overseas delegates and, if so, do they all speak English or is there a need to provide interpretation facilities?

It also refers to the speakers who may be involved, either for presentations to plenary sessions or as leaders for workshops or 'breakout' sessions. Are there outside speakers to be invited, and will they require a fee as well as travel expenses?

'Who?' should also include the organising team, which may be just one person or a dedicated group of people, some of whom could include intermediary agencies as described in Chapter 2. When there is a team involved, not all of them will necessarily participate from the initial planning stage right through to post-event evaluation, but their degree of involvement is something which will need to be thought through early on. The more complex the event and the numbers involved in organising it, the more the need for some form of critical path analysis, mapping out the sequence of events in a logical order and within a realistic time-frame.

What?

What kind of conference is being organised? Is it a corporate or association event? Is it a management retreat, training course, incentive event? A conference to update delegates on new developments in a scientific or medical field? A launch to dealers and trade media, or some other kind of event? Will delegates be listening and passive, or is there a high degree of participation, perhaps involving team-building or outdoor activities?

What kind of message is the conference designed to convey? The organiser may have little or no control over this, as it may be something determined by senior managers or an organisation's 'conference committee', but it is imperative that he understands this clearly.

When?

Timing is another major consideration. All too often inadequate time is allowed to plan and prepare for a conference. The conference organiser may simply be given the conference dates and asked to ensure that it happens. He may have made little input to the decision, even though his perspective is vital. The corporate sector, in particular, is notorious for allowing insufficient 'lead time'. Perhaps this is a reflection on the work that still needs to be done to raise the status of conference and event organisers to one which is on a par with an organisation's senior management team. In the final analysis, it is a company's reputation, not simply that of the conference organiser, which is in jeopardy if an event is poorly run.

Some flexibility on dates can also be helpful in securing the best possible rates from the chosen venue. The venue may be able to offer more favourable rates if the dates selected assist in its maximisation of yield.

Timing also needs to take into consideration the likely diary commitments of delegates. Are there any other events happening at the same time, or around that time, which might have an impact on delegate numbers? Is the conference occurring in a busy work period, or during holidays, or in winter months and, if so, what impact might any of these factors have?

Where?

Location needs to be determined at an early stage, whether this is expressed in rather broad terms such as The Midlands, Scotland, or 'no further north than Manchester', or quite specifically such as Cardiff, Nottingham, or 'within a 20-mile radius of Bristol'. When deciding the ideal location, easy access to a motorway may be desirable (unless the event requires a venue off the beaten track). If many delegates are to use the train, location near a mainline station will be necessary, unless sophisticated local transport arrangements can be made easily.

When events have an international dimension, with delegates arriving by plane, it is usually important to select a venue within reasonable travelling time of an international airport. Several hours sitting in a long-haul jet followed by several hours in transit around Britain is not a recipe for a successful start to what will be a prestige event.

Does the location need to be a particular kind of venue to accommodate the event? Is there scope to explore an unusual venue, possibly to link in with the theme of the conference? The checklist below gives some of the principal factors for consideration in venue selection.

Venue Choice Checklist

Having decided upon the general location, the next step is to draw up a shortlist of potential venues. Some of the main points to consider are listed below:

1. Type of Venue

There may be a very wide choice, including: purpose-built conference or convention centres, civic halls/rooms and council chambers, hotels, universities and colleges, management training centres, or one of the many unusual venues now becoming increasingly popular (stately homes, castles, sporting venues, tourist attractions, even a lighthouse or two). Chapter 2 gives further details of the numbers and characteristics of the different venue types. The range of venue options can, of course, be increased dramatically when the search parameters extend to overseas, as well as British, locations.

2. Conference Rooms and Facilities

● Is there the correct combination of rooms available for plenary sessions, syndicate groups, catering, possibly an accompanying exhibition?

▷

Figure 6.1 Some conference room layout options.

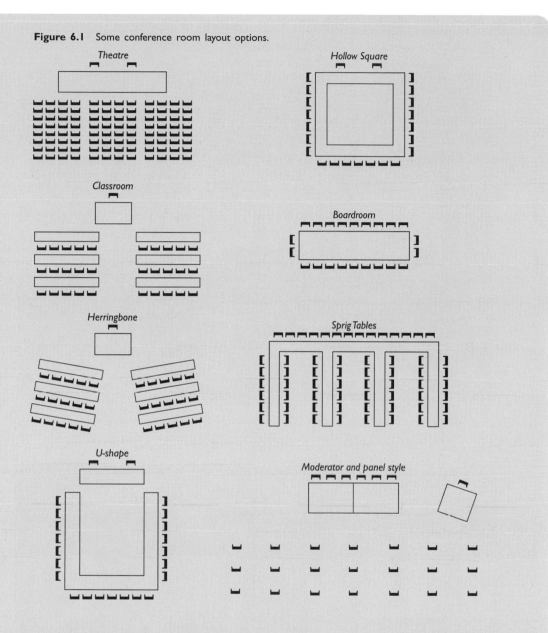

- Is there good access for disabled delegates? Is the venue equipped in other ways to meet the many different disabilities which delegates may have?
- What style of seating will be needed? U-shape, boardroom, theatre-style, classroom, hollow-square and herringbone are just some of the options (see Figure 6.1). For the purposes of calculations, a room which seats 100 delegates theatre-style will seat 50 classroom-style, 25 hollow-square/ boardroom/U-shape, and about 75 for dinner/lunch at round tables/top table with sprigs.
- Do the meeting rooms have natural light and, if not, can the room be blacked out satisfactorily?
- How noisy is the heating and air conditioning system?

Figure 6.2 shows a conference room arranged in a U-shape seating layout.
Figure 6.3 shows a conference room in boardroom format.

Venue Choice Checklist continued

Figure 6.2 Conference room arranged in U-shape seating layout.

Source: The Manor House Hotel and Castle Combe Golf Club Ltd

Figure 6.3 Conference room suitable for boardroom meetings and banquets.

Source: Skibo Castle (Skibo Ltd)

Carey (1997) provides a series of checklists for conference organisers. An example of one of these, a 'Meeting Room Checklist', is given in Fig 6.4.

Figure 6.4 Meeting room checklist.

Meeting Room Checklist

To attend a site inspection without a checklist is a recipe for extra work, as vital questions will remain unasked and important features remain uninspected. Every conference brings its own demands but if you investigate the following you will be halfway there.

A. Location
- Independent access[1]
- Freight access[1]
- Easy to find? (well signed?)
- Proximity to:[2]
  - Main entrance & car park
  - Meal areas & kitchens
  - Fresh air
  - Lifts
  - Toilets & cloakrooms
  - Telephones
  - Break-out rooms
- Disabled access

B. Fixtures
- Decor
- Wall & floor materials[3]
- Pillars/obstructions
- Room shape and partitions[4]
- Location of doors
- Where doors lead to[5]
- Fire exits[6]
- Natural light/Views
- Chandeliers & mirrors[7]

- Stage area and access to it
- Registration area
- Light switches or regulators
- Power & telephone points[8]
- Temperature controls (location)[9]
- Blackout curtains
- Acoustics
- Ceiling height[10]

C. Non fixtures
- Chairs (comfort factor)
- Tables (size & coverings)
- Table furniture[11]
- Signage

D. General
- Cleanliness
- Overall comfort
- Capacity
- Ambience
- Pre function space
- Smell

Notes
1. Direct onto concourse, foyer or street.
2. Explore for yourself.
3. Should be sound absorbent, not bright and not 'busy'.
4. Are partitions really soundproof?
5. Beware doors that open onto kitchens or garbage areas.
6. Are they blocked or locked?
7. Chandeliers can impede projection. Mirrors toss light from projectors and lecterns indiscriminately around a room.
8. You may need lots for PCs, modems and fax machines.
9. Are they in the room?
10. High enough for maximum screen height.
11. What is provided? E.g. Water, cordials, note pads, mints.

Did you hear about the organiser who checked the dimensions of the access doors with the venue (over the phone) and computed that the car would fit through them? Sadly, he was unaware until the day of the launch that the room he had booked wasn't on the ground floor!

Source: Carey, T. (1997) *Crisis or Conference?*

Venue Choice Checklist continued

3. Accommodation and Leisure Options

● Is the event residential and, if so, is it important for all delegates to sleep under the same roof? Or can they be accommodated in different hotels and transported to the conference venue?

● Will delegates require single bedrooms, or will some double or twin rooms be needed?

● Are delegates expecting a venue with its own leisure facilities?

● What are the options for social activities in the vicinity, if there is time in the conference programme for these?

4. Venue Staff

● Does the venue have a dedicated conference co-ordinator who can assist with the detailed planning and arrangements?

● Are there other venue staff with whom you will be working and, if so, when will you be able to meet them? At what stage will the sales manager – usually the organiser's initial point of contact – pass on the booking details to colleagues, who then become the main points of reference?

● Are there in-house technical staff to operate audio-visual equipment? If so, is there an additional charge for using their services? If there are no such staff on site, what arrangements does the venue have with independent audio-visual companies, and what do they charge? What audio-visual equipment is needed during the event? (Normally this can be decided quite close to the event, unless the requirements are quite specialised.)

● Is there a high turnover of staff in the venue, which might create problems in the build-up? Does the venue team give the impression of being experienced, professional, easy-to-work-with?

Cardinal rule: never book a venue without visiting it first – a site inspection is a must!

The choice of location may be taken out of the organiser's hands. He may be told to hold the event in a particular destination, or the conference may rotate around specific destinations/venues in a regular sequence. The organiser's role may simply be to draw up a shortlist of potential venues from which other people will make the final selection.

Why?

Maitland suggests that:

> The 'Why?' is almost certainly the most crucial question that needs to be asked at this stage. Don't ignore or underestimate it. You must be able to answer it well if you are going to proceed with your plans. Is 'because we always do it at this time of year' a good enough reason? It could be a huge waste of time and money if it is held for this reason alone. Are you staging it because it is the quickest and easiest way of putting across your important message to many people in a friendly and personal manner? That's a better motive. Consider carefully if a conference is really necessary. Are there less time-consuming and costly ways to achieve the same goals – perhaps a sales report, a promotional brochure or a press release?

How?

The format and duration of a conference are also very important factors, which will have an effect on some of the preceding considerations. Events requiring lots of syndicate rooms, as well as a main auditorium, plus exhibition space and catering areas will have a much more restricted range of options than events needing just one room with theatre-style seating for 75 people. Duration will also impact on venue availability, rates charged, accommodation requirements and other factors.

'How?' should also take into account the way in which an event fits into a company's overall marketing or training programme. Where a membership organisation is involved, such as a professional association or a trade union, how does a conference contribute to its communication links with members, and facilitate links between the members themselves? Are there ways in which these could be improved?

Budgeting and Financial Management

Whether the conference is being organised for a corporate organisation or for one in the 'non-profit making' sector, financial management is equally important. There are, however, some key differences:

- within the corporate sector, the budget is set by the company. Budgets may be allocated per event or as an annual total which needs to be used effectively to finance a number of events. The budget is required to cover delegate expenses as well as the other costs associated with planning and promoting the event

- within the not-for-profit sector, conferences have to be income-generating with delegate fees being charged to defray costs. The events are designed to cover their own costs and perhaps make a small profit which, in some cases, is used as a start-up fund to pay for the initial promotion and planning of the next event

- within the government and public sectors, either of the above approaches may apply.

Even so, the same principles hold good for all types of organisation: budgets must be drawn up to show projected income and expenditure, systems need to be in place to manage income and expenditure flows and, at the conclusion of the event, a balance sheet should be prepared to show actual income against expenditure. This balance sheet then forms the basis for planning the next event, particularly if it is one in a sequence of conferences taking place on a regular basis.

Income streams will vary according to the nature of the organisation and the event. With corporate events, the income source will be the company itself, but there may also be scope for attracting sponsorship for certain elements. With associations and other organisations in the not-for-profit sector, income will come primarily from delegate fees, although there may also be substantial opportunities to offset the costs of the conference by running an associated exhibition. Trade union, political party and medical conferences, for example, often have concurrent exhibitions which attract exhibitors wishing to promote their products to delegates. Opportunities also exist to attract sponsorship, as typified by pharmaceutical companies sponsoring aspects of medical conferences.

Many destinations are prepared to host a civic reception or banquet for delegates, as a form of welcome and expression of gratitude that the event is being held in their town or city. Convention and visitor bureaus (CVBs) may offer interest-free loans, particularly for events with a lead time of several years: the event organiser may incur expenses, especially promotional costs, well before any income is received from delegate fees. Loans are designed to assist with cash flow but will have to be re-paid once the event is over (and, if the conference has made a profit, the CVB may require a share of the profits).

Expenditure projections have to cover a whole host of items, but the main ones are:

- venue hire
- catering costs
- accommodation costs: delegates, partners, speakers/invited guests, organisers
- speakers' expenses: travel costs, fees, subsistence, presentation materials
- social programme costs: entertainment, transport, other venue hire, food and beverage
- conference production costs: audio-visual equipment and technical staff to stage manage the event plus, when appropriate, set construction
- promotional costs: leaflets and publicity material, press releases, possibly advertising and/or direct mail
- miscellaneous costs: event insurance, security, couriers, interpreters and many others.

Maitland (1996) provides a cashflow forecast form (see Table 6.1, opposite) which can be computerised (spreadsheet software handles this very easily) or in paper format. This is a recognised way of keeping an overview of what is happening with the finances for an event, and helps to flag up any potential problem areas at an early stage.

Sourcing a Venue

There are many sources of information and advice to assist with choosing the venue most suited to a particular event. These include directories and brochures, computer software, trade exhibitions, trade press and specialist agencies. References in this section are primarily to sources of information on British conference and meeting venues but similar types of information exist for many other countries.

Directories and brochures

Several annual directories are available which provide a very useful reference source. Among the most widely used are the following.

Conference Blue and Green Books published by Miller Freeman Information Services. The *Conference Blue Book* lists some 600 venues, by region, and gives detailed meeting room specifications with black and white photographic illustrations. It also contains listings of 5000 venues, by town, with brief capacity details for each. The *Conference Green Book* lists around 200 venues and describes their meeting and sports/leisure facilities, with full colour photographs. It also contains a listing of 1500 suppliers by product/service. The 1998 two-volume price of £76.00 + p&p includes a complimentary CD-Rom version of the books with fast search options.

Contact: Miller Freeman Information Services, Miller Freeman Plc, Riverbank House, Angel Lane, Tonbridge, Kent TN9 1SE (tel: 44 (0)1732–377586).

British Conference Destinations Directory, published by the British Association of Conference Destinations. This provides an overview of the main attractions and facilities of the major British conference destinations (all BACD members), supported by key facts and figures and details of services available from the conference office or convention bureau, as well as full contact details (a sample page from the 1998 edition is shown as

Table 6.1 Cashflow forecast form

| | Month | | Month | | Month | | Month | | Month | | Month | |
	Estimated	Actual	Estimated	Actual	Estimated	Actual	Estimated	Actual	Estimated	Actual	Estimated	Actual
Income												
Sponsors												
Delegates/Partners												
Other sources												
Self												
Total Income (A)												
Expenditure												
Venue												
Overnight accommodation												
Speakers/Partners												
Delegates/Partners												
Publicity												
Outside Assistance												
Rehearsals												
The programme												
Post-conference activities												
Other												
Total expenditure (B)												
Net cashflow (A–B)												
Opening Balance												
Closing Balance												

Source: Maitland, I. (1996)

Figure 6.5 An entry from the 1998 BACD Directory.

Derry

Question: Looking for an exciting alternative location for your small to medium-sized conference?

Solution: Go west to the historic walled city of Londonderry and experience a place where the quality of the conference facilities is surpassed only by the warmth of the hospitality. Easy access, high quality hotels and business support services and Derry's reputation as an historic and cultural centre par excellence, all go towards making your conference, meeting or event an unqualified success.

Attention to Detail

You'll also enjoy the professional support of the Derry Visitor and Convention Bureau who will ensure that, from the moment you step off the plane at the ultra-modern City of Derry Airport, you realize why attention to detail is recognised as one of our greatest strengths.

History

Away from the conference chamber, explore a city replete with sumptuous Georgian architecture and crowned with the only complete city walls left in Ireland. The beautiful St Columb's Cathedral (1633) is a storehouse of historical artifacts, while the distinctive Tower Museum was recently cited by The Times as one of the Top Ten Museums in the UK.

Shopping

Londonderry's shopping facilities are second to none and range from top quality specialist outlets to £65 million shopping malls. And as you'd expect from a city renowned for its hospitality, the nightlife is exuberant and varied and is sure to become one of the highlights of your stay.

The Great Outdoors

Fishing, golf, sailing and riding are all available locally and, whichever direction you set your compass, the scenery is outstanding. The Giant's Causeway and the mystical hills of Donegal, for example, lie only a short distance away by car.

The Promise

From residential conferences to one-day events, commercial conventions to academic seminars, we'll match our services and facilities to your needs.

Call now for a free copy of Derry: Conference City

Derry by night

Please mention the BACD Directory when contacting BACD member destinations

Catherine O'Connor
Manager
Derry Visitor & Convention Bureau
44 Foyle Street
Derry
Northern Ireland BT48 6AT
Tel: 01504 377577
Fax: 01504 377992

Areas Represented
Derry

Access
Air: City of Derry (10KM)
Rail: Northern Ireland Reilways, Waterside
Road. M2, A6

Conference Venue Capacity
Max. seating of major conference venue 450

Exhibition Venue Capacity
Max. exhibition space
390 sq. m in one venue

Accommodation
274 hotel/venue bedrooms with ensuite facilities
57 bedrooms in largest hotel
141 hotel/venue bedrooms within 1 mile radius of main venue
137 hotel/venue bedrooms within 5 mile radius of main venue

Services/Advice
● Venue selection
● Accommodation booking
● Delegate Information
● Access and local transport
● Tours/social programmes
● Familiarisation visits
● Local support services

Source: British Conference Destinations Directory, 1998

Figure 6.5). Venue capacity charts and detailed maps are also included. Free to conference organisers, £11.00 + p&p to others.

Contact: BACD, 1st Floor, Elizabeth House, 22 Suffolk Street, Queensway, Birmingham B1 1LS (tel: 44 (0)121–616–1400).

Venue – The Worldwide Guide to Conference and Incentive Travel Facilities, published by Haymarket Business Publications. Entries are listed by country and then in alphabetical order by destination, with a summary description of the destination, and also include details of the conference venues in each destination. As well as the UK section, the 1997–98 edition includes similar information on 66 other countries worldwide, contact details for over 2000 suppliers to the conference and travel industry, indexes for selecting venues by price and delegate rates, and a listing of international purpose-built centres. *Venue* has a controlled free circulation and copies may also be purchased at £60.

Contact: Haymarket Business Publications, 174 Hammersmith Road, London W6 7JP (tel: 44 (0)171–413–4165).

Other more specialised directories are available, such as Johanssens *Recommended Business Meeting Venues Guide*, which features over 160 UK hotels and other meeting venues, *Worldwide Convention Centres Directory*, with full-page entries for over 60 centres and listings by country of over 500 (published by CAT Publications), and the *Official Meeting Facilities Guide* (published by Reed Travel Group). Venue consortiums of the kind listed in Chapter 5 publish listings and/or directories of their member venues.

All venues produce some form of promotional brochure and conference organisers should keep up-to-date copies of such information for places used on a regular basis. However, because of the number of available venues (between 4000 and 5000 in the British Isles alone), it would require a huge filing system to maintain a comprehensive set of brochures, many of which are designed in different shapes and sizes. It would also be a full-time occupation to keep these up to date.

A better use of limited filing and storage space would be to obtain a set of *destination guides*, produced by all conference destinations and mostly updated annually or biennially. These tend to be produced in A4 format, and describe all of the venues in a destination as well as summarising attractions, communications, support services and other features. A set of 120 or so destination guides could easily be stored in a single filing cabinet, and would give detailed coverage of most British conference facilities.

Computer software

Computer software packages, listing conference venues, have been in existence since the early 1990s, although it is fair to say that they have struggled to achieve widespread acceptance among conference organisers and, in fact, none of the early versions has survived. Since the mid-1990s two packages, in particular, have established a presence in the marketplace.

Viewpoint Conference Guide was launched in 1993 and is updated twice yearly. This guide, in CD-Rom for Windows format, contains 500 fields of data on 4000-plus venues in the UK, plus detailed accommodation and leisure information on over 3000 business hotels (RRP £129.95 + VAT). There is also a *Viewpoint Conference Guide Worldwide* (RRP £199.95 + VAT), launched in 1997, containing 500 data fields on over 10 000 4-star and 5-star hotels and conference centres.

Contact: CID Publishing Ltd, Unit 1, 125 Battersea High Street, London SW11 3HY (tel/fax: 44 (0)171–801–0011; or tel: 44 (0)181–341–6455; fax: 44 (0)171–801–0099).

The Venue Directory for Windows is a venue finding software package for conference and event organisers containing extensive information on approximately 4000 UK properties. Updated every four months, it is available free of charge on both diskettes and CD-Rom. The system can also be found on the Internet (www.venuedirectory.com) where it includes a short-term availability section updated daily. *The Venue Directory* has been developed in conjunction with professional organisers.

Contact: Berry Marketing Services Ltd, Berry House, 11–13 Stone Street, Cran-brook, Kent TN17 3HF (tel: 44 (0)1580–715151; fax: 44 (0)1580–715588; e-mail: bms@venuedirectory.com).

Other specialist software is also coming onto the market, including a package which enables organisers to design the layout of a meeting room 'on screen', and virtual reality software which gives guided tours of venues. It is important for organisers to keep abreast, and evaluate the benefits, of such innovations.

For those conference organisers who prefer to source their own venues, rather than use an intermediary organisation, computer software packages and venue brochures and directories are a useful way of whittling down the options to a manageable shortlist. They do not, however, obviate the need to visit venues before making a final choice. Computer or printed images and text can help, but they do not replace the need to see a venue at first hand and meet the staff.

As Cotterell says, inspection visits

> *are important because there is much that cannot be ascertained from a brochure. The experienced organiser will travel to a venue the way most delegates will, to experience at first hand any problems with finding it or reaching it. Judgements will be made on the overall first impressions, the attitude of the staff, the quality, colours, style and condition of furnishings, the ease of getting from one area to another, and so on. Many experienced organisers make a check-list of points they need to cover . . . It is sometimes easier to attend one of the group inspection visits organised by hotels, tourist boards, convention bureaus, trade associations and some trade magazines. These give an opportunity, often over a weekend, to inspect a variety of venues within a location in the company of other organisers, an aspect that can be a most valuable opportunity to add to one's own personal network.*

Trade exhibitions

There are a number of trade shows and exhibitions specifically designed for conference organisers and meeting planners, where the exhibitors include conference venues and destinations, conference service suppliers, intermediary agencies, transport companies and trade magazines. The advantage for conference organisers is that an exhibition enables them to make contact with potential suppliers, all under one roof – people it would be very expensive and time-consuming to contact individually away from the show. Exhibitions are a good way of updating information files, making personal contacts, finding out about new developments and facilities. Many exhibitions also have a seminar programme running alongside, covering topics of relevance to conference organisers in their every-day work.

Major industry exhibitions include:

1. *Confex* – the largest of the British shows which is held at Earls Court Exhibition Centre, London (usually late February/early March over three days). Exhibitors are British and overseas companies and organisations.

2. *Meetings and Incentive Travel Show* – held at Olympia Exhibition Centre, London (late June over two days). Exhibitors are British and overseas companies and organisations.

3. *Confer* – held in Kensington Town Hall, London (one-day event in October). All of the exhibitors are British conference destinations (and members of BACD).

4. *EIBTM* (European Incentive and Business Travel and Meetings Exhibition) – a truly international exhibition (see Chapter 1) held at Palexpo, Geneva (in May over three days). Several thousand buyers are hosted to the show each year by the organisers, who provide complimentary flights and overnight hotel accommodation.

For conference organisers interested in university and college venues, both the British Universities Accommodation Consortium (BUAC) and Connect have their own one-day exhibitions, again held in London, normally in October and April/May respectively.

Trade press

Conference industry trade magazines are a valuable source of up-to-date news and feature coverage on conference venues and destinations, both national and international. As well as articles reviewing the facilities and attractions of specific areas, some magazines also include case studies of events which illustrate how other organisers have staged events in particular locations.

Readers of trade magazines need to bear in mind that all of the magazines depend for their survival on attracting advertising support from conference venues and destinations, a fact which can influence editorial content. Despite this caveat, trade magazines are an important source of information and provide a service which does not exist elsewhere. They also contain many other features, for example on trends and statistics and new legislation, which provide essential background for professional buyers.

A list of the main trade magazines is given in Appendix B.

Agencies

Various agencies provide specialist venue-finding services. These include venue-finding agencies, professional conference organisers (PCOs), conference production companies, and destination management companies (DMCs) (see Chapter 2). Agency services are usually free to buyers (unless the agencies are also involved in the planning and organisation of a conference), with commission being charged to the venues where business is placed. Some agencies have been criticised from time to time for recommending to their clients those venues which will pay them the highest levels of commission, rather than putting forward the venues which are best suited to clients' needs. Such a practice is, however, short-sighted as a disappointed client is unlikely to make use of those services again.

A different kind of agency service is that provided by the British Association of Conference Destinations (BACD) through its Venue Location Service, administered in partnership with the members of the Association. The service, which is free of charge, operates to a published code of practice (to which all BACD members are required to sign up annually) and guarantees an impartial response within a specified timeframe. Its unique feature is that the service is delivered via BACD members around the British Isles who have personal knowledge of all the venues within their destination and with whom they are in contact on a regular, often daily, basis. No other venue-finding service has a similar network of destination contacts who, between them, are able to provide information on over 3000 venues countrywide.

Whichever source(s) of information organisers choose to use, they will need to have at their finger tips the answers to various questions which will be posed by venue staff or intermediary agencies. The Enquiry Form used by BACD's Venue Location Service (see Figure 6.6, overleaf) lists the most common questions.

Figure 6.6
BACD venue
location service
enquiry form.

CONTACT NAME   DATE
_____

POSITION
_____

ORGANISATION
_____

ADDRESS
_____

                                        POSTCODE
_____

TELEPHONE   FAX
_____

MAIN BUSINESS ACTIVITY
_____

AGENCY   YES/NO   COMMISSION   YES/NO   _____%
_____

TYPE OF EVENT [CONFERENCE, EXHIBITION, TRAINING, SEMINAR, PRODUCT LAUNCH, ROADSHOW] OTHER:
_____

LENGTH [ARRIVE, DEPART, NUMBER OF DAYS, TIME OF WEEK, ANY SETUP TIME]
_____

PROPOSED DATE(S)
_____

NUMBER OF DELEGATES/EXHIBITORS
_____

PREFERRED LOCATION(S)

_____

TYPE OF VENUE [PURPOSE BUILT CENTRE, CIVIC HALL, HOTEL (3*/4*-URBAN/RURAL), ACADEMIC, UNUSUAL]
_____

SPACE REQUIREMENTS
MAIN ROOM
NO. OF DELEGATES _____ SEATING [BOARDROOM, HORSE SHOE, THEATRE, CLASSROOM]

STAGE/RAISED PLATFORM/PODIUM/LECTERN [YES, NO, MAYBE, SIZE]

SYNDICATE ROOMS
NUMBER OF ROOMS _____ NO. OF DELEGATES IN EACH _____ STYLE [BR, HS, TH, CL]

EXHIBITION SPACE [YES, NO, SIZE OF SPACE REQUIRED]

Figure 6.6
(*cont.*)

AV EQUIPMENT [OHP, SCREEN, BACK/SLIDE PROJECTION, MICROPHONE/PA, FLIPCHART, VIDEO] OTHER:

CATERING [BREAKFAST, BUFFET: FINGER/FORK, SITDOWN/STANDUP LUNCH, DINNER, MORNING/AFTERNOON TEA/COFFEE, FULL]

SPECIAL ARRANGEMENTS [COCKTAIL/CHAMPAGNE RECEPTIONS, BANQUETING, ENTERTAINMENT] OTHER:

PRIVATE DINING [YES, NO]

ACCOMMODATION
NUMBER OF NIGHTS [NIGHT BEFORE/NIGHTS OF]

NUMBER OF BEDS [SINGLE, DOUBLE, TWIN]

BUDGET

DEADLINE FOR RESPONSE

WHEN IS DECISION/BOOKING LIKELY TO BE MADE

OTHER INFORMATION: [EG. HOW WILL DELEGATES BE TRAVELLING TO EVENT, DISABLED ACCESS, PREFERENCE FOR RECEIVING RESPONSES]

HOW DID YOU HEAR ABOUT THE VENUE LOCATION SERVICE
[ADVERT – WHICH PERIODICAL, DIRECTORY, RECOMMENDATION – MEMBER, TOURIST BOARD] OTHER:

ARE YOU USING THE FREEPHONE NO. [YES, NO] FOR FUTURE REFERENCE: 0500–140–100

WHICH LEVEL OF RESPONSE DO YOU REQUIRE [TIER ONE, TIER TWO]

PLEASE FAX (PREFERABLY) OR POST TO THE ADDRESS GIVEN BELOW:

BRITISH ASSOCIATION OF CONFERENCE DESTINATIONS
1st Floor, Elizabeth House, 22 Suffolk Street, Queensway, Birmingham, B1 1LS
Freephone: 0500–140–100   Fax: 0121–616–1364

Source: British Association of Conference Destinations

Negotiating with Venues

Once a shortlist of suitable venues has been produced and inspection visits made, the process of negotiating a final rate or package with the preferred venue takes place. Conference organisers should be aware of a venue's need to maximise yield from its bookings (as described in Chapter 5) but, nevertheless, there is almost always scope to negotiate on a venue's published delegate rates.

Carey suggests that:

> *As a professional conference organiser, you are in a powerful position to negotiate a good deal with your chosen venue and it can be tempting to bully the management into ridiculously low room, food and beverage rates. This may make you feel good and impress your Finance Director but it will almost certainly jeopardize the vital relationship between you and the venue. As a rule, it is better to pay a reasonable rate for facilities and accommodation and then negotiate added value and service.*

Some flexibility on the part of the organiser can assist in the negotiation process, particularly if this can help to make a booking even more attractive in the eyes of the venue. The following points should also be borne in mind:

- If the event is to be held midweek, rates charged are likely to be higher than at weekends. Significant reductions can be achieved by holding an event at least partially over a weekend when occupancy levels, especially for hotels, are generally lower.

- The scope for negotiation will also depend on the time of year (Autumn and Spring are the peak seasons for conferences, and so the busiest for the venues), the number of delegates, nature of the organisation (lower rates may be available for non-profit making organisations, especially from civic venues and sometimes from purpose-built conference centres).

- Published rates do not (yet) cover the same package from venue to venue. It is, therefore, important to examine what the rates do actually cover. The provision of audio-visual equipment is one of the areas where wide variations can exist.

- While most venues (and certainly almost all hotels) promote a delegate package (expressed either as a non-residential or eight-hour or day delegate rate *or* as a residential or 24-hour delegate rate), it is also possible to ask for room hire and catering charges separately, and sometimes these may be cheaper than an integrated package.

Cotterell (1994) puts forward a number of strategies to be used by conference buyers in the negotiation process, including:

- prepare – for example, know the prices charged by the venue to other clients, and know the prices charged by similar venues in the area
- be nice, but gain respect
- don't lie
- be flexible
- never reveal deadlines
- name drop
- hint at other business to be placed
- be patient

- disclaim responsibility (for the final decision)
- don't underestimate the sellers.

Carey (1997) produces a further checklist of 'potential areas of negotiation with a venue', reproduced in Figure 6.7.

Figure 6.7
Potential areas of
negotiation with
a venue.

Potential areas of negotiation with a venue

I. Here are some areas of expense that you might consider asking the venue to waive or reduce.

- Partner rates
- Single supplements
- Early check in and late check out
- Deposits
- Meeting room charges
- Set up and break down days
- A-V equipment
- Technical staff
- Corkage charges
- Live music
- Use of amenities (E.g. disco, sauna, etc.)

- Bar licence extension
- Newspapers
- Use of office equipment
- Flowers and table settings
- Storage facilities
- Signs
- Extra porters/bell staff
- Local telephone calls
- Parking
- Airport transfers
- Room for organiser after the event

2. And here are some items that you might ask the venue to include in their terms.

- Complimentary rooms
- Room upgrades
- A turn-down service
- Fruit and flowers in rooms
- Variation of payment terms
- Service charges
- Gratuities
- Cost of mains water and power
- Table furniture in meeting rooms
- Storage facilities
- Extra staff
- Continuous tea/coffee service

- Pastries with coffee
- Soft drinks
- Menu upgrade
- Wines upgrade
- Welcome cocktail
- Dry snacks
- Menu and place card printing
- Welcome letter
- Special service for VIPs
- Use of an office
- Extra bedroom amenities
- A total invoice rebate

Any conference organiser who attempts to negotiate all of the above items has totally misunderstood the concept and would be better employed as a debt collector for the Mob!

Source: Carey, T. (1997) Crisis or Conference?

Travel Arrangements

There is not always a requirement for conference organisers to involve themselves in the travel and logistical arrangements for their delegates. As shown by research in the German conference industry (see Chapter 4), most delegates travel by car, rather than relying on public transport. However, when significant numbers of delegates are likely to make use of public transport, there can be good PR reasons, as well as financial benefits, for organisers to offer travel package options.

It is possible for organisers to liaise directly with airlines, although it is often the case that British airlines confuse conference travel with group travel, requiring conference delegates to travel in groups (usually a minimum of ten) to qualify for discounted air tickets. The airlines fail to grasp or, in a buoyant market, seem unwilling to adapt their reservation systems to the fact that, in most cases, conference delegates travel as individuals from many different destinations to the same final destination, and do not travel in groups. Organisers may, therefore, find it easier to obtain discounted rates by working through a business travel agency, PCO/DMC, or a convention and visitor bureau to make airline reservations.

While there may be scope for British airlines to improve their products for conference delegates (other national airlines have already progressed further in this area), their shortcomings are as nothing when compared with the almost complete lack of recognition of conference travellers by the rail companies. It should be said, in fairness, that all of the train-operating companies established after the break-up of British Rail are still in their infancy but it is disappointing that, among the half dozen or so 'intercity'-type service providers, few, if any, products have yet been developed specifically for conference delegates. Again, there is usually a possibility of discounts for 'group travel' but, as already stated, this is to misunderstand the nature of conference travel.

There is the possibility of transport assistance, often on a complimentary basis, for transfers between airports or railway stations and the conference venue. Many larger hotels have minibuses or small coaches to ferry delegates from and to the airports or stations. Transport within a selected destination is also an area where a convention bureau or conference office can usually assist, recommending and booking coach firms and, for a very high-profile conference, investigating the possibility of financial support from the host city towards the cost of coach transfers.

Programme Planning

It is of prime importance that the conference programme matches the overall objectives. The content, style and pace of the programme will, of course, vary from event to event. In general terms, however, there is a stronger business orientation to most conferences than was the case in the 1980s, plus a noticeable trend for even larger conferences to be more participatory, inviting delegate contributions to plenary presentations and, particularly, through a greater use of syndicate sessions. There is also a requirement for programmes to cater for different delegate needs: this may be less of a concern for corporate conferences where delegates' levels of experience and expertise can be checked and controlled, but a challenge for association conferences where delegates are self-selecting to a much greater extent and will have disparate levels of experience.

The choice of speakers, and leaders of syndicate or workshop sessions, is crucial to the success of any event. In some cases, decisions about speakers may be imposed upon the organiser by senior managers or a conference committee. Where this is the case, the organiser's role is to ensure that speakers are properly briefed about the aims for the conference as well as for their own presentation, and that all of the technical and environmental factors (room layout, audio-visual facilities, introductory speeches) are carefully planned to create a successful 'performance'.

When the organiser has to source speakers himself, imagination and recommendation should be uppermost in his mind, probably in equal proportions. It is often stimulating for delegates to listen to a speaker with new ideas or controversial views, and a rousing opening session which generates discussion and debate may be just the spark needed to ensure a lively and productive conference. But few organisers will be willing to put their own reputations on the line by inviting relatively unknown speakers to the platform, unless they come recommended by others. Colleagues are clearly an important source of such speaker recommendations. Other sources can include trade associations, editors of trade magazines, university or college departments, and professional conference organisers.

Some conferences are strictly business events with little or no free time. Others, particularly in the association sector, combine a business programme with a social programme. The social itinerary is another area where an organiser has an opportunity to display his creativity and really make the conference memorable. The social programme should allow delegates to mix informally and network (for many, this is often the most worthwhile part of the event), but also to experience something of the destination in which the conference is being staged. It may be possible for social activities to extend, in a lighthearted way, the theme of the conference. Invaluable assistance in the design of social programmes is available from the local convention bureau or conference office, as well as from PCOs and, especially, DMCs. Examples of social events at BACD conferences in recent years have included:

- a tour of the Whisky Heritage Centre in Edinburgh, followed by dinner, concluding with a late-evening guided tour of the narrow streets around Edinburgh Castle by a 'ghost' (Adam Lyal Deceased) – a truly haunting experience!

- a banquet in the splendour of Cardiff Castle featuring Welsh dancers and a male voice choir

- a Caribbean evening in Leicester, with delegates in Caribbean costume being entertained by steel bands and cabaret

- a torchlit drinks reception in the Roman baths in Bath, followed by a banquet in the Pump Room

- a formal whisky tasting, under instruction, at Glamis Castle near Dundee, followed by a tour of the Castle and a sumptuous banquet

- a boat trip to the island of Sark (from a conference in Guernsey) with rides by horse-drawn carriage and bicycle (there are no cars on Sark), followed by dinner.

Each of these gave the event a unique character and made it an enjoyable and memorable experience.

Conference Management and Production

The general management of a conference requires, in Carey's (1997) words, 'common sense, forethought, meticulous planning and attention to detail, team work and sometimes crisis management'. Much of the administration can be enhanced by the use of event management software packages, which are designed to handle delegate registrations and correspondence, itinerary planning, invoicing, report production, and other aspects.

Examples of such software packages include:

- *Event Master*, designed and written for a Microsoft Windows environment, and available in different program versions, in modular format, for use by large organisations or small companies with a limited budget.

  Supplied by Mission Business Systems Ltd, Enterprise House, Foleshill Enterprise Park, Courtaulds Way, Coventry CV6 5NX (tel: 44 (0)1203–688448; fax: 44 (0)1203–684468).

- *Visual Impact*, also written for a Microsoft Windows environment, is designed to assist managers control the administration of all aspects of events and meetings. The core program can be supplemented with a number of optional modules covering flights, accommodation, delegate sponsorship, payments, abstract management, exhibitors and speakers and other features. Other software systems are also available covering venue management, exhibition management and event evaluation.

  Supplied by: Event Management Systems, 5 Bucklersbury, Hitchin, Hertfordshire SG5 1BB (tel: 44 (0)1462–420780; fax: 44 (0)1462–422335).

- *ConQuest 2000*, which can handle multiple events simultaneously, covering attendee management, extensive reporting, payment advices, receipts and more, and links directly to Windows word processing software.

  Supplied by: DeBoyce Ltd, Suite A, Squires House, 81–87 High Street, Billericay, Essex CM12 9AS (tel: 44 (0)1277–632022; fax: 44 (0)1277–632023).

- *confoRM*, written in Microsoft Access for the Windows environment, has modules to cover delegate registration, company/organisation details, event set-up and session management, accommodation, flight and travel details, reports, inventory management of all bookable components, and full multi-currency sales accounting.

  Developed originally by a PCO and now supplied by: Infocentre Travel Systems, Meon House, College Street, Petersfield, Hampshire GU32 3JN (tel: 44 (0)1730–303000; fax: 44 (0)1730–231810; e-mail: info@infocentre.com; Internet: www.infocentre.com).

It is useful to provide delegates, either in advance or at the registration desk, with a printed itinerary detailing the timing and location of individual sessions, particularly important when there are a number of sessions running concurrently. When this is the case, delegates will normally have been asked to pre-select the sessions of most interest to them and it is worth producing a reminder list of these sessions for them, perhaps with a list of the other delegates who have chosen the same sessions.

It should be remembered that a conference is an event which needs to be stage-managed and which requires a very professional approach to its production and presentation on the day. Through familiarity with television programmes and other broadcast media, delegates now expect the same high standards of presentation in their working environments. Poorly produced slides or overheads, problems with projectors or microphones, ill-prepared chairmen, intrusive air conditioning, uncomfortable seating are just some of the all-too-frequently voiced criticisms of conferences in the late 1990s, and all are less and less acceptable. What is more, all can and should be avoided with proper planning.

While the message is, of course, more important than the medium used to convey it, the message may get lost or misinterpreted if not presented in a way which holds delegates' attention. For this reason, the appropriate use of audio-visual technology should be discussed with speakers, who will usually have their own ideas about how best to make their presentations. If something more than just an overhead projector and flipchart is to be used, and certainly once computer-generated presentations, back-projection and video are being discussed, an organiser should look at employing a specialist conference production company. The services of such companies are not cheap, but their costs can be built into the budget and will minimise the risk of embarrassing crises, as well as reassuring speakers that their presentations will not be plagued by technical hitches.

Wherever possible, speakers should participate in rehearsals, both to familiarise themselves with the room and technical equipment to be used, and also to run through the sequence of introductions and cues to be used with the session chairman.

Event Evaluation

Once the conference is over, an evaluation of the event needs to take place as soon as possible. Ideally, delegates should complete assessments for each session as soon as it ends or shortly afterwards. Delegate itineraries can include evaluation questionnaires (a sample from a BACD conference is shown at Figure 6.8) for each session, as well as an

Figure 6.8
BACD evaluation questionnaire.

Session Title:					
Session Date:					
Presenter:					

The following is a general questionnaire, some statements may not be applicable to this session. If so, please omit.

Please indicate the extent to which you agree or disagree with the following statements regarding this session. (5=strongly agree, 1=strongly disagree; circle one number only.)

	Strongly Agree				Strongly Disagree
The speaker demonstrated knowledge of the subject	5	4	3	2	1
The speaker was effective in communicating the subject matter	5	4	3	2	1
The subject matter was of relevance and interest	5	4	3	2	1
The visual aids/handouts formed a useful part of the presentation	5	4	3	2	1
The question and answer session was of benefit	5	4	3	2	1
I learnt new skills/gained new insight and understanding	5	4	3	2	1

● My overall impression of the session was:

_____

_____

_____

● Additional Comments:

_____

_____

_____

Source: British Association of Conference Destinations

overall evaluation sheet for completion at the end of the conference. Feedback from delegates is crucial in assessing the success of the conference. It is also very important as a means of gathering ideas for future events.

In some cases, of course, a fully objective appraisal of the conference will not be possible until months later, as the outcomes of the event are translated into improved sales, enhanced performances, a more effective sharing of information, or whatever objectives were set in the first place.

The organiser will also want to evaluate how, from his perspective, the conference was managed and to what extent it met the set objectives. Ideas for improving those aspects which did not work well should emerge, and the more successful elements can be developed further in the future.

An appraisal should also take place with the venue. In the author's experience, this is an area where many venues lose marks. Discussions with the client after the event seem to be the exception, whereas they should be the norm. Even when an event appears to have run smoothly, there will always be scope for further improvement. Venues should take the initiative in following up with clients to assess all aspects of their performance. Unfortunately, few seem to bother.

Summary

- The planning of a conference involves steps which are similar to those involved in the staging of many other events. It demands a logical approach and great attention to detail on the part of an organiser, but also affords scope for creativity and imagination.

- At the outset, clear objectives for the conference should be set and as much information collected as possible about the participants, programme, timing, location and format. Financial aspects are another important part of the planning process: budgets need to be drawn up and, where appropriate, cashflow forecasts prepared.

- The selection of a suitable venue is crucial to the success of any event, and time and resources should be allocated to ensuring that the right choice is made. Various forms of assistance in venue finding are available, including directories, brochures, computer software, exhibitions, magazines and specialist agencies. Once a shortlist of the most suitable venues has been completed, inspection visits are made and negotiations take place between organisers and venues to determine an agreed package.

- Planning the detail of the conference programme should always take account of the objectives set for the event from the start. The choice of speakers is a critical factor in delegate perceptions of the event. Social programmes present an ideal opportunity for organisers to bring something distinctive and memorable to an event.

- No conference ends with the closing session. Organisers should spend time evaluating the event through feedback from delegates and other interested parties. Ideas for improving future events will emerge from this evaluation process.

Review and discussion questions

1. From the perspective of an event organiser, compare and contrast the various information sources (directories, brochures, computer software, magazine features, Internet sites) for a chosen conference destination. Evaluate the strengths and weaknesses of each source.

2. Re-read the sections on 'Negotiating with Venues' and 'Yield Management' from Chapter 5. Describe the characteristics of a 'win win' negotiation which both organiser and venue would consider a success.

3. You have 12 months to plan a new medical association conference for 300 delegates (plus partners). There is no previous event history. Produce a schedule which details the actions and decisions required on a month-by-month basis in the planning and staging of the conference. The schedule should include a budget and cashflow forecasts. The conference committee has given you an initial promotional budget of £3000 and asked you to make a profit of £5000 which can be used as a start-up fund for the following year's conference.

4. A venue charges £30 per delegate as a non-residential or day delegate rate, to include room hire, lunch, and morning and afternoon teas/coffees. Alternatively, these may be bought as separate items at a cost of £600 for room hire, £16 per person for lunch, and £2.00 for each tea/coffee consumed. Calculate the best way of buying for 40, 70, 100 and 150 delegates.

References

● Carey, Tony (1997) *Crisis or Conference!*, The Industrial Society.
● Cotterell, Peter (1994) *Conferences: An Organiser's Guide*, Hodder & Stoughton.
● Maitland, Iain (1996) *How to Organize a Conference*, Gower.

Further Reading

● Burton, C. and Micheal, N. (1992) *A Practical Guide to Project Management*, Kogan Page.
● Jay, A. (1993) *Effective Presentation*, Pitman.
● Mandel, S. (1993) *Effective Presentation Skills*, Kogan Page.
● Owen, John and Holliday, Pat (1993) *Confer in Confidence*, Meetings Industry Association.
● Polivka, Edward G. (ed.) (1997) *Professional Meeting Management*, 3rd edn, Professional Convention Management Association.
● Seekings, D. (1992) *How to Organise Successful Conferences and Meetings*, Kogan Page.
● *The Sharp Guide to Presentations* (1994) Sharp Electronics (UK) Ltd.
● Torrence, S. R. (1991) *How to Run Scientific and Technical Meetings*, Van Nostrand Reinhold.
● Watson, W., Pardo, L. and Tomovic, V. (1994) *How to Give an Effective Seminar*, Kogan Page.

Chapter 7

A People Industry

Introduction

The conference industry depends for its success and future profitability on attract-ing people with the highest quality inter-personal and organisational skills. Such skills are equally important to both the buying and supply sides of the industry. Education and training opportunities specific to the conference sector are now beginning to emerge. Stimulating and rewarding careers can be enjoyed, although clear entry routes and progression paths do not yet exist.

Objectives

This chapter examines:

- the importance of people skills
- education and training opportunities
- National Vocational Qualifications for the events industry
- careers in the conference industry
- career profiles of leading industry figures.

The Importance of People Skills

The conference industry is, by definition, about people. The word 'confer' implies a discussion or meeting involving two or more people. It follows, therefore, that those wishing to make their career in the industry need to be 'people' people. They need to have very good inter-personal skills and enjoy mixing with a very wide range of people. Diplomacy, flexibility, tact, patience, friendliness, approachability, a sense of humour, the ability to be a team player, are just some of the skills needed for success. A variety of other skills is also required depending upon the actual position occupied.

The following job vacancy descriptions are based on actual advertisements which appeared in national newspapers and other sources (in Summer 1997) and are quoted to highlight the types of skills needed for different posts:

● *Conference administrator*: Small, high-profile conference company seeks an administrator to organise prestigious events. Computer literate, well organised, meticulously accurate team player required. Competitive salary according to experience.

● *Conference and publicity coordinator*: Are you a graduate with experience of organising major high-profile conferences and publicity events? Do you have proven knowledge of media and public relations? Have you at least two years' experience of project management and budgetary control? If you fit this description, you could be responsible for the planning, marketing and coordination of events, an Annual Conference and Exhibition and public relations for [a professional medical association]. You will lead a small dynamic team and, in addition to the stated skills, will be able to prioritise and juggle tasks and will have excellent oral, written, presentation, negotiation and decision-making skills. The post is likely to attract candidates who are computer literate, are ambitious, have established media contacts and enjoy UK travel. Salary circa £22 000 plus benefits.

● *Event coordinator (with a conference centre)*: Acting as principal contact between the Centre and the client, developing, organising and managing events to ensure client requirements are carried out to the highest standard with the main objective of securing repeat and increased business. It is essential that the successful applicant has proven experience of organising events where the focus is on high quality customer care/service, possesses excellent communication skills together with the ability to produce detailed and accurate documentation. Applicants must be team players who are organised, thorough, able to work in a pressurised environment and possess a high level of motivation. This is a role for a dedicated and highly committed individual. Salary circa £17 500.

● *Conference organisers*: An international company, based in London, seeks two people to join its training and seminars office. We produce high-level seminars for ministers and senior officials of foreign governments. Skills required: an analytical mind, ability to work under pressure, attention to detail, experience of seminars or courses, interest in world affairs, knowledge of languages (especially Spanish, Russian, French), excellent written skills and ability to deal with senior people.

● *Trainee conference producers*: Is business research your forte? Are you ambitious, entrepreneurial, analytical and quick to grasp new and complex topics? If a career producing and devising influential, international, high-level business conferences is your aim, you'll need a good degree/PhD in Science/Geography/Surveying/Law, proven business experience (minimum one year) and financial acumen. European languages desirable. Salary £16 000–£20 000.

● *Senior manager – convention bureau*: Due to a promotion we have a vacancy in one of our key posts for a talented individual who will be a commercially oriented team player who understands the need for a high level of operational support to sustain a division within a highly competitive conference marketing and sales environment. Reporting to the Director for the successful coordination and implementation of a target-led marketing and sales programme, including production of print, development of operational systems, coordination of research, membership recruitment and the motivation and management of a sales and operational team of 8 people. Highly developed leadership, communications and excellent organisational skills plus computer literacy and a full appreciation of the conference industry are pre-requisites for this position. Salary £20 781–£25 770.

● *Marketing assistant – conferences, events and promotions (local authority confer-ence office)*: As a Marketing Assistant in a small team, you will be ideas-oriented and have sound organisational ability. A practical person, with exceptional communica-tion skills, you will be keen to become fully involved in planning, coordinating and implementing all factors of a project and work well in a team. You will need at least two years' marketing experience in order to meet the level of respons-ibility required, and previous involvement in events organisation or conference marketing would be an asset. A tourism or marketing qualification is not essential, but would be an advantage. Salary £12 171–£15 264.

A number of skills and personal characteristics recur in this small selection of advertise-ments. Some also re-appear later in the chapter, identified by leading conference indus-try figures as important requirements when they outline their own career profiles. The industry is broad enough to accommodate people with various working backgrounds and educational qualifications, but the common thread is the ability to build productive relationships with a wide variety of people (colleagues, clients and customers, suppliers, the media, and others) and to enjoy doing so.

The importance of people skills was well illustrated by research into a possible clas-sification and grading scheme for conference venues undertaken in 1996–97. Sponsored by the Scottish, English, Northern Ireland and Wales Tourist Boards and undertaken by Travel and Tourism Research, the research found that where conference organisers had problems with venues it was not, for the most part, with the facilities and equipment but with staff service, specifically lack of professionalism and friendliness.

As the physical attributes of conference venues become more standardised and of a generally acceptable level, it is likely to be the quality of the staff which will differenti-ate one from another. This point was expressed very lucidly in a report published by the Department of National Heritage (DNH – now Department for Culture, Media and Sport) in 1996. Entitled *Tourism: Competing with the Best – People Working in Tourism and Hospitality*, the report said that:

> *The quality of personal service is perhaps more important to tourism and hospital-ity than to any other industry. Consumers who buy one of this industry's products will often have made a significant financial investment, but also an emotional investment and an investment of time. Of course the* physical *product – the facilit-ies of the holiday village, the distinctiveness of the tourist attraction, the appointments of the hotel, the quality of the restaurant's food – is very important to them. But during the period customers are in the establishment, they will have many inter-actions with* people*: some indirect, with the management and chefs and cleaners; and many direct, with the front-line staff. The quality of those interactions is an integral part of the experience and has the potential to delight or disappointment the consumer. We do not believe that this potential is there to the same extent in any other employing sector.*

The DNH report rightly claims that:

> *Excellent service at a competitive price can only be provided by competent, well-managed and well-motivated people. This means recruiting the right people in the first place, equipping them with the skills they need, managing staff well to create motivation, job satisfaction, and high productivity.*

The report analyses some of the tourism industry's shortcomings in respect of these object-ives, specifically:

The threat of a self-perpetuating vicious circle that is harmful to profitability and competitiveness. In some parts of the industry a number of characteristics reinforce each other: recruitment difficulties, shortages of skilled and qualified staff, relatively low pay, high staff turnover and a relatively unattractive image as an employing sector.

The report then gives examples of good practice, and makes some proposals for future improvements to overall standards, through better dissemination of good practice, a greater understanding of customer needs and improving quality, improving the image of the industry, and improving the supply of skills to the industry.

The conference sector of the tourism and hospitality industry is not immune from these criticisms. While they apply specifically to the supply side of the industry, it is undoubtedly the case that there is also scope to improve the training and professionalism of those on the buying side. Perhaps there is a need for a 'Code of Practice' for buyers, in the same way that conference venues now offer quality-assured branded products delivered with customer guarantees. In the author's experience, familiar failings on the part of buyers include:

- ludicrously short lead times for planning events and booking venues and services
- 'no shows' or last-minute cancellations from buyer familiarisation trips, when flights have been paid for and hotel rooms booked
- a failure to evaluate events. Research by American Express (summarised in *Meetings & Incentive Travel Magazine*, February 1997) found that 35 per cent of corporate organisers did not obtain delegate feedback and evaluate the effectiveness of their meetings
- making reservations for, say 40 delegates, but only half this number turning up, leaving the venue with unsold rooms
- a failure to provide fully comprehensive technical and organisational specifications
- a tendency to assume too much about a venue's capabilities and responsibilities
- failing to inform bureaus and agencies which have provided them with a venue finding service of bookings made, and then complaining when they get follow-up calls.

The conference industry is a wonderful, dynamic, seductive industry but one which still fails to command the recognition it deserves. For it to achieve its full potential and be appreciated as a major benefactor to the national economy, both sides of the industry must embrace and maintain the same high standards of integrity and professionalism. The status of the conference organiser must be raised to that of a real profession, of equal standing with solicitors, accountants, sales or production managers.

There is a need to invest in education and training programmes for buyers (a few are now available and others are slowly coming on stream, but there is still a long way to go), to develop career structures so that experience and expertise are retained within the meetings industry, to enhance college and university courses to give appropriate coverage to conference and business tourism, and to provide recognised qualifications in line with other professions.

Buyers and suppliers are interdependent, neither can succeed without the other. Effective collaboration and partnerships should be born of respect for the skills and knowledge of each other, built on mutual trust and confidence.

To translate such needs and aspirations into reality will depend to a great extent upon developments to education and training programmes. The next section looks at the opportunities for education and training currently available within the conference industry, some of which are appropriate to those looking to make a career in the industry, others are for those already employed within it.

Education and Training Opportunities

College and university courses

As will be made clear later in this chapter in the section on careers, it is *not* essential for those looking to make a career in the conference industry to have pursued a particular educational course, although certain courses can provide skills and knowledge which are readily applicable to the industry.

For those wishing to study a course which is directly relevant to a future career, the best options are probably hotel and catering courses and, particularly, courses involving tourism and tourism management. Since the late 1980s there has been an explosion in tourism courses in the United Kingdom, with several hundred colleges now offering full-time courses (including GNVQ, Advanced GNVQ, Higher National Diploma, degree). The 1998–99 UCAS Handbook lists 58 universities and colleges running tourism courses at degree level, while a number of universities also offer post-graduate tourism-related courses.

Until very recently, conference and business tourism did not feature strongly on any of these courses. This is beginning to change as an increasing number of educational institutions offer 'conference management' and 'event management' modules as part of tourism and hotel and catering courses. A typical module outline is shown in Figure 7.1, reproduced by permission of Birmingham College of Food, Tourism and Creative Studies, where the module is designed as background for students looking for careers in the hotel industry.

It seems that most modules are designed for those expecting to work on the supply side of the industry, as conference or event coordinators in venues, for example. There has been little provision for people looking to find employment as conference buyers or in a conference agency.

In part to address this need, Leeds Metropolitan University launched a new degree course in Events Management in 1996, believed to be the only course of its kind in Europe. Available for study as a four-year sandwich course, three-year full-time course, or on a part-time basis for those in employment (as well as a one-year top-up degree for students who have gained a Higher National Diploma in a related discipline or have relevant experience). The areas studied include conference and meeting planning, convention and trade show organisation, concert and event planning, security and law and contracts and tendering. To underpin these essential areas, there is further academic study exploring financial management within the event industry, strategic management and strategic human resource management. The principles of marketing are also studied in depth. There is a placement opportunity in Year 2 lasting 48 weeks, which provides a learning experience for students to develop their skills while working in the event industry.

Contact: Julia Tum, Course Leader, The School of Tourism and Hospitality Management, Faculty of Cultural and Education Studies, Leeds Metropolitan University, Calverley Street, Leeds LSI 3HE (tel: 44 (0)113–283–3478; fax: 44 (0)113–283–3111).

AIMS

One of the features of recent years in the hotel and catering industry has been the continuing development of the conference and exhibition market and the increasing provision of hotel facilities and services to accommodate this market. While the main focus is on conference and exhibition topics, consideration is also given to related areas such as business tourism and incentive travel; both of which are frequently interrelated with conference and exhibition provision. The final year module, Conference and Exhibition Management, affords the student the opportunity of studying this area in depth.

It is also intended that the module will act as an integrating mechanism across the other final year modules. Many of the concepts of Hotel Operations Management can be applied to the provision and organisation of facilities and services for the conference and exhibition market. Increased targeting and development of facilities for this market segment is, for many hotel companies, a key feature of their Organisation Development strategy. Finally, conference and exhibition providers have to compete within the international arena for custom and International Marketing techniques are, therefore, of particular relevance.

SYLLABUS

Conference and Exhibition Market

The nature of the conference and exhibition market and related areas of business tourism. Segments of the market. Size and significance of the markets to hotels. Characteristics of the conference and exhibition product. Determinants of demand for, and supply of, conference and exhibition facilities. Competitor analysis. Comparison of facilities/venues in U.K. and Europe.

The Consumer of Conference and Exhibition Products

Market segments and characteristics of organisers and delegates. Satisfying needs and expectations. Factors affecting choice (including analysis of facilities). Effective marketing and selling techniques to secure potential bookings. Significance of the conference agent. Working with agents.

Planning, Organisation and Control

Planning the organisation and deployment of resources to stage conferences and exhibitions. Problem identification, analysis and diagnosis. Reservations and charting systems. Computerised conference reservation and information systems. Communication – with client and internally within the hotel. Timing and scheduling. Working within budget parameters. Analysis of constraints. Working with service contractors and production companies. Contractual obligations of hotel and client. Dealing with cancellations. Other terms and conditions. Current developments and trends in the conference and exhibition sector.

MODULE LENGTH

45 hours total learning support, approximately two-thirds of which will comprise the formal lecture/seminar programme.

ASSESSMENT

The balance of assessment will be 60% coursework and 40% end of year.

TEACHING AND LEARNING STRATEGY

Lectures, case studies and student-led seminars. It is also intended to arrange for industry-based speakers during the course of the module.

Source: Birmingham College of Food, Tourism and Creative Studies

Figure 7.1
Conference and exhibition management module, Birmingham College of Food, Tourism and Creative Studies BA/BA (Honours) in Hotel Business Management – Year 4.

At the time of writing (August 1997), a course specific to the conference industry is seeking support for a commencement date in 1997 or 1998. This is an HNC in Business for Conference and Event Management, designed by the Association of British Professional Conference Organisers (ABPCO) in partnership with the University of Westminster and

City of Westminster College, London. This two-year part-time course is designed to equip students with:

- an understanding of the practical and theoretical applications of conference and event management
- an awareness of the general principles within which conferences are managed
- an awareness of the legal and financial implications in the context of conferences and events.

Contact: Caroline Roney, ABPCO Education and Training Co-ordinator, Congress House, 65 West Drive, Cheam, Surrey SM2 7NB (tel: 44 (0)181–661–0877; fax: 44 (0)181–661–9036).

'An Introduction to Conference Management'

Designed for relative newcomers to the field of conference organising and those who undertake event management as a secondary role, 'An Introduction to Conference Management' was first held in 1985 and is claimed to be the longest-running training course of its kind in the British Isles. The course is led by Tony Carey, a well-known speaker and writer on the conference industry, assisted by specialists from different sectors of the business. The course is held over three days, normally at a central London venue, at least once a year. Subjects covered include: sources of information, venue selection, site inspections, negotiation, programme planning, speaker management, hospitality planning, budgets and accounts, preparing delegates. The course fee of £450 (1997) includes tuition, materials, daily lunch and refreshments.

Contact: Tony Carey, Campaign Management Associates Limited, Sydney Vane House, St Peter Port, Guernsey, Channel Islands, GY1 2HU (tel: 44 (0)1481–728007; fax: 44 (0)1481–713789; e-mail: tonyccma@itl.net).

ACE courses

The Association for Conferences and Events (ACE) holds several short courses each year designed for those working as conference organisers or seeking to find employment as such. The two regular courses are:

1. 'Principles of Meetings Planning': a three-day residential course (usually Friday–Sunday) held in different locations and covering: the strategy of meetings, venue sourcing, venue evaluation and selection, administration, programming meetings, speakers and presentations, food and beverage fundamentals, delegate care. Course fee of £285 + VAT in 1997, with a discount for ACE member organisations.

2. 'Meetings Planning and Organisation': an intermediate level course (which can also serve as a follow-on to 'Principles of Meeting Planning') which is also three-day residential (Friday–Sunday) and covers: programme design, budgeting and controlling costs, finding suitable locations, getting the best deal in negotiation, creative catering, social and formal function planning. Course fee of £330 + VAT (in 1997), with a discount for ACE member organisations.

Contact details of these and other ACE courses: Association for Conferences and Events, ACE International, Riverside House, High Street, Huntingdon, Cambridgeshire PE18 6SG (tel: 44 (0)1480–457595).

IAPCO courses

The International Association of Professional Congress Organisers (IAPCO) runs courses at several levels through its Institute for Congress Management Training. The best known is the annual IAPCO Seminar on Professional Congress Organisation, popularly known as the Wolfsberg Seminar, first staged in 1975. This is a week-long seminar held in Switzerland in late January and provides a comprehensive training programme for executives involved in conference organisation, international conference destination promotion or ancillary services. Topics covered include: introduction to the industry, the role of the PCO, conference promotion and sponsorship, meeting programmes, on-site management, PCO office structure, marketing, finance, communications, technology. Attendance at the seminar can earn points towards the 'Certificate in Meetings Management' (see below). Cost of the Seminar (1998): 4000 Swiss francs for IAPCO members, 4800 Swiss francs for non-members.

In addition IAPCO runs senior and middle management seminars especially focusing on conferences as a service industry. It also arranges an annual Forum of International Conferences, which uses Open Space Technology and provides a platform for interactive discussion on the latest trends and techniques (in 1997 the Forum focused on medical meetings). Open Space Technology is a recent innovation which entails staging meetings with no pre-set programme: discussion leaders are on hand, if required, but essentially the agenda is determined by participants. Delegates choose which sessions they want to attend, with the freedom to move around from one group to another.

Contact: IAPCO, 40 rue Washington, 1050 Brussels, Belgium (tel: 32–2–640–71–05; fax: 32–2–640–47–31; e-mail: iapco@agoranet.be or iapco@pophost.eunet.be; Internet: http://www.iapco.org).

'Certificate in Meetings Management'

The 'Certificate in Meetings Management' (CMM) is the first university-certified qualification for meeting professionals in Europe, and a major step towards encouraging and recognising professionalism in meeting and conference management. The unique partnership between Meeting Professionals International (MPI), the largest meeting industry association in the world, and the Institut de Management Hôtelier in Paris, one of the most prestigious educational institutions in Europe, guarantees the validity of the programme both from an academic and a meeting industry perspective. The CMM qualification is designed for all those involved in the industry, including:

Planners (buyers)	*Suppliers*
Corporate planners (full- or part-time)	Hotels and conference centres
Association planners	Staff of convention bureaus
Professional conference organisers	Audio-visual/production companies
	Airlines
	Destination management companies, etc.

In order to obtain the CMM certificate, candidates must complete a self-assessment form which documents their professional and educational background, work and meeting management experience, language skills and professional contributions. The CMM courses, as well as many other educational programmes offered by MPI and other associations (such as ICCA, IAPCO) contribute to the final points score on the self-assessment form. Candidates with a minimum of 85 points (out of a maximum possible of 110) are eligible to sit for the CMM examination.

The programme requires a major commitment from applicants, both in time (each course is a full immersion week) and financially (course costs approximately £845, exam costs £410), but does provide a professional qualification of high international repute.

Contact: MPI European Bureau, Boulevard St-Michel 15, B-1040 Brussels, Belgium (tel: 32-2-743-15-44; fax: 32-2-743-15-50).

EFCT Summer School

The European Federation of Conference Towns (EFCT) has been running an annual Summer School since 1987, held in a different country each year (normally end of August/ early September) over three to four days. The programme aims to give an overview of the conference industry, emphasising the role of convention bureaus and conference centres, but also catering for related hotel, airline and PCO/DMC personnel. Topics at the 1997 Summer School (held in Barcelona) included: marketing a destination, working with the European Community, surveys and statistics, the role of the PCO, the marketing mix and working with the press, simultaneous interpretation, new conference technology, successful bidding for a conference, future expectations for the industry. The cost of the 1997 Summer School was ECU1000 for EFCT member staff and ECU1100 for others (approximately £700–£800), excluding travel costs to the host city.

Contact: EFCT, BP 182, 1040 Brussels, Belgium (tel: 32-2-732-69-54).

The International Meetings Academy

The International Meetings Academy (IMA) is the title of a series of education and training programmes being developed by the International Congress and Convention Association (ICCA) to meet the needs of the *international* conference and exhibition industry in all sectors, in all regions of the world, and at all levels. The initial programmes are targeted at suppliers, while later programmes are expected to address the needs of buyers. They are tailored to provide personal growth and enable individuals to advance from basic to advanced professional knowledge.

IMA programmes include:

- *Young Executive Programme*: a full week intensive course concentrating on conference management and marketing skills for those with a minimum of two years' industry experience. The course covers: market segments, clients' expectations, development of a marketing plan and competitive analysis, budgeting and finance for meetings, presentation skills, group work, trends in the industry. Cost: US$1900 for ICCA members, US$2000 for non-members (in 1997).

- *Middle Management Programme*: a four-day programme based on developing personal skills, further in-depth knowledge of marketing techniques, marketing communication techniques, management skills, presentation techniques. Designed for those who have already completed the Young Executive Programme as well as for others in a middle management position with some three to four years' working experience. 1997 costs: US$2695 for ICCA members or for those who have completed the Young Executive Programme, US$2895 for non-members.

- *New Executive Programme*: a four-day programme for experienced managers who are new to the conference industry. The curriculum is based on case materials as well as in-depth exchange of hands-on experiences. Supplier, client and market analyses as well as competitive analyses of the principal conference destinations are part of the programme. 1997 costs: US$2250 for ICCA members or US$2450 for non-members.

Other courses are being planned as part of the IMA. Contact: Ms Quirine Laman Trip, Head of Faculty, International Meetings Academy of ICCA, Entrada 121, 1096 EB Amsterdam, The Netherlands (tel: 31–20–690–1171).

One-day courses and workshops

One-day courses, workshops and seminars are run by several trade associations, as well as other organisations. These include:

- the British Association of Conference Destinations (BACD) runs a series of Winter Workshops (some of which are open to non-members) on topics such as: Setting Up and Running a Conference Bureau, Direct Marketing, Effective Communication/ Rapport Skills, Advertising and Print Production, Designing a Client Database (typical cost approximately £200 + VAT). The BACD educational programme also includes a three-day residential Summer School on different aspects of conference destination marketing.

  Contact: British Association of Conference Destinations, 1st Floor Elizabeth House, 22 Suffolk Street, Queensway, Birmingham B1 1LS (tel: 44–(0)121–616–1400; fax: 44–(0)121–616–1364; e-mail:bacdassoc@aol.com).

- the Meetings Industry Association (MIA) runs an annual one-day Presentation Skills seminar, and half-day training seminars on the use and availability of audio-visual equipment (open to both members and potential members). The MIA has also produced two training videos designed for staff working in conference venues: a) 'Comprehending Clients', b) 'Meeting on Good Terms', priced at £150 + VAT and £125 + VAT respectively, with discounts for MIA members.

  Contact: Meetings Industry Association, 34 High Street, Broadway, Worcestershire WR12 7DT (tel: 44 (0)1386–858572; fax: 44 (0)1386–858986).

- the Society of Event Organisers runs half-day, one-day and two-day courses on a wide range of topics, including the strategy of conferences and meetings (why you run them), choosing destinations and venues, how to negotiate with venues, how to programme meetings, food and beverage selection, administration, and trouble shooting. Costs range from £50 to £200 depending upon duration. Courses are also run for venues by The Meetings Forum on how to market themselves effectively to the conference market.

  Contact: Peter Cotterell, Society of Event Organisers/The Meetings Forum, 29a Market Square, Biggleswade, Bedfordshire SG18 8AQ (tel: 44 (0)1767–316255; fax: 44 (0)1767–316430).

It is perhaps not suprising that a number of high quality education programmes are available in the United States and Canada, the real birthplace of the conference industry. Particularly noteworthy are those run by the Professional Convention Management Association (PCMA) and the International Association of Convention and Visitor Bureaus (IACVB), especially its 'Certified Destination Management Executive' programme. However, with the exception of MPI's 'Certificate in Meetings Management' (described earlier in this chapter), no cost-effective way has yet been found to export these programmes to other regions of the world.

National Vocational Qualifications for the Events Industry

In addition to the education and training opportunities described in the previous section, work has been under way since 1993 to establish recognised occupational standards for the events industry. These occupational standards are the first major stage in the programme to develop National and Scottish Vocational Qualifications (N/SVQs) for almost everyone involved in the events industry, whether they are working as organisers, in venues, as suppliers or as exhibitors. N/SVQs are competence-based, measuring employees' actual ability to complete work tasks successfully. The efforts to establish N/SVQs have been spearheaded by the Events Sector Industry Training Organisation (ESITO), on which the following ten trade associations are represented: Association of British Professional Conference Organisers, Association for Conferences and Events, Association of Exhibition Organisers, British Exhibition Contractors Association, British Exhibition Venues Association, Incentive Travel and Meetings Association, Meetings Industry Association, National Exhibitors Association, National Outdoor Events Association, The Event Services Association.

Contact: ESITO, Riverside House, High Street, Huntingdon, Cambridgeshire PE18 6SG (tel: 44 (0)1480–457595).

1997 saw the launch in Britain of a new seminar entitled 'Conference Care' (not strictly speaking a National Vocational Qualification), built on the framework of the highly successful Welcome Host scheme. Conference Care is designed to improve the standards of service and hospitality to all visitors to an area, especially conference and business travellers. Developed originally in Glasgow to prepare the city for hosting two major international conventions, Conference Care is now being extended to other parts of the country and delivered through Welcome Host Local Coordinators, with places often being subsidised by Local Enterprise Companies and Training and Enterprise Councils.

Contact: Glasgow Tourism Training Unit, c/o Greater Glasgow and Clyde Valley Tourist Board, 11 George Square, Glasgow G2 1DY (tel: 44 (0)141–204–4480).

Careers in the Conference Industry

Unlike many other professions, the conference industry does not yet have clear entry routes or easily identified career progression paths. It is one of the facets which illustrate its relative immaturity as an industry. This lack of structure may be somewhat frustrating and confusing for those, both within and outside the industry, who have set their sights on reaching a particular career goal but are uncertain about how best to get there. At the same time, however, this lack of precedent and structure can encourage a greater fluidity and freedom of movement between jobs. There is often no set requirement to progress in a particular way, or to have obtained specific qualifications before being able to move on.

Many of those now working in the industry have come to it as a second or third career. This is not surprising in view of the need to be at ease in dealing with a wide range of people, or in coping with a last-minute crisis in the build-up to a high-profile conference – situations which require a reasonable maturity and some experience of life.

Previous experience in hotel and catering, sales and marketing, business administration, secretarial work, financial management, local government administration, training, travel and transport, or leisure and tourism could be advantageous, depending upon the position being considered. But many other backgrounds and disciplines can also give very relevant skills and knowledge, as shown in the job vacancies quoted earlier in this chapter, provided that these are combined with a natural affinity for working with people.

For those looking to find employment straight from university or college, vacancies do arise in conference agencies (e.g. administrative posts, assisting in venue finding, computer work) and in conference venues (as assistant conference and banqueting coordinators, or in venue sales and marketing). It can be possible for new graduates to obtain posts in conference offices and convention bureaus, although more often one to two years' previous experience in sales and marketing or local government administration is desirable.

Relatively few buyers, especially within the corporate sector, are full-time conference organisers and meeting planners. They are first and foremost secretaries/PAs, marketing assistants/managers, training managers, or public relations executives, who find themselves asked to organise events on behalf of their department or company. Their role in conference organising may, of course, develop if they prove to have the right talents and enthusiasm and if this meets the company's own development needs.

Other openings arise, from time to time, in conference industry trade associations and, for those with an interest in publishing, in the industry's trade magazines (either in advertising sales or, for those with some journalistic background, as part of the editorial teams).

Before beginning a career within conferencing, it is probably helpful to know whether one's interest is primarily in the buying or supply side of the industry (see Chapter 2). It is, of course, quite possible at a later stage to switch from one side to the other, and an understanding of how both buyers and suppliers operate is obviously important and beneficial. It is a moot point whether intermediary agencies are best described as buyers or suppliers. Their activities certainly revolve around venue finding and event management, but they do this by providing a service to their clients, the actual buyers.

It should be stressed that most companies and organisations operating within the conference industry are small, employing limited numbers of people. This is true of most corporate and association event departments, convention bureaus, conference venues, agencies and trade associations. They cannot offer multiple career opportunities and endless possibilities for progression. But their smallness does often ensure that there is a great variety of work with considerable responsibility and lots of scope to display initiative. It does also mean that it is possible, quite quickly, to get to know many of the players in the industry, building friendships and networks of colleagues nationally and, indeed, across the world.

Finally, sources of job vacancies. There are not a great many to choose from at present, but in the author's experience the following can be helpful:

- The Association for Conferences and Events (ACE) produces a 'Job Spot' vacancy list every few weeks.
- National newspapers (broadsheets) are a reasonable source, with *The Guardian* being especially useful (Monday and Saturday editions).
- The industry's own trade magazines have occasional vacancies, usually with conference agencies.
- Tony Carey, PR consultant and conference industry writer and trainer, has launched a website to help meeting planners. It contains hints for organisers and a job spot listing vacancies in the industry. *Contact: http://user.itl.net/~tonyccma.*
- If financial/personal circumstances permit, would-be entrants to the industry should aim to get some work experience in the industry, even if this means working unpaid for a short time. The experience itself will be invaluable (and count for a lot on CVs), and it may also be the source of contacts for full-time posts.

Career Profiles of Leading Industry Figures

The last section of this chapter contains a series of career profiles written by well-known personalities within the British conference industry. They each describe their current jobs and those aspects of their work which they find rewarding and fulfilling. Some also outline the parts of their work which they find less enjoyable. And previous career experiences, including education and training, are touched on. It is hoped that these profiles will be instructive and maybe inspirational, encouraging some of the readers of this book to want to follow in the footsteps of these people and forge their own careers in the infinitely varied and endlessly stimulating conference industry.

Pat Neville, British Association of Urological Surgeons

In 1997 it rained! Delegates with long memories said it was the first time in 12 years but, however successful the conference was, it will be remembered for the weather.

I joined the British Association of Urological Surgeons (BAUS) as Administrative Secretary in 1986, coming from a Medical Faculty where I had been responsible for small-scale courses and meetings, mainly in-house. My first encounter with the medical field had been a stint with a market researcher at the North West Regional Health Authority, assessing the efficacy of postgraduate training of general practitioners. Spending six months carrying out telephone interviews with everyone concerned, from laboratory technicians to professors of medicine, gave me a serious grounding in medical terminology.

When I came to BAUS the Annual Meeting attracted around 300 delegates with an associated exhibition covering little more than 100 square metres. Ten years on, delegate numbers have risen to over 1000, the exhibition spreads over 900 square metres and many additional features have been introduced to the programme. What has really changed in the organisation process?

In those far-off days of 300 participants, a wide choice of venues was available: Buxton, Jersey, Scarborough, even London. Now the need for two large lecture theatres, extensive exhibition space, room for lunches, poster displays, video booths, company-sponsored satellite meetings, and so on restricts the conference to four or five UK locations, with three- to four-year lead times for bookings.

When I took over, both the conference and the exhibition were contracted out to a PCO. Within one year I brought the conference in house followed, a year later, by the exhibition. I can recall watching, with barely disguised amazement, as two young women from the PCO company spent the equivalent in hours of about three weeks 'organising' our exhibition and, after the event, their company retained 55 per cent of the income! Like many associations we are financially dependent upon the surplus from our main exhibition. I had assumed until then that anything to do with exhibitions required a great deal of technical knowledge but saw, by keeping my eyes open, that the only necessities were, as with most things, common sense and an attention to detail. I am convinced that one of the reasons for the growth of our exhibition is the fact that the exhiting companies know that the profits are coming to BAUS, a registered charity, and not to a PCO. Also, the fact that we deal with them personally, as individuals, means that mutual respect and friendship have been the cement with which the success of the exhibition has been built. Free-build stands have replaced shell scheme for many of the exhibiting companies with a constant stream of innovative ways to attract delegates: cocktail bars, go-karts, virtual reality golf, and many more.

The only aspects of the conference now handled by outside agencies are hotel bookings and the accompanying persons programme, once the content has been agreed.

Thanks to our audio-visual consultants we have stayed, if anything, ahead of the game in presentation technology with multiple projection, multimedia capabilities, computer-generated images and live satellite links.

Life in the office has recently been made easier by the introduction of a computer system which integrates the membership database of the Association with the registration and financial reporting requirements of the conference. This is beginning to prove its worth after a somewhat turbulent and lengthy introductory period – par for the course, I am told.

The staff of the Association has grown over ten years from two to four, including myself, with additional help brought in for the Annual Meeting. The work of the Association has expanded dramatically over this period with a twofold increase in membership and the commensurate work in collecting subscriptions, additional meetings and courses – some in other EU countries – and taking on the administration of an additional association, the British Prostate Group, with 300 members and its own calendar of meetings.

Several years ago, I gave up having a job title printed on my business cards, 'Jack (or Jill) of all Trades' would be the only appropriate description.

Skills necessary for a conference organiser? Firstly, an almost obsessive attention to detail is a prerequisite for meticulous planning, coupled with the creative vision to turn vast empty spaces into attractive areas for both the professional and social aspects of the meeting. Infinite patience helps, together with negotiating skills, tact, and a diplomatic ability which would put the Foreign Office to shame! It goes without saying that the ability to walk quickly, holding parallel conversations on a mobile phone and a walkie-talkie, while simultaneously eating a baguette, is a technique every conference organiser acquires over time.

My personal likes:

● Taking a blank piece of graph paper, making a scale drawing of a hall and producing an exhibition floor plan which, months later, becomes reality. I believe that computer programmes can now do this but I do enjoy letting out the draughtsman in me.

● Researching venues for dinners and social events. I love using venues not normally available to the public, getting to know Lord this or Lady that in the process, meeting wonderful, interesting people is so much part of the fun. Of course, there is also the hard work involved in having wine tastings and eating test meals!

● Seeing a large project through, from booking the venue, preparing a budget, planning all printed material, and so on, right through the actual event and (hopefully) receiving many kind letters of thanks afterwards, is particularly fulfilling for all concerned.

And dislikes:

● Delegates registering on site, nobody on my staff is psychic!

● Being asked at the end of a conference 'what do you do for the rest of the year?'

I would advise anyone involved in organising meetings to attend events arranged by other associations/companies. There is always something to learn, even if it is how not to do it. It is especially illuminating to see a conference or exhibition through delegates' eyes.

So in 1997 it rained. The exhibitors loved it and asked if I would kindly arrange rain for next year. Who said the impossible takes a little longer?

Martin Peters, Head of Marketing and Development, Leicester Promotions Visitor and Conference Service

There are certain events in life that stick in the memory. My first foray into the tourism industry is one such occasion.

A cold, wet November morning in 1982 saw me taking up a post on the counter at the City Information Bureau in Leicester. This was not part of a highly developed life-plan that had my goals mapped out for the next 25 years! The post was taken as a stop-gap while post-A Level options were considered and, as for many people, it was always going to be a temporary arrangement.

This almost accidental introduction to tourism has subsequently proved to be a most valuable training and development opportunity.

Skipping over the intervening years, my career has included Tourist Information Centre (TIC) management, overseas marketing, travel trade, short-breaks and business tourism.

A couple of other milestones bring the story up to date. In 1990, as part of an English Tourist Board Tourism Development Action Programme (TDAP), conference tourism was put much higher on the agenda for Leicester. I had the opportunity to work with a number of key professionals locally and further afield, to understand the principal elements of successful conference city marketing and how to apply them to Leicester.

Secondly, in 1993, I was able to be part of the team establishing a fully independent company, Leicester Promotions Ltd, to which the marketing and promotion of the city would be contracted in the future.

And so to today. My post as Head of Marketing and Development with Leicester Promotions Ltd allows me to play an active role in the fortunes and success of the city and our company. The post operates on a number of levels:

- *Corporate*: Having a senior position in a private destination marketing company is no different from the corporate responsibility of any other business. Reporting to a Chief Executive and Board of Directors, ensuring tight and accurate budgetary control, constant and consistent monitoring of performance and effectiveness, looking for new and better business opportunities, are a few of the demands.

- *Functional*: A traditional team leader role. The team in this case is 12 staff, covering all aspects of a destination-based tourism operation. A full-service visitor and conference operation deals daily with conference buyers, travel trade and independent travellers. A highly developed and respected TIC operation handles around 200 000 customers a year and is operated with a tight commercial focus. A very successful short-breaks promotion continues to attract ever-increasing numbers.

- *Product*: There comes a point when a critical look at the product being marketed is needed. The dynamics of a city, the plethora of partners involved, the barriers which sometimes seem to have been created to prevent development, are some of the challenges faced. But it is a highly rewarding aspect when success is achieved. This responsibility manifests itself in many guises including working constantly to put the needs of visitors higher up the agenda, identifying and helping to break down barriers to development, and overseeing the research and implementation of a long-term development strategy.

● *National*: Decisions and policy at a regional level through regional tourist boards and at a national level through national tourist boards, trade associations and government have a major impact on all of the above categories and a watching brief must be kept at all times. Lobbying to ensure the needs and importance of the industry are recognised, fighting for appropriate division of funding, influencing structures and priorities will all pay dividends in achieving local success. Increasingly, the influence and consequences of European legislation and policy need regular review.

Delivering the above takes many forms. From overseeing the implementation of a new merchandising strategy for the TIC, to advising on a five-year development plan for short breaks. Staff reviews and appraisals, presentations to current and potential clients and working with a local university on a five-year corporate development plan. Meetings with regional tourist board colleagues, BACD and other association colleagues, local councillors and government ministers. Reviewing the strategic marketing objectives of the tourism operation, setting performance targets and objectives. Speaking at conference and industry events and providing consultancy services to other destinations. All of these activities, and many more, have been in my diary in the last few months.

So what do you need to do the job? A broad-based experience of the tourism industry, an understanding of the dynamics of a city, powerful negotiation skills. Clear, strategic thinking and a calm, lateral approach to problem solving. The ability to motivate and lead, lobby and influence. Sound experience of researching, implementing and monitoring marketing campaigns and a thorough understanding of finances.

But don't forget a lot of energy, masses of enthusiasm and a sense of humour!

Sue Potton, Sales Manager, Queen Elizabeth II Conference Centre, London

I am responsible for managing the sales team as well as developing the business and sales strategy long-term for the Queen Elizabeth II Conference Centre [QEIICC]. The strategic planning is vital; it has to be implemented and constantly maintained and I continually monitor performance against targets.

I specialise in the North American market and the larger national and international events. My role includes developing new business and maintaining and developing business with existing clients. I visit America quite often: in June [1997] I was in New York and Boston for a week, meeting with clients, industry contacts such as the British Tourist Authority, and making presentations to potential clients. I spend about 10 per cent of my working life abroad on the Centre's behalf.

I have direct line management for four people and oversee their daily activities. We work closely together and I am their coach and mentor as well as their manager. In a service industry, it's important that staff are well-trained and the QEIICC has a strong emphasis on training. I conduct in-house seminars for my own staff as well as others in the Centre and I also recommend external courses. Training sessions cover a variety of subjects, such as 'Effective Sales Visits', to help increase confidence.

It's important to maintain the focus and motivation of the sales team because we are very pro-active in following up sales leads and contacts. We also pride ourselves on our responsiveness to clients, so our reactions to incoming enquiries are equally important and we try to make sure that enquiries are dealt with quickly and efficiently, with materials sent out the same day.

We develop creative ideas to bring new clients into the Centre and conduct joint marketing events with organisations like the Institute of Public Relations. We have regular meetings with other departments to exchange ideas, priorities, and views and their feedback helps us enormously, particularly in developing high-spend clients.

A major part of the job is building our relationships with existing and potential clients and understanding their business needs. This function drives the Centre's business so it's a role that my team and I take very seriously. This often involves entertaining two or three clients a week at the Centre – Leith's catering is one of the star attractions, so clients welcome the opportunity to sample new dishes while discussing business. I often invite someone from Leith's at the Centre to the meeting, which helps their sales too.

I particularly relish the opportunities the industry presents and the wide range of fascinating people I meet. In any given day I could talk to a heart transplant specialist, a professional conference organiser, a PR representative, or a chief executive. Developing strong working relationships with our clients is always enjoyable. The cross-section of events makes the job rewarding too: from international association conferences of several thousand, to prestigious awards ceremonies, exhibitions or press launches, there is always something different happening and new challenges to meet.

It's a very sociable industry and I am a gregarious person, a firm believer in the advantages of networking and getting involved in other areas of the industry. I work closely with many industry organisations such as the London Convention Bureau, the British Tourist Authority and Conventions Great Britain. I am also Chairman of the European Council for Education for Meeting Professionals International (MPI).

The downside is when you don't get a piece of business that you know was tailor-made for the venue or when something is cancelled, through no fault of your own, after you have put a great deal of work into it. And although the travel sounds glamorous, it's not much fun driving around on your own in a snowstorm in Boston – or spending six days in a darkened hotel room with a perforated cornea!

My route into the conference industry was via the hotel industry and sales. While I was at school, I worked in hotels during the summer and at weekends and I knew that's what I wanted to do when I finished my 'A' levels. I started as a management trainee with Goodhews, a small hotel chain, and worked in every department from housekeeping to front of house, then at the Spiders Web in Bushey helping to oversee banqueting events and room bookings.

My first real introduction to sales was with Drake Personnel, where I helped set up their executive recruitment division, then with Abraxas, the computer recruitment specialists as a recruitment consultant making presentations to big companies. In the early 80s high level computer appointments were burgeoning, so it was extremely competitive and gave me great experience of front-line selling.

But my first love was hotels. With the sales experience under my belt, I became assistant manager at the Anglo-Swiss Hotel in Bournemouth, part of the Quadrant Group, and was responsible for all their sales activity; I was subsequently promoted to group sales manager for Quadrant.

In 1991 I joined the Bournemouth International Centre as sales executive. Everything I had learned previously seemed to fall into place; it was wonderful to have this huge facility with capacity for 4000 delegates, concerts and all types of events. I had my first taste of bidding for international events, trade shows, the North American market and bringing business to Bournemouth. We worked closely with organisations like the British Association of Conference Destinations and it was also my first exposure to the wider network of conference venues and convention bureaus around the world. It's also where I met Gill Price, who is now Commercial Director of the QEIICC.

It's hard to say what is the best, or the right way into the industry, but sales, tourism and hospitality experience and training are all relevant. There are some excellent courses in the hospitality industry now throughout the UK, but Bournemouth University seems especially good. A specialised conference industry training course has more value once you are in the job, such as NVQs, which the QEIICC has been involved in developing.

If you are applying for a job in the industry, ask what sort of training and career development opportunities there are with the job. Most importantly, you have to have the right attitude. All the people I have recruited have different backgrounds but they are all positive, forward-thinking, open to new ideas and adaptable. You have to be a 'people' person and enjoy forging new relationships. You have to work with a wide range of people in different positions, from suppliers to senior executives, so you have to be able to think on your feet and work under pressure, be self-motivated *and* be a team-player.

Penny Hanson, Managing Director, The Hanson Organisation (exhibition organisers and consultants)

I have always thoroughly enjoyed organising exhibitions for a number of reasons. Firstly, there is a great deal of contact with all types of people. From the exhibitors to contractors, hall owners, sponsors and trade associations to VIPs and the famous. As a director of many exhibitions over the years, I have met, or hosted on tours, princesses, prime ministers, MPs and showbiz stars on the one hand, while dealing with cleaners, caterers and standbuilders on the other.

Secondly, every exhibition is different and, no matter how successful an exhibition is, there is always a need to reflect, review, change or improve things for the next one. Complacency can be a fatal mistake for both the show and the organiser.

Thirdly, the work itself varies enormously throughout the year. Depending on the precise role of the organiser and the type of company structure they work within, they could be responsible, with support staff, for managing the entire event, from venue selection and liaison through to sales and marketing, technical organisation and overall administration.

When organising an exhibition, an eye for detail is absolutely essential, as well as an organised approach to everything you do. No stone can be left unturned as even the slightest error made in the office can lead to major problems on site.

Being able to manage people is an important skill, as organising exhibitions is very much a team effort, relying on the varied talents of the sales team, the marketeers, the public relations specialists, plus of course the venue and appointed outside contractors. Clear, effective and efficient communication with all these people is essential to ensure that all aspects of the show are well organised.

In essence, it is the variety of exhibition organising that I truly enjoy, in addition to the great sense of satisfaction one achieves after a year or more of organising a successful show from start to finish.

Probably one of the most frustrating aspects of the job is the amount of administration involved. Anyone wanting to become an exhibition organiser must be prepared to spend a large part of their time on basic, but essential, administration.

After my school education, I studied a bi-lingual secretarial course at London Polytechnic. I started work in 1974 as a bi-lingual secretary in the Economic Directorate at the EEC in Brussels. I quickly became disillusioned with the work and moved back to London in 1975 where I started my career in exhibitions with a company called Brintex Exhibitions. In 1979 I was appointed director responsible for running their fashion shows. In 1985 I joined a newly formed company called Queensdale Exhibitions as director responsible for the development of new exhibitions. Queensdale Exhibitions, together with its sister company Dresswell Ltd, went public in 1986 and formed the Blenheim Exhibition Group. In 1990 I was made Managing Director of Blenheim Queensdale Ltd and left in 1991 to set up on my own.

Since I started my own business I have combined exhibition consultancy work primarily with the organisation of the 'Meetings & Incentive Travel Show'. As far as possible, I fit my consultancy work into the quieter part of the year for the exhibition. This type of work ranges from researching new events through to providing advice and information on all aspects of exhibition organising (venue selection, sales, marketing, public relations, management, organisation and administration). All consultancy work is fee-based and varies according to the nature and length of the contract. Fees can be based on hourly, daily or negotiated long-term rates.

The consultancy service is supplementary to my work on the 'Meetings & Incentive Travel Show' which, as it expands, takes up an increasing amount of my time, particularly during the last six months before the show. In 1997 the 'Meetings & Incentive Travel Show' occupied 2250 square metres, with 235 stands and 350 exhibitors, generating a total revenue of approximately £575 000.

With the exception of specific sales training courses, I have never received any formal training in organising exhibitions. In fact, it is only within the last few years that colleges have introduced exhibition organising as part of certain courses. My organising skills have been developed by working up through the ranks, by working across the board on all aspects of exhibition organisation, by hard work and experience.

People can enter the world of exhibitions from many different angles: through exhibition sales, marketing, publishing or maybe because they have the expertise in a specific market. Working for small organisers can be very different from working for large companies. Working for a small organiser might offer the opportunity to obtain a greater breadth of experience in a short period of time, whereas a larger company may separate its organisational functions so one only works on a specific aspect of the show, such as sales or marketing or organisation. However, a large company can also offer the possibility to move from department to department.

Above all else, exhibitions are not for those looking for a regimented 9–5 job. Flexibility, adaptability, stamina, an ability to think on your feet, a positive attitude to hard work and a desire to succeed are all essential qualities of a good exhibition organiser.

Martin Lewis, Managing Editor, Meetings *&* Incentive Travel *magazine*

Diversity of activities, products and services. That's what has made this industry fascinating for me.

After all, how do you produce a magazine to interest as eclectic a group of people as a personnel manager for a tyre company, a brand manager for a confectionery company, the chairman of a computer company, an hotelier, an audio-visual producer, a travel agent, an after-dinner speaker, the secretary of the National Union of Teachers, a professional conference organiser . . . need I go on?

It's more like producing a consumer magazine than trade publishing – the only common denominator is that all our readers are involved in the events business as a part of their lives. Some are involved for every working minute of their professional lives in organising meetings or incentive travel programmes, product launches, training programmes and the like. Others do it as just a small part of a wider professional brief – personnel management, marketing and association managers, for example, are the part-time professionals. But all need to know how, where, when and why they should do things to be efficient and successful.

That's our brief – to produce a magazine to interest men and women, from chairman to secretary, from full-timer to part-timer, from corporate man to association woman. It's an interesting challenge and one which I often think can only result in degrees of failure. After all, *any* subject can alienate *part* of the target audience so we start from that position. My aim has always been modest: to persuade readers there is at least *one* item in the magazine that will interest, inform and/or entertain them. If they happen to find more than one, we have reduced the degree of failure still further.

If the diverse nature of the readership is the challenge, it is the diverse nature of the business that is the reward. When I left newspapers where I had worked as a reporter and sub-editor on news and sport for the apparently lush and cushier pastures of travel trade newspapers, I was initially attracted by the travel opportunities but then bored by the mind-numbing sameness of it all.

When I then joined a magazine called *Conference & Exhibitions* 17 years ago, it was because I was out of work and needed a job rather than out of any sense of professional calling. I joined my old mate Rob Spalding and, having done so, immediately wondered what on earth I was doing up this particular career cul-de-sac. But gradually the conference business wooed me and won me over. Yes, I liked the people and, yes, I liked the business – the idea of a business dedicated to better communication between people appealed to my naive and romantic view of a worthwhile industry. But the real reason I have stayed in it is because of the diversity – and it is constantly changing and totally international.

Even I, with the attention span of a two year-old and the concentration level of a squirrel, cannot be bored in this business.

In *Meetings & Incentive Travel* we cover venues and destinations at home and abroad, technical equipment from simultaneous interpretation to back-screen projection, marketing methods from exhibitions to the Internet, event management methods from sponsorship funding to event software, staff movement from agencies to hotels, case histories of actual events from a BT roadshow to the Hong Kong handover ceremony, price surveys of hotels and conference centres, legal requirements at home and abroad, government policy at home and overseas and the trading results of the leading agencies.

We also organise an exhibition once a year called the 'Meetings & Incentive Travel Show'.

We talk to tourist offices, airline people, conference producers, video designers, graphic artists, hoteliers, travel agents, interpreters, motivators, trainers, corporate entertainers, after-dinner speakers – the list is endless. We meet people of every nationality and every cultural background.

How could I be bored?

It is interesting to see how many others stay in the business and how many of those who leave, then return and are delighted to be back. Rob Spalding once called it a 'global village hall' and the phrase has stayed with me. The meetings and incentive travel business is bigger and more international than ever but still it is a tight community of old friends.

It has meant we have published things that some of my friends (I mean contacts) haven't liked and some of them are no longer friends. But, on the whole, a fairly 'shoot-from-the-hip' editorial style has won more friends than it has lost.

My first ever editor told me on my first day's work as a reporter: 'Martin, don't get too close to your contacts.' I didn't understand the advice then, but I do now and he was right. Unfortunately, in this business I have not been able to follow his words. I'm afraid it just isn't possible.

The meetings and incentive travel business is just too social, just too darned friendly and just too much fun.

Summary

- Excellent inter-personal skills are essential to anyone looking to make a career in the conference industry. A range of other qualities will also be needed, including organisational ability, computer literacy, a facility for working well under pressure, and oral and written communication skills.

- As the quality of the physical conference product (venues, equipment, infrastructure) reaches a generally acceptable standard, it will be the quality of service delivered by the industry's employees which will distinguish one venue or destination from another.

- The conference industry and the education sector have been slow to develop appropriate education and training opportunities for the industry's current workforce and for potential new entrants. This situation is now changing as educational institutions and professional associations begin to develop full-time, part-time, and short course programmes.

- There is a lack of professional qualifications specific to the conference industry, although initiatives are under way to address this need, both at national and international levels.

- The industry is broad enough to welcome into its ranks people from diverse employment backgrounds and disciplines. The lack of clear career structures and progression routes can be confusing and frustrating, but also stimulates greater fluidity and freedom of movement between jobs.

Summary continued

● The conference industry offers a rich diversity of employment opportunities. Few people will become millionaires, but the rewards in terms of job satisfaction, fun, creativity, and building friendships around the world are rich indeed.

Review and discussion questions

1. Re-read the job advertisements and career profiles in this chapter and use these to write a 'person specification' for three vacancies which are about to be advertised: a) a conference organiser (with a company or association), b) a conference sales manager (with a venue), c) a destination marketer (working for a conference desk or convention bureau).

2. The hotel sector has a reputation for high staff turnover, with insufficiently trained staff and limited career opportunities. To what extent is this an accurate description of the UK hotel sector today? What measures should be taken to change perceptions of the sector and ensure that it really does attract, and retain, the highest calibre of personnel?

3. What image does the conference industry have among the general public? Design a questionnaire and carry out a survey among friends, family, colleagues to establish their understanding of what the industry is like, whether it is important and why, their experience of attending conferences, and to clarify their overall impressions of the industry. Use the findings to make recommendations for changes which could lead to greater recognition for the industry and for the people it employs.

4. The Department of National Heritage (DNH) report quoted in this chapter says that:

   The quality of personal service is perhaps more important to tourism and hospitality than to any other industry . . . The quality of interactions (with industry employees) is an integral part of the experience and has the potential to delight or disappoint the consumer. We do not believe that this potential is there to the same extent in any other employing sector.

   Compare tourism and hospitality with another service industry and give reasons why you would agree or disagree with the DNH report.

References

● *American Express UK Meetings Market Survey* (1997) American Express Card Division.
● DNH (1996) *Tourism: Competing with the Best No. 3 'People Working in Tourism and Hospitality'*, Department of National Heritage (now Department for Culture, Media and Sport).
● *A Quality Assurance Scheme for Conference Venues: Exploratory Research* (1977) Scottish Tourist Board, English Tourist Board, Northern Ireland Tourist Board, Wales Tourist Board.

Chapter 8

A Twenty-first Century Industry

Introduction

Tourism is on the verge of becoming the world's largest industry. As a sub-sector of tourism, conference and business tourism is also showing sustained growth. This chapter looks at whether this growth is likely to continue into the twenty-first century by examining current trends and the impact of new communications technology. It also discusses many of the key issues facing the industry on the threshold of the new millennium, issues for which appropriate solutions must be found if the industry is to continue to progress. Finally, it concludes with an optimistic prediction for conferencing in the twenty-first century.

Objectives

This chapter covers:

Market trends

- the tourism market
- the conference market
- conference and meeting trends
- impact of new technology
- research needs.

Issues and developments

- what role for government and government agencies?
- funding for business tourism
- the design of conference facilities
- the needs of disabled delegates
- environmental issues and sustainable tourism.

In conclusion

- an optimistic forecast.

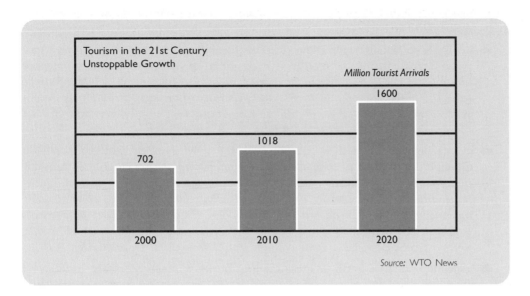

Figure 8.1
World Tourism
Organisation
forecast for
tourism growth
to the year 2020.

Market Trends

The tourism market

Tourism is set to become the world's largest industry in the course of the next few years, according to all expert opinion. The World Tourism Organisation (WTO) suggests that the 'growth of the tourism industry will be unstoppable in the twenty-first century, soaring to 1.6 billion international arrivals annually by the year 2020' (*WTO News*, 1997). Preliminary findings of WTO's *Tourism Vision 2020*, announced in March 1997, predicted that, globally, the tourism industry would continue strong growth of about 4 per cent a year through the first two decades of the next century. It forecasts that there will be 702 million international arrivals in the year 2000, over one billion in 2010, reaching 1.6 billion by 2020, nearly three times the number of international trips (592 million) made in 1996.

Other findings from *Tourism Vision 2020* are that the twenty-first century will see a higher percentage of the total population travelling, especially in developing countries, and people will be going on holiday more often, sometimes two, three or four times a year. Tourists of the twenty-first century will also be travelling further from their homes, with one out of every three trips by 2020 predicted to be long-haul journeys to other regions of the world. Long-haul travel is expected to increase from 24 per cent of all international tourism in 1995 to 32 per cent by 2020.

Figure 8.1 summarises WTO forecasts for international tourism growth up to the year 2020.

The conference market

But what of conference and business tourism? Is there likely to be the same exponential growth in this sector of the industry? Or is the pessimistic forecast of Munro (1994), who predicts the demise of the conference industry within 50 years, nearer to reality?

Munro's (1994) scathing attack on the value of conferences includes the following reasons why delegates like to attend conferences (my comments are shown in italics):

- international 'first class' air travel: *In reality, only a small proportion of delegates travel first class.*

- luxury hotel rooms 'with a chocolate on the pillow': *This ignores the fact that many large conferences require a wide range of accommodation, from guest house provision to 5-star facilities. Luxury is an over-used word. While it may be true to say that accommodation standards have risen significantly over recent years, and are expected to continue to rise, only a very small percentage of hotel rooms could be described as luxurious.*

- events being scheduled to coincide with the 'Olympics' or 'British Open Golf Championship': *This is completely to misunderstand the scheduling of international conventions and the bidding processes which determine their actual locations. International sporting and cultural events can themselves generate new meetings and conferences. But few, if any, organisers of association conferences would deliberately try to arrange their conferences to coincide with such events, not least because hotel accommodation would simply not be available.*

- 'delegates spend a lot of time putting together their itinerary to take in as many events as possible in a round-the-world trip': *No organisation could possibly afford to employ a 'professional conference-goer' when ever higher levels of employee productivity and performance are expected.*

Munro outlines a typical conference day as starting at 9.30am and finishing by 4pm – explain that to the corporate executive who is still in session at 10pm and is then given work to prepare in time for an 8.30am start the following morning! Munro suggests that organisations will no longer be willing to waste time and money on sending their employees off to attend conferences where only a small part of the whole conference will be relevant and beneficial. Video conferencing is put forward as the panacea for company communications, and as the great destroyer of the conference centre building boom of the late twentieth century. 'With a little imagination, the whole conference interaction can be handled without leaving home', concludes Munro.

There is no doubt that video conferencing has, and will continue to have, a significant role to play in the evolution of the conference industry into the twenty-first century, although current estimates suggest that it only accounts for around 1 per cent of the meetings market. Almost certainly, other developments in technology, many as yet quite unforeseen, will affect the style and quality of interaction in the conference of 2020 and beyond (a description of current applications of new technology is given later in this chapter under 'Impact of New Technology'). But will they decimate the conference industry in the way that Munro suggests? Four years on from when Munro was writing, let us look at what is happening, and what seems likely to happen during the early years of the twenty-first century.

The American Society of Association Executives (ASAE) and Meeting Professionals International (MPI) produce an annual 'Meetings Outlook Survey', based on interviews with 100 meeting professionals (50 association planners, 40 corporate planners, and ten independent planners or PCOs). While the findings relate primarily to the US market, it is worth noting that 58 per cent of those polled plan meetings outside the United States, the three most popular destinations being, in ranking order, Canada (with meetings ranging in size from 100 to 10 000), Mexico (with meetings from 85 to 400), and England (with meetings from 50 to 400).

The *1998 Meetings Outlook Survey*, published in August 1997, predicted a 24 per cent growth in the number of meetings to be held in 1998. In more detail:

- 16 per cent of association planners expected to hold more meetings, 76 per cent the same number, and only 8 per cent fewer meetings

- 30 per cent of corporate planners expected to hold more meetings, 68 per cent the same number, and just 2 per cent fewer

- 40 per cent of independent planners (or PCOs) expected to hold more meetings; 60 per cent the same number.

Of those predicting increases, 18 per cent were expecting to conduct more regional meetings, 21 per cent more national meetings, and 14 per cent more international meetings.

This prediction for strong market growth replicates the findings of the 1997 ASAE/MPI 'Meetings Outlook Survey' which suggested that there would be an increase of 39 per cent in the numbers of meetings held during 1997, compared with 1996.

The number of conferences held by international organisations has continued to show substantial growth. An analysis of the conferences recorded by the Union of International Associations (see Chapter 1) reveals a growth of 85 per cent between 1983 and 1996. There is nothing to suggest that further growth cannot be sustained into the twenty-first century.

A growing internationalisation in buying trends was noted in the 1997 survey of hotel chains carried out by *Conference and Incentive Travel* magazine (July/August 1997). An article entitled 'Hotels Brand Wars' quotes Paul Hussey, Director of Sales Development for conference agency Banks Sadler, as saying: 'We are doing more overseas business than ever before. Companies are settling down with EMEA (Europe, Middle East and Africa) structures and a lot of internal meetings now are for the whole of that area.' The article suggests that 'under these new pan-European structures, an executive in London is as likely to be working on a project with a colleague in Madrid as with someone in the next door office. It is no wonder, therefore, with economies revitalising in most places . . . that both bookings and optimism are on a dramatic upward curve for the conference industry.'

The European Federation of Conference Towns, in its annual review of the European conference industry, *A Report on Europe 1996* (1997), confirms this trend towards a more international conference sector:

> *The Common Market of the European Union has, despite some setbacks, boosted the European conference scene. The freer movement of people, capital, goods and services across fifteen participating nations has simplified many aspects of meetings marketing and management. It has created new sales and operational opportunities for destinations as business expands, bringing new meetings, conferences, seminars, and other events.*

The confidence and buoyancy of the conference and meetings industry in the late 1990s does seem set to continue. Downturns in national and global economies will, of course, have repercussions for the industry, but history has shown how resilient the conference sector can be. The underlying trend remains one of consistent growth combined with increasing international competition.

Conference and meeting trends

Conferences in the late 1990s are now much more active and participatory in style than was the case just a few years ago. The emphasis is on dialogue rather than declamation, networking and sharing rather than on passive listening, getting hands-on experience and forming workgroups so that conference themes can be understood and digested.

This means delegates spend less time in plenary sessions in the main conference auditorium, and much more time in smaller groups and syndicates. There is still a requirement to bring delegates together for keynote presentations, whose aim may be motivational or inspirational, or to provide an opportunity to present new corporate strategy, or to give leadership and direction.

But meetings and conferences now have a much clearer business focus. They are probably more intensive events than in the 1980s, using an interactive approach through personal computers and multi-media technology. In the words of Peter Berners-Price, past Chairman of Spectrum and now a Director of Carabiner Europe (speaking at a BACD conference in 1994):

The strength of multi-media, the result of technology that is based on transmitting text and pictures digitally through telephone wires, or rather through microwave technology off satellites and down fibre optic cables, is that it will revolutionise interactive learning. It will be far more efficient in communicating information than listening to someone speaking from a stage or a teacher in a classroom.

Why? Well, firstly it will go at the speed at which you want to go. It will ask questions depending on how you have answered the last one. It will appeal to the creative imagination through colourful video, and dramatic animation. It will speak to you. It will play you music. And yes, of course, it will test you! So why is this technology good for the conference industry? Primarily because the technology will bring an amazing dimension of interactivity right into the conference room itself.

Large association conferences typically involve a combination of plenary and workshop sessions. Many have poster sessions (displays of reports or scientific/academic papers put up by authors, sometimes with a short presentation or question-and-answer session between the author and interested delegates) and a concurrent exhibition, often used by conference organisers as a way of generating income to defray the costs of the business sessions. In an increasingly commercial climate, with convention centre managers now under pressure, often for the first time, to achieve operational profits, the requirement is much greater for hall hire charges to be set at market rates, even for non-profit making organisations. This, in turn, brings pressure on association organisers to keep a much closer eye on the 'bottom line' and to be imaginative and creative in obtaining sponsorship, or finding other ways to generate funds which can help to keep delegate fees at affordable levels.

Forecasting the likely structure and format of conferences in ten or fifteen years' time is a sure way to invite questions as the pace of change continues to accelerate. It is clear that technology will have a major influence, as is shown in the summary of new technology applications and trends in the next section.

Impact of new technology

Some 52 per cent of respondents to the ASAE/MPI *1998 Meetings Outlook Survey* (to which reference was made earlier in this chapter) anticipated that technology would be the cause of the most significant changes to the meetings industry over the next two years, particularly the use of satellite audio/video conferencing, online education access via the Internet, online delegate registration via the Internet, and online venue selection 'Hot Dates/Hot Rates', again via the Internet. Almost 90 per cent of planners use computer-controlled multi-media/LCD (Liquid Crystal Display) panels for meeting production on-site and for educational instruction.

Certain applications of modern communications technology, both inside the conference auditorium and elsewhere in the convention centre, are well illustrated in the following excerpt reproduced from *Meeting Planner International* magazine (Spring 1997), describing the contributions of Professional Conference Organisers (PCOs) to the planning and staging of large conventions:

> *At McGill University in Montreal, Canada, PCO Joan Gross and experts in the university's computer department developed an interactive system which could receive, process and publish some 3000 abstracts on the World Wide Web. The system was also fitted with conference management systems and various programs which allowed participants, using any operating system, to contact the congress Web site, type in their abstract and register for the congress all at the same time. During the congress, which attracted 5000 scientists, computer terminals and printers, distributed throughout buildings where events took place, enabled delegates to print out any documents they needed. Because papers were available before the congress even started, Joan Gross said that, in the actual sessions, there was a completely different kind of dialogue at a much higher level than would normally be expected.*
>
> *Similarly, in Amsterdam, at the 1996 meeting of the Société Internationale de Chirurgie Orthopédique et de Traumatologie, the local PCO came up with some new ideas which changed the whole environment of the conference. Again, computer workstations were distributed around the venue so that participants could access the programme and plan their own schedules. In addition, each pariticipant received a CD-Rom containing a full set of abstracts and the list of participants. The second innovation was to show 1500 posters and cut out literally hundreds of free-paper presentations.*

It is very important for conference presentations to be visually attractive and stimulating. Video and digital technology and large format video projectors that approach the quality of big screen slide presentations will increase the visual impact of presentations. An article entitled 'Meetings Outlive the Millennium' in *Conference and Incentive Travel* magazine (May 1997) quotes conference production companies using video conferencing, multi-media (the merging of telecommunications, video and computers to give a completely new communications medium), the Internet and Intranet as ways of conveying the information and knowledge content of conferences for their clients. However, it predicted that companies will still need to bring their employees together, face-to-face, for the motivational aspects of communications, in order to inspire delegates to want to do something with the knowledge they have acquired. There is likely to be greater use of audience response systems to provide an immediate feedback from delegates to issues under consideration.

The same article describes the potential of virtual reality as an interactive medium, citing car manufacturers giving customers 'an immersive experience in a new product at a launch', while a financial services company could 'demonstrate a new service by allowing people to interact with it'. Virtual reality is also in use in CD-Rom venue-finding software, taking users on guided tours around the rooms and facilities of venues.

The 'virtual conference' is expected to be with us within two years, according to an article in *Meetings & Incentive Travel Magazine* (September 1997, p.12) reporting on a presentation by Stephen Dowd of Ashleigh Consultants. By 1999 video cameras will be built in as standard on desk-top computers, so that no additional hardware will be needed. Dowd forecasts that the arrival of remote or virtual conferencing will mean that a modem and a web browser are all that will be needed to attend a conference via the

Internet. Microsoft has already launched a product called 'Meeting Net' for this market. A 'virtual delegate' will be able to choose which view of the speaker or audience he wants and will be able to listen in any language or watch subtitles. Other advantages of the virtual conference are listed as:

- savings on travel and hotels, as well as the time involved in travelling
- the ability to download a presentation in full
- the ability to access a list of delegates
- savings on full delegate fees
- the ability to pay per module accessed
- no limit on attendance levels
- the ability to visit a virtual exhibition
- the facility to ask questions and vote without physically attending.

Such developments might seem to lend weight to Munro's predictions for the early demise of the conference industry. Dowd forecasts, however, that they will not signal the end of the live conference industry and, indeed, will make little impact on the existing habits of the industry. Instead, the virtual conference and remote conferencing will 'add opportunities for people to attend sessions "virtually" through their computer on a more selective and cost-effective basis'. There is also some evidence, as yet unquantified, that video conferencing has actually stimulated new 'live' events, as participation in a video conference has confirmed the need for delegates to meet face-to-face.

As well as the use of new technology in the conference (or 'virtual' conference) auditorium, other developments are taking place which may impact on access to conferences. For example, the Department of Trade and Industry decision to license parts of the radio spectrum, allowing mobile phone companies airwave capacity to provide highly improved services – known as Universal Mobile Telephone Services – is expected to lead by the year 2002 to a new range of mobile phones enabling users to access the Internet, send e-mail, watch films and participate in video conferencing.

Research needs

It is vital that the conference industry keeps abreast of market trends and new developments in order to anticipate and respond pro-actively to client requirements. Research is the key to meeting such objectives.

Certain shortcomings in available research and market intelligence are outlined in Chapters 1 and 4. Weaknesses identified include an inadequate statistical base, lack of standardised terminology, lack of agreed economic multipliers and, consequently, no truly reliable estimates of the industry's value. Initiatives are under way which will address some of these deficiencies.

There is also a need for new research in other areas, including:

- a study of the 'national association' market in the United Kingdom to confirm the numbers of associations by segment (professional association, voluntary association or society, trade union, religious organisation, and so on), by volume and type of business to be placed, and by rotational pattern in site selection.
- ongoing economic impact studies to monitor the direct and indirect benefits to communities arising from conferences and delegate expenditure, with implications not just for the UK but also worldwide.

● projections into future trends and the needs of delegates and organisers. Most research tends to be retrospective. Difficult though forecasting is, there is a need to make predictions about the industry's requirements in ten to fifteen years' time, and such predictions should be based upon the best possible statistical foundations. Organisations looking to invest in new conference and exhibition centres need accurate and well-informed projections in order to make long-term plans and have some confidence in achieving a reasonable return on their investments.

Issues and Developments

The second half of this chapter examines some of the principal issues and developments facing the conference industry as it gears up to the challenge of the new millennium.

What role for government and government agencies?

A seminar organised jointly by the World Tourism Organisation's Commission for Europe and the European Travel Commission, held in Salzburg in April 1997 (and reported in *WTO News*, 1997) discussed what should be the role and responsibilities of European governments in the face of increasingly global competition and structural changes in tourism markets. The seminar's main conclusion was that governments should assume the role of catalyst, bringing together all the different public and private sector players involved in tourism. The seminar found that, although governments have traditionally played a key role in the development of their countries as tourism destinations, there have been increasing signs of disengagement over the past decade – at least in Western Europe. To some extent, the trend has been a natural consequence of decentralisation which, in many countries, has resulted in powers of decision-making being shifted to provincial and local authorities. Budget constraints have also been a major contributing factor to governments' increasing withdrawal from tourism development and marketing.

Two speakers at the seminar (Peter Keller, Switzerland and Egon Smeral, Austria) identified the following as the core tasks of governments vis-à-vis the tourism industry:

● definition and elaboration of the fundamental principles of tourism policy

● creation of a tourism-friendly environment

● acting as a catalyst for promotion and marketing

● stimulating innovation and international cooperation

● creation and protection of 'brand image'

● regular upgrading of tourism infrastructure

● providing support for the accommodation sector.

In their keynote address to the seminar, they suggested that:

As destinations now compete worldwide through globalisation, we have to ask our-selves with increasing frequency why some destinations succeed in international competition and why others fail. The focus of tourism is no longer on air travel, hotel rooms, and meals, but rather the experiences of fantasy worlds connected with specific destinations. It seems that the old thinking does not work any more and that there is a growing need for a new paradigm in tourism policy to influence the competitive position of a destination under the conditions of global competition.

A market-oriented approach makes it easier to integrate matters relating to tour-ism policy with economic policy. A consistent market-oriented approach can make

it easier to prepare and implement tourism policy measures, because it forces those responsible for tourism policy to concentrate on what is essential and feasible. This in turn makes the task of allocating funds for carrying out tourism policy easier. Even so, the need to fight for the thinly stretched budget available to governments today is certain to make an obstacle course out of anything to do with tourism policy.

When attempting to put market-oriented policies into practice, it is important always to bear in mind the peculiar nature of the tourism sector. Unlike the manufacture of watches, in which state participation is nil, in tourism the state is co-producer, an active partner in the creation of tourism products. Is it not the state which ensures the availability of such basic necessities as education, the essential infrastructure of airports, railways, roads, supply and disposal networks, and such all-important 'soft' factors as peace, order and security? Tourism is the marketing of a location. It, therefore, relies on the ability of the state to provide a full complement of modern services.

While the presentation by Keller and Smeral concerned itself with tourism in the broadest sense, with perhaps a bias towards leisure tourism, the principles which they outline, as the role for government, apply equally to business and conference tourism, although it may be helpful to clarify that, in the case of the United Kingdom, government operates both centrally and locally.

There does need to be a greater recognition by government of the contribution that business tourism plays in the economic prosperity of communities, at national and local levels. Generally speaking, local government has woken up to the potential which this young industry offers, but central government is still not fully committed. The launch of 'Success through Partnership – A Strategy for Tourism' by the Conservative Government in February 1997 was at least a start and, almost for the first time in a government paper, mention was made of 'the business/conferences/exhibitions and events sector as a . . . high-value market'. There is here the glimmer of recognition – it is to be hoped that it does not lead only to a false dawn.

Central government has a role to play in bringing together in true partnership – with shared investment, risk and benefits – the industry's major players, public and private sectors, venues and hotels, trade associations and airlines, buyers as well as suppliers, to formulate policies and marketing strategies, to create a strong brand for 'Conference UK' which will make an impact in domestic and international markets.

There is much creativity and enthusiasm waiting to be harnessed within the British conference industry. The Labour administration has the opportunity to adopt this catalytic role and, in alliance with the industry, to forge a cohesive national policy for business tourism. By providing leadership and direction, it can also help the industry to confirm a long-term vision and strategic objectives, and thus assist in overcoming the short-termism and need for immediate return displayed by some sectors (in varying degrees by hotels, certain airlines, and local authorities) which threaten to thwart the growth of this high-earning sector.

There are also anomalies which demand the attention of central government, such as the wide divergence in funding for business tourism among the UK national tourist boards (see Chapter 3), although the devolution policies now in vogue are likely to make this less achievable. At the same time, the non-statutory nature of local government responsibility for tourism has also created tremendous variations in local authority participation in tourism development and marketing – a factor which does little to harmonise the quality of product and service delivery from area to area.

Perhaps there is a role here for the new Regional Development Agencies, in England at least, in their objectives of 'providing for effective, properly coordinated regional economic development, underpinning wider regeneration, and enabling the English regions to improve their competitiveness' (Department of the Environment discussion paper). The re-alignment of Regional Tourist Board boundaries in line with those of the Regional Development Agencies is a hopeful portent of productive partnerships.

Local authorities in Scotland do have a statutory responsibility to support tourism by co-funding (in conjunction with the Scottish Tourist Board and the private sector) the 14 area tourist boards established in April 1996. However, the level of funding is left to the discretion of each local authority, a policy which has created many problems for the area tourist boards which have often found themselves constrained by reduced financial support from their local authority partners. This is an outcome directly opposite to that envisaged when the legislation was being drawn up by the Scottish Office.

It is to be hoped that central government, through the Department of Trade and Industry, will develop a more consistent policy in its support for British participation in overseas conference-sector trade shows than was the case during the early 1990s. Then, frequent changes in support policy made long-term planning difficult and contributed to a British presence at shows such as EIBTM in Geneva of inferior quality to those of its international competitors.

Discussions have taken place from time to time about the establishment of a National Convention Bureau for Britain and, while no consensus has yet emerged on the merits and demerits of such a development, now is the time for a proper evaluation to take place. Any assessment of whether a National Convention Bureau should operate at a pan-Britain level, or at the level of individual countries, needs to examine the structures and systems in place in other international destinations, developing the best ideas and adapting them to the British context.

In the final analysis, most discussions and proposals come back to the question of funding, and it is to this issue that attention must now turn.

Funding for business tourism

Reference has been made in the previous section (and in Chapter 3) to variations in the levels of funding for tourism across the United Kingdom. It is clearly unrealistic, in the political climate of the 1990s, to expect a major increase in funding from central government, although there is scope for some additional, well-targeted financial support. Seedcorn funding of key infrastructure projects and marketing initiatives will pay for itself many times over. Glasgow, for example, can demonstrate that every £1 it spends on marketing the destination to business and leisure visitors generates a return of well over £30 in economic benefit, and many other destinations can produce similar figures.

Money has been available from the European Union to fund tourism projects in certain parts of the UK which meet eligibility criteria, and this funding has been important. However, significant EU support for the tourism industry across Europe is not likely to be forthcoming in the near future. A programme entitled 'Philoxenia' (Greek for 'hospitality'), which would have boosted the industry's promotional activities, was due for ratification in 1996 but, in the end, it was not approved. While lobbying continues to try to reverse this decision and to achieve greater recognition for the economic and social importance of tourism, it seems unrealistic to expect the European Union to play the role of Father Christmas by providing new funding regimes at an early stage.

So what is the solution?

In a 1995 analysis of Scottish tourism development, Eddie Friel, Visiting Professor at the University of Strathclyde's Scottish Hotel School, put forward a radical solution for future funding, based on systems already operating successfully in the USA. In a paper entitled 'Tourism in the "Ace" Age', he wrote:

We need to make Scottish tourism more accountable and more results oriented. The idea that local authorities will be able to sustain the present level of funding for the new Area Tourist Boards beyond 1996 is not realistic. We have to devise a system that exports the tax burden to the end-user as is the case in most US cities and some European and Asian destinations. The present system of funding, which is based on the annual begging-bowl principle, will reduce tourism to a modern day Lazarus, picking through the crumbs in order to survive. Managers currently spend 85% of their time trying to persuade those who hired them why they should be given the tools to do the job! Is this the proper way for Britain, let alone Scotland, to fund the most competitive, largest, fastest-growing industry in the world today? I do not think so.

Perhaps a local bed tax is the key. How would this work in practice? Fundamentally the customer pays a bed tax levied by the city government. In cities across the US who have established Visitor and Convention Bureaus, which are predominantly not-for-profit organisations, revenues generated for their operations range from $500 000 to $80 000 000.

Applying the principle of a tax of £1 per bednight on the total available hotel stock in Scotland would generate £9 147 032 operating at an annual occupancy level of 50%. The total amount of local authority funding to Area Tourist Boards for the 1994/5 financial year was £7 672 300.

The introduction of a bed tax would have the following results:

- *concentrate the focus of tourism on the development of staying visitors*
- *provide a consistent basis for funding destination marketing agencies*
- *create a dynamic result-oriented tourism sector*
- *permit the establishment of measurable objectives*
- *allow performance measurement*
- *attract and develop professional, competent managers*
- *dictate through accommodation availability and recognisable brand identities what the geographical boundaries of the area tourist board should be*
- *remove the burden of funding from local authorities*
- *allow an independent state of the tourism nation assessment*
- *produce more meaningful data that would inform business of development opportunities, and*
- *improve the quality of customer care.*

In a subsequent presentation on the relevance of a bed tax to destination marketing organisations, Eddie Friel asserted that it 'exports the tax burden to the end-user and frees local authority funding for social programmes. It also turns destination marketing organisations into businesses rather than bureaucracies and makes them masters of their own fate.'

Of course, no government wants to be seen as an instigator of further taxes, risking the unpopularity which would go with such actions. Organisations like the Confederation of British Industry (CBI) would probably oppose the introduction of a bed tax, in the light of their published policy statement: 'It is neither in line with overall CBI object-ives on tax nor in the interests of the (tourism) industry's competitiveness for specific additional taxes to be levied on its operations' (*Visitors Welcome – Tourism in the third millennium*).

Yet the evidence is that bed taxes work and do not lead to major competitive disad-vantage. The City of Vienna has levied a bed tax of 2.8 per cent since 1987, but still suc-ceeds in occupying second place in the 1996 UIA rankings of international convention cities.

Philip Cooke, in 1991 deputy leisure services officer for Gloucester City Council, under-took a study of tourist taxation in three US cities. He describes the benefits of the Transient Visitor Tax (bed tax):

> *[It is] a system which surcharges the tourist directly at the point of consumption – the hotel bill. The tourist pays the tax to the hotel. The hotel collects the tax and pays it to the local authority which then uses it for tourism promotion and for capital projects. This results in more tourists, who pay more tax revenues, which funds more promotion and investment, which produces more tourists.*

He concludes:

> *While the tourist industry in Britain is being starved of funds for destination mar-keting, the Transient Visitor Tax provides American cities and regions with finance, not just for tourism marketing but for the cost of constructing conference centres and arenas.*

In the author's view, it is now time for widespread consultations to take place over the introduction of such a system in the United Kingdom.

The design of conference facilities

Projecting the design requirements of conference centres and facilities to be constructed in the twenty-first century is not easy, especially as the pace of technological and social change continues to gather momentum. Flexibility is likely to remain a key considera-tion, enabling maximum use of venue rooms and space in order to maximise occupancy, through increased demand, by allowing different types of events to take place and, indeed, a number of mutually exclusive events to take place simultaneously. While few of the major, purpose-built conference centres have been run at a profit hitherto, there is now increasing pressure on centre managements to achieve operational profits, as confirmed by the European Federation of Conference Towns in 'A Report on Europe in 1996', their annual survey of the European conference scene published in April 1997.

The principles of good design which apply to conference facilities in the 1990s seem likely also to apply through the early years of the next millennium, at the very least. The exposition of these principles in the following paragraphs is based on the experiences and expertise of venue design consultancy, The Right Solution Limited.

> *The designer of conference facilities, whether a major convention centre or a new conference room for a hotel, needs to consider the same basic principles.*
> *Firstly and most importantly, who will be using the facilities and for what pur-pose? The target markets and the likely occupancy of the facilities are crucial to their viability and must be considered carefully at every stage of the design. In other words, form should follow function, not the other way round, which is so often the case.*

Figure 8.2
Edinburgh
International
Conference
Centre.

Source: Edinburgh International Conference Centre

The basic shape of conference rooms determines their ease of use, their flexibility, and the degree to which they can accommodate different seating layouts. Plenary sessions, for example, usually require a large room, often with raked seating. However, the plenary frequently lasts only a short time, with the rest of the event being split into breakout sessions. Normally, fixed-seating auditoriums are inflexible. In the case of the Edinburgh International Conference Centre (EICC) (see Figure 8.2), one of the newest purpose-built centres in the United Kingdom which opened in 1995, two sections of the main auditorium revolve to transform a 1200-seat theatre into three rooms, of 600, 300 and 300 seats.

The most flexible shape is the 'shoebox' – a rectangular space with adequate ceiling height. The key to this type of space is access. Access is one of the most important criteria – it needs to be easy for delegates, equipment and staff. The larger the space, the more important this becomes. Direct vehicle access into a conference room or hall is frequently required. A loading bay, under cover and large enough to accommodate several articulated lorries at a time, is a useful feature, especially with a lift to enable goods to be moved easily and quickly to the stage of the auditorium.

Getting equipment in and out quickly reduces set-up and breakdown times and leaves more time for the events themselves, which for venues means maximising the opportunities to sell food and beverages. For the client, venues that enhance flexibility of event production are popular because there are no technical constraints. If the technicians can install and remove a production in half the time it would take in a poorly designed venue, this will save enormously on labour, equipment and room hire costs.

Delegate access is also a prime consideration. It has to be remembered that delegates do not necessarily know the layout of a venue, so simplicity of circulation is important. A main entrance giving direct access to a spacious foyer, for delegate

*registration and access to stairs, escalators and lifts, will facilitate delegate move-
ment around the building while, at the same time, enabling the organiser and
venue staff to monitor and control the flow, for security and safety's sake.*

*The configuration of facilities can greatly influence the easy running of the
conference schedule. Particular issues are the proximity to the main auditorium
of breakout rooms and catering areas. It also helps event organisers to site an
exhibition area where people will naturally walk through without having to make
a huge detour. This will encourage the sale of stands (often a pre-requisite of
financing major conferences). Office facilities and other essential services should
also be easily accessible. If a speaker arrives five minutes before he is due to start
presenting and needs his notes photocopying several hundred times before he has
finished speaking, it does help if the organiser does not have to walk half a mile
to the office.*

*Ensuring a plentiful supply of toilets close to the function room, enough tele-
phones, large enough cloakrooms and plenty of space in the reception area, are
points not often appreciated if they are well thought through. However, they will
cause a barrage of complaints if they are inadequate.*

*The meeting rooms should have a good ceiling height so that screens, sets and
presenters are above the audience and clearly in view of everyone. This also helps
the lighting to point downwards, rather than at the presenter, which both dazzles
and causes shadows. To enhance the staging possibilities, it is worth building load-
bearing points into the ceiling to hang lighting, sound and video equipment.*

*If a room is used for special dinners and occasions requiring either an intim-
ate or a grand ambience, as well as more functional meeting uses, then good
lighting systems will help create the necessary flexibility. It is possible to install
chandeliers with electric motors so that they can be raised into roof recesses, and
to add variations into the lighting to suit all types of event. In the EICC's Cromdale
Hall, a grid of hanging bars ensures that lighting can be hung anywhere in the
room. This means that each table in a banquet can have a pin spot illuminating
it, reflecting the shining cutlery and glassware – a spectacular effect. It also has
a practical application. Standard table layouts are quickly achieved by simply
putting the spotlights on and aligning each table under the pool of light on the
floor. In this way, room set-up can be completed speedily and accurately.*

*The general decor of facilities also affects their adaptability. It is possible, with due
thought and consideration, to design interiors so that they are attractive enough
for gala dinners and practical enough for conferences. The most common errors
are lining the walls with mirrors, which causes a lot of reflection and is not good
for acoustics; windows which cannot be blacked out for audio-visual presentations although they are of obvious benefit for social occasions, if there are attractive grounds or views; and colours that could potentially clash with set designs and
company logos. With neutral decor, a room can be decorated to suit any event.*

*Chairs always need to provide adequate comfort for delegates who are seated
for long periods of time. They may also need to be sufficiently attractive to suit
the setting for wedding receptions. Adequacy of comfort is defined, in conference
terms, as 8-hour sittings. Standard banqueting chairs found in most venues are
usually comfortable for a couple of hours. Then that well-known medical condi-
tion appears: NBS (for the less medically informed, 'Numb Bum Syndrome'). This
can only lead to dissatisfaction and is clearly a pain in the . . . neck!*

*On a more technical note, an efficient and well-designed cabling infrastructure,
to include water and compressed air services as well as the provision of electrical*

power and cabling for multi-media communications, will assist a venue to respond efficiently to the many-faceted demands of today's event organisers. It will also prevent the need for the all-too-common yet dangerous and unsightly practice of having cables running all over the floors which can trip people up, cross fire exits and mean that doors have to be propped open – adding to the concerns of the fire officer. The use of tie-lines – built-in cabling to link sound, video and lighting in various parts of a room – can easily prevent these problems. The provision of a large power supply will always stand a venue in good stead. Communications technology today means that telephone, data and broadband video can all be sent down one set of cabling – if it has been installed in the first place.

The present conference climate demands high levels of both tele- and data-communications facilities. This demand will increase, as more and more bandwidth, at ever-increasing speeds, is required to relay information required within conferences. Equipment exists today to send a presentation 'down the line' from anywhere, direct into a video projector, to support a presenter on stage. Before long, a presenter will be able to image 35 mm slides digitally, and instantly transform the presentation into a flexible, manipulable format. This is only possible if the communications medium – the way of getting from point A to point B – is available.

Peter Berners-Price also emphasises the importance of wiring and cabling for conference venues:

Any new investment in conference facilities, whether building anew or adapting what already exists, must take into account the wiring needs. There may still be differences between the compatibility of computer hardware, and the intelligence of computer software, although problems of incompatibility are now far less than they were. But information signals will be fed to and from the facility via a dish on the roof, or by a single ISDN (Integrated Services Digital Network) telecommunications socket, which can carry signals throughout the country and throughout the world. New exhibition halls have made allowances, but conference rooms, whether they be in hotels or so-called purpose-built centres, are still remarkably unfriendly when it comes to wiring up equipment within the room itself. Flexibility is the watchword, and wiring is the key. Wiring for sound, wiring for lighting, and wiring for the new technology that will drive multi-media.

The Right Solution suggest that:

Clients will not always want to use the in-house cabling – outside broadcast being a prime example. In this instance, integral temporary cable routes can mean a fast and safe installation. Where routes pass through walls, fire-protected cable pass-throughs can ensure that fire exit doors are not propped open by errant cables.

Sound systems are also one of those areas that are taken for granted if they work well but cause much dissatisfaction among delegates or guests if they cannot hear, or if sound is broken or disrupted. This is particularly the case if poor partitions and inadequate sound-proofing mean that they can hear what is happening in the next room, or can hear plates being cleared in the kitchen.

The design of conference facilities should be driven by users and operators, rather than by designers. All the decisions taken during the design stage of venue planning can impact its revenue-earning potential and, in many cases, that of its home city. Large numbers of happy delegates will tend to spend more in hotels, restaurants and shops. Ultimately, this is the reason any city builds a convention centre. Extra care and consideration taken at the concept stage and followed through in the development of the design will, undoubtedly, be paid for many times over by higher occupancy, increased revenue and maximum profitability.

The needs of disabled delegates

The recently introduced Disability Discrimination Act gives disabled people rights of access to buildings, transport, work, services, decision-making and all the cultural, commercial and social activities of a modern and civilised society. It provides the legislative backbone to a growing movement which seeks to ensure that disabled people can play the fullest possible part in society, including participation in meetings and conferences.

For conference venues it means that access and facilities should be designed in a way that takes full account of the needs of people with disabilities. These include wheelchair users, those with hearing and visual impairments, but also many others such as people with cerebral palsy or facial disfigurements and those with learning difficulties. All will be delegates at some time, all with differing losses but also with differing gifts, and all at different stages of coming to terms with their particular disabilities.

Venues are gradually adapting their facilities to meet the needs of their disabled guests, but much work remains to be done, no only in the design and equipping of buildings but also in the education of their staff. The following incident, relayed at the BACD annual conference in 1996 by Dr Scott Hutchison, a disabled person for 49 years, epitomises the challenge faced by the industry:

> *Some time ago, I was told by a fairly reliable source that a certain Glasgow hotel was ideal for the disabled. However, as always, I first 'phoned up. 'Is your hotel accessible for wheelchair users?' 'Yes, sir, we have a portable ramp at the front and all is on the level inside.' Just to make sure about things, I asked: 'Now about the portable ramp. Being portable it's not likely to be in position when I arrive?' 'No problem, sir, just come into Reception and we will get a porter right away to put it down for you.'*

The national Holiday Care Service charity provides consultancy to venues on the needs of disabled people. Their advice to conference venues and destinations includes the following:

- in general terms, extend the same positive approach to disabled clients as you would to others. In other words, do not treat disabled clients differently.
- have a copy of destination information available in large print, braille or even on audio tape. Or, if you use a promotional video, ensure that it has commentary and text description. It should also describe facilities that have been designed to be accessible.
- keep an up-to-date list of 'British Sign Language' interpreters, available from the Council of Advancement of Communication for Deaf People (tel: 44 (0)191–374–3607).
- if you book accommodation for wheelchair users, ensure that it has been inspected under the 'TOURISM FOR ALL National Accessible Scheme', and that it has an access category and facilities appropriate to your clients' needs.
- where an induction loop/inductive coupler system has been fitted for hard-of-hearing delegates, the appropriate symbols should be prominently on display – for example, at the reception desk, in the conference room and beside the public telephones. A public telephone should be placed at desk height: 700 to 800 mm.

Figure 8.3
West Park
Centre, Dundee.

Source: West Park Centre, University of Dundee

- venues should try to place posters/display/merchandise that specifically express a welcome to people who use a wheelchair at a height of 900 mm, for example at registration points. At this height it also remains accessible for delegates who can stand up. Print styles should be large and clear for delegate packs and signage.

- where practical, venues should allow 800 mm minimum aisle width for people using wheelchairs, with a turning circle at the end of the aisle of 1500 mm minimum. Is there a ramp available up to the stage?

- venues should avoid placing items where they may be a danger to, or become easily dislodged by, delegates who are blind or partially sighted.

- try to put yourself in a disabled person's position. How 'user friendly' would your destination or venue appear if you were seated at a height of 400 to 500 mm, or if you had your eyes closed?

A proposed 'National Accessible Scheme' standard is being considered for introduction in 1998 or 1999. A working party has been formed to review draft criteria.

Contact: The Holiday Care Service may be contacted at 2nd Floor, Imperial Buildings, Victoria Road, Horley, Surrey RH6 7PZ (tel: 44 (0)1293–771500; fax: 44 (0)1293–784647.

Catering professionally and in a caring way for the needs of disabled delegates is not only good from an ethical standpoint. It also makes sound business sense. There is a huge potential market for venues which can provide the correct combination of well-designed facilities and well-trained staff. Training in disability awareness is a sensible investment for destination managers and venue operators. The Holiday Care Service is able to supply details of suitable training providers.

Figure 8.3 shows the University of Dundee's West Park Centre, the only conference centre in the British Isles, in the author's experience, designed specifically for use by disabled people.

Environmental issues and sustainable tourism

Reference has been made in Chapter 1 to the fact that conference and business tourism has far fewer negative impacts on the natural environment than mass leisure tourism. Nevertheless, there is still enormous scope within the conference sector to minimise waste and introduce policies which are genuinely 'green'. The World Travel and Tourism Council's 'Green Globe' programme and the International Hotels Environment Initiative are just two examples of ventures which aim to encourage those working in the tourism and hospitality industries to adopt environmentally friendly practices and thus create sustainable tourism.

The organisers of EIBTM, one of the conference industry's major exhibitions held in Geneva, have for a number of years given their support to environmental initiatives by publishing an annual 'Green Directory' and sponsoring 'Greening of Business Tourism' Awards. The overall winner of the 1997 Awards was The Ministry of Tourism, Nassau, Bahamas, selected

> *for the example set by their sustainable tourism strategy which incorporates marketing, hotel and resort green management, environmental impact assessment, natural and cultural resource protection and enhancement, and the establishment of a sustainable tourism development unit. The unit has also introduced an ecotourism policy and initiated ecotourism awareness months. (EIBTM Newsletter, Summer 1997)*

Whether at the macro level of a broad strategy for a destination or international hotel chain, or at the micro level of, for example, avoiding over-production of brochures to promote a new meeting venue and thus reducing the wastage element, green issues will be increasingly important in the years ahead. The limited research so far carried out suggests that suppliers are taking environmental concerns more seriously than buyers. But this is clearly another area where a positive espousal of green practices makes good business sense, both in eliminating waste (and so reducing costs) and in being seen to support policies which protect the earth's fragile ecology (and thus enhancing the public image of the company or organisation).

In Conclusion

An optimistic forecast

The author makes no claim to have covered all of the topical issues facing the conference industry on the eve of the new millennium. Reference has been made to other important issues – the need to improve the industry's statistical base, the desirability of rationalising the number of trade associations, the importance of enhancing education and training programmes, for example – but, no doubt, some issues have been overlooked.

Readers must, and will, draw their own conclusions on whether this great conference industry faces future expansion or contraction. In the author's view, and in the opinion of many leading figures in the industry, the importance of face-to-face contact and physical networking will continue to sustain the conference and meetings industry. People are social, gregarious creatures by nature, and conferences are a wonderful way of bringing people together in beneficial interaction, and for communicating through educational and inspirational experiences.

To those working in this dynamic industry, buyers and suppliers, it offers variety, stimulation, scope for creativity and imagination, travel, fulfilment, excitement, enjoyment, constant challenges, the chance to build friendships around the world, and so much more. Few other industries can offer as much. Surely, none can offer more.

The Congress of Vienna marked the beginning of a long period of peace and stability for Europe in the nineteenth century. Conferences have the potential for ensuring a permanent peace for the world throughout the twenty-first century and beyond, as they provide the framework for discussion rather than conflict, for uniting rather than dividing communities and nations, and for encouraging the sharing of ideas and information for the benefit of all mankind. Whether 'conference' will still be the most appropriate word to describe what the industry will become in the next millennium is another matter, and perhaps a keynote topic for a twenty-first century congress!

Summary

- The international tourism industry is set for 'unstoppable growth' over the next 25 years, almost tripling in volume. Predictions for the conference industry, as a segment of the tourism industry, do not exist on a similar long-term timescale. Short-term forecasts, however, confirm the present health and buoyancy of the conference market and their likely continuation into the early years of the next century.

- The format of conferences and meetings has undergone a significant change of emphasis in recent years, with much greater active participation on the part of delegates. The application of new multi-media technologies in conference venues is revolutionising communication systems and learning methods, but not reducing the need for delegates to confer on a face-to-face basis.

- The rapid pace of market change underlines the importance of regular research to keep abreast of new developments and emerging trends, and to ensure that suppliers are able to anticipate the needs of future customers.

- The role of governments vis-à-vis the tourism industry has been changing. The UK government can play an important catalytic role, both in giving impetus to public and private sector partnerships and in helping the industry set strategic objectives for its long-term development. There is also a need for government to address a number of anomalies and key issues currently facing the conference sector, and to implement appropriate systems for funding future product development and destination marketing.

- The design of conference facilities should be based on the requirements of conference organisers and venue operators rather than on the whims of architects and designers. The principles of good practical design are likely to be as relevant in the next century as they are today.

- In responding positively and promptly to other contemporary issues, such as the needs of disabled delegates or the concerns for environmental conservation, the industry can demonstrate its growing maturity and sense of social responsibility. It should also see that there are good business reasons for adopting an ethical approach to these issues.

- The conference industry faces an exciting future as it enters the twenty-first century. The potential is huge, the competition is immense, the rewards in terms of enjoyment and job satisfaction are incalculable.

Review and discussion questions

1. Television, computers and the Internet have had a dramatic effect on society and on the lives of individual people. Television, in particular, has been accused of creating a generation of 'couch potatoes'. Is the home, therefore, likely to become the conference venue of the future as we all become 'virtual' delegates? Or are people's social and gregarious instincts strong enough to ensure that face-to-face communication remains the pre-eminent form of human interaction? Outline the arguments for and against both scenarios, with specific reference to the conference industry.

2. Should governments disengage from tourism development and marketing, as the speakers at the WTO seminar suggested has been happening in Western Europe over the past ten years? Or is a greater 'hands-on' approach by governments to be preferred? Support your conclusions by analysing two European states, with particular reference to the conference and business tourism sector.

3. Summarise the arguments for and against the introduction of a bed tax as a means of funding tourism infrastructure development and destination marketing in the UK. Is a bed tax a realistic and desirable way of funding this industry's future growth, or are there more attractive alternatives?

4. Arrange to visit two conference venues and assess the degree to which they meet the principles of good design described in this chapter. To what extent could their design be said to be customer and operator-driven, rather than architect-driven?

References

- ASAE (1997) *1998 Meetings Outlook Survey*, American Society of Association Executives and Meeting Professionals International.
- Berners-Price, Peter (1994) *Looking Ahead . . . The Conference Industry in the 21st Century*, presentation at the BACD Annual Conference.
- Cohen, A. 'Hotels Brand Wars' (1997) *Conference and Incentive Travel Magazine*, Haymarket Marketing Publications, July/August.
- Cooke, P. W. (1992) The American System of Tourist Taxation and the Financing of Visitor and Convention Bureaux, unpublished report.
- DNH (1997) *Success Through Partnership – A Strategy For Tourism*, Department of National Heritage, February.
- DoE (1997) *Regional Development Agencies – Issues for Discussion*, Department of the Environment, Summer.
- European Federation of Conference Towns (1997) *A Report on Europe in 1996*.
- Friel, Eddie (1995) *Tourism in the 'Ace' Age*, The Scottish Hotel School.
- *Meetings & Incentive Travel Magazine* (1997) CAT Publications, September.
- 'Meetings Outlive the Millennium' (1997) *Conference and Incentive Travel Magazine*, Haymarket Marketing Publications, May.
- Munro, D. (1994) 'Conference Centres in the 21st Century', in A. V. Seaton (ed.) *Tourism: The State of the Art*, John Wiley.
- 'PCOs – You Either Love Them Or Don't Even Know They Exist' (1997) *Meeting Planner International Magazine*, Hallmark Communications Limited, Spring.
- *Visitors Welcome – Tourism in the Third Millennium* (1996) Confederation of British Industry.
- *WTO News* (1997) World Tourism Organisation, May.

Appendix A: List of BACD Members

Scotland and Northern Ireland

Aberdeen
Ayrshire & Arran
Belfast
Derry
Dundee & Angus
Edinburgh
Greater Glasgow
 & Clyde Valley
Highlands of Scotland
Perthshire
St Andrews & Fife

North West England and Isle of Man

Blackpool
Bolton
Chester & Cheshire
Isle of Man
Lake District (South)
Lancaster
Manchester
Manchester/Trafford
Merseyside
Morecambe
Preston
Southport
Warrington

North East England

Bradford
Bridlington
Calderdale
Doncaster
Durham
Harrogate
Hull
Kirklees
Leeds
Middlesbrough
Newcastle-upon-Tyne
Rotherham
Scarborough
Sheffield
Tees Valley
Wakefield
York

Wales

Cardiff (Caerdydd)
Llandudno
Newport
Powys – mid Wales
Swansea
Tenby, Pembrokeshire

Midlands

Birmingham
Buxton
Cheltenham

Coventry & Warwickshire
Derby
Gloucester
Herefordshire &
 Worcestershire
Leicestershire & Rutland
Malvern
Northamptonshire
Nottingham
Oxford
Shakespeare Country
Staffordshire/
 Stoke-on-Trent
Telford & Shropshire

Eastern Counties

Bury St. Edmunds
Cambridge
Grantham & Stamford
Great Yarmouth
Ipswich
Lincoln
Norwich
Peterborough
Skegness
Suffolk Coastal

South West England and Channel Islands

Bath
Bournemouth

Bristol
Chippenham & North
  Wiltshire
Devon
English Riviera
Exeter
Guernsey
Jersey
Plymouth
Poole
Swindon
West Wiltshire
Weston-super-Mare
Weymouth

Home Counties and South East England

Basingstoke
Brighton & Hove
Canterbury
Eastbourne
Eastleigh
Essex
Folkestone
Guildford
Hastings
Isle of Wight
London

London Gatwick
Luton
Maidstone
Milton Keynes
Portsmouth
Reading
Rochester-upon-Medway
Southampton
Southend-on-Sea
Surrey
West Berkshire
Winchester
Worthing

Appendix B: Leading Conference Industry Trade Magazines

Association Executive	Courtleigh, Westbury Leigh, Westbury, Wiltshire BA13 3TA
Association Management	ASAE, 1575 I Street, NW, Washington, DC20005-1168 USA
Association Manager	1a Tradescant Road, London SW8 1XD
Association Meetings	63 Great Road, Maynard, USA MA 01754
Association Meetings International	CAT Publications Ltd, Ashdown Court, Lewes Road, Forest Row, East Sussex RH18 5EZ
Conference & Exhibition Fact Finder	Pembroke House, Campsbourne Road, Hornsey, London N8 7PE
Conference & Incentive Travel	Haymarket Publishing, 174 Hammersmith Road, London W6 7JP
Congresos Convenciones e Incentivos	C/Princesa, 1, Torre de Madrid, Planta 27a – Of.1, 28008 Madrid, SPAIN
Convene	100 Vestavia Parkway, Suite 220, Birmingham, Alabama 35216, USA
Corporate Entertainer	Hedley Molyneux Ltd, The Cromwell Centre, Minerva Road, London NW10 6HJ
Executive Travel	Reed Travel Group, Church Street, Dunstable, Herts LU5 4HB
Expo News Magazine	Groupe Expo News, 5 rue de Chazelles, 75017 Paris, FRANCE
Incentive Today	Blenheim Group Plc, Blenheim House, 630 Chiswick High Rd, London W4 5BG
Incentive Travel & Corporate Meetings	Market House, 19–21 Market Place, Wokingham, Berkshire RG40 1AP
Meeting & Congressi	Corso S Gottardo, 39, 20136 Milano, Italy
Meeting Facilities Review	60 Neville Road, Uckfield, East Sussex TN22 1NJ
Meeting Planner International	Hallmark Communications, Unit B-5 Enterprise Point, Melbourne Street, Brighton BN2 3LH
Meetings & Incentive Travel	Ashdown Court, Lewes Road, Forest Row, East Sussex RH18 5EZ

Meridian	15 Keeble Court, Fairmeadows, North Seaton, Northumberland NE63 9SF
Quality Travel Magazine	Corso Porta Romana, 20122 Milano, ITALY
Successful Meetings	355 Park Avenue South, New York, USA NY 10010
The Organiser	Media Products Internat'l, 5 Ella Mews, Cressy Road, London NW3 2NH
Travel GBI	3rd Floor, Foundation Hse, Perseverance Works, 38 Kingsland Road, London E2 8DD
TW Tagungs-Wirtschaft	Mainzer Landstrasse 251, D-60326, Frankfurt-am-Main, GERMANY

Appendix C: The UK Conference Industry – SWOT Analysis

An analysis of the strengths and weaknesses of the UK conference industry, and of the opportunities and threats facing the industry.

Strengths

- The UK has a very diverse and mostly high quality conference product, located within a small geographical area with an excellent communications infrastructure.

- The UK is recognised internationally as one of the world's leading conference destinations.

- Conference business is conducted throughout the year. The peak seasons are Autumn and Spring, complementing the leisure tourism sector which peaks in Summer.

- The industry sustains full-time employment.

- Where good conference facilities exist, the profile of the area can be raised and inward investment is stimulated by hotel development, tourism attractions, and communications infrastructure improvements.

- It is complementary to the exhibitions sector.

- The conference industry has recognised portable skills for personnel. It attracts and accommodates people with skills and expertise from a wide range of other industry sectors (hotels and catering, marketing, travel and transport, public administration, even engineering and scientific disciplines where a structured, logical approach is engendered).

- English is recognised as the primary language for the international conference industry.

- The UK's rich cultural, architectural and artistic heritage provides a wealth of opportunities for exciting social programmes for delegates and partners, as well as for additional spend through pre- and post-conference tours.

- The UK conference trade media are among the best in the world, and command an international readership.

- The UK is famous for the quality of its creative skills, particularly in media and communications technologies.

Weaknesses

- There is a perception of the industry as low paid, non-skilled, especially that part represented by hotels (which account for approximately two-thirds of the total conference venue product). This can make it difficult to attract and retain the high calibre of staff required. There is a high turnover of personnel in the hotel sector.

- Conference/event management, conference venue/destination marketing, have no set career entry routes or specific professional qualifications.

- The industry is characterised by a proliferation of trade associations, each representing different segments.

- The construction of major new venues such as the International Convention Centre in Birmingham and the Edinburgh International Conference Centre is reliant upon public sector funding at a time when such funds are more difficult to secure than before.

- There is an irrational situation with regard to the availability of development grants: seedcorn funding is available to a country house hotel in Wales but not for a major conference centre in London. Likewise, a car factory in England can be funded but an hotel cannot.

- There is a scarcity of purpose-built facilities in some of the larger cities (Bristol, Manchester, Leeds, Newcastle, for example). Such facilities are essential to compete for bigger national and international high-spend conventions.

- Some of the more traditional seaside resorts have venues which can accommodate quite large events (e.g. Southend, Bridlington, Margate, Skegness) but they are struggling to attract investment from hotel developers to bring new 3-star and 4-star hotels into the resorts, thus reducing their suitability for many of the larger 'association' events

- The UK as a conference destination could be marketed in a more dynamic, creative and cohesive way overseas

- The industry lacks a weighty profile in commercial and political circles

- Not enough intelligence is available to the industry – statistics on trends, size, and value – to which industry and government could respond.

Opportunities

- The buoyant national economy is creating higher activity levels within the conference and events sector.

- The success of the UK in attracting inward investment (from Japan and the Far East, North America, and Europe especially) creates opportunities to attract more delegates from these countries to events held in the UK.

- Representation of the UK as a destination for conferences could be improved through the support and involvement of government bodies.

- Proposals for new facilities in the UK will act as a stimulus to local economies and will also help to attract more overseas visitors.

- A 'One-Stop Shop' enquiry service for the industry (representing over 3000 venues, 110 destinations, and myriad service suppliers) already exists (via BACD), but is in need of greater resources (staffing/technology/marketing) to realise its full potential. While the existing 'Venue Location Service' is probably an industry leader when compared with what is available from other countries, there is scope to develop it much further and ensure that it maintains its competitive edge internationally.

- The explosion in travel and tourism courses in schools, colleges and universities provides an excellent platform for informing and educating a future workforce about career opportunities within the conference/business tourism sector, and for ensuring that curricula/qualifications match the industry's future needs.

- The introduction of a bed tax (as already exists in the USA) would bring much needed additional funding, for tourism development and marketing, to local communities, with the burden being carried by those using and enjoying the services/facilities of a destination rather than being borne by local citizens.

- There is considerable scope, nationally and internationally, for strategic alliances to be forged by trade associations and other bodies, improving still further the professionalism of the industry and maximising the use of available resources.

- Improvements in air and rail communications (including the Channel Tunnel) are bringing increased opportunities to attract more overseas delegates and partners to conferences in the UK.

- Videoconferencing has led to increased communication opportunities which, in turn, have generated numbers of new events. The wider application of multi-media technologies may provide additional opportunities for the creation of new, live events.

Threats

- It is not a level playing field. Many overseas governments provide substantially higher levels of resources/funding than those given to the industry in the UK. That is something clearly demonstrated by the quality of exhibition stands that even developing countries can present at shows such as European Incentive and Business Travel and Meetings (EIBTM) exhibition in Geneva (a show, incidentally, organised by a British company). Within the UK, England is the poor relation in terms of its spend through the English Tourist Board and Regional Tourist Boards on conference/business tourism compared with the other three countries.

- Strong emerging competition from foreign competitors, especially in the former East European block and Pacific Asia.

- Insufficient purpose-designed facilities could prevent the UK responding to international demand.

- The introduction of new tax regimes, including airport and bed taxes, could militate against the UK's competitiveness unless similar tax policies are adopted by competitor countries.

- Higher VAT charges than in most other European countries make the UK seem more expensive.

- Planning and environmental regulations are restricting the development of new conference facilities in some destinations, especially heritage cities.

- New communications technology (video conference and teleconferencing, virtual reality, the Internet) may reduce the need for face-to-face meeting.

- Changing social patterns are impacting on conferences, with more partners going out to work and thus reducing partner attendance at conferences (especially 'association' events).

- Reduced public sector funding for tourism marketing.

- Improved transport communications (airlines and railways) also make it easier for delegates to travel to overseas locations for events that might previously have taken place only in the UK.

Appendix D: Abbreviations and Acronyms

A list of some of the more commonly used abbreviations and acronyms in the conference industry.

AACVB	Asian Association of Convention and Visitor Bureaus
ABPCO	Association of British Professional Conference Organisers
ACE	Association for Conferences and Events
AEO	Association of Exhibition Organisers
AIIC	Association Internationale des Interprètes de Conférence
AIPC	Association Internationale des Palais de Congrès
ASAE	American Society of Association Executives
BACD	British Association of Conference Destinations
BECA	British Exhibition Contractors Association
BITOA	British Incoming Tour Operators Association
BTA	British Tourist Authority
BUAC	British Universities Accommodation Consortium
CHA	Corporate Hospitality and Event Association
CLC	Convention Liaison Council
DCMS	Department for Culture, Media and Sport
EFCT	European Federation of Conference Towns
EMILG	European Meetings Industry Liaison Group
ESAE	European Society of Association Executives
ETB	English Tourist Board
EVA	Exhibition Venues Association
IACVB	International Association of Convention and Visitor Bureaus
IAPCO	International Association of Professional Congress Organisers
ICCA	International Congress and Convention Association
ITMA	Incentive Travel and Meetings Association
JMIC	Joint Meetings Industry Council
MIA	Meetings Industry Association
MPI	Meeting Professionals International
NICB	Northern Ireland Conference Bureau
NITB	Northern Ireland Tourist Board
PCMA	Professional Convention Management Association
RTB	Regional Tourist Board

SCB	Spain Convention Bureau
SEO	Society of Event Organisers
STB	Scottish Tourist Board
SITE	Society of Incentive Travel Executives
UIA	Union of International Associations
WTB	Wales Tourist Board
WTO	World Tourism Organisation

Appendix E: Meetings Magna Carta

MIA Minimum Components of Residential/ Non-Residential Conference Packages

A schedule of the minimum 'components' which MIA venues are expected to provide in their conference packages.

This has been developed in consultation with the Meetings Industry Advisory Board, a panel of experienced corporate and association buyers. It reflects the needs of 95% of researched buyers.

The MIA Minimum Components of a Residential Conference Package

1. Accommodation with private bath or shower in rooms for single or twin/double occupancy.
2. Full breakfast.
3. One service of morning coffee or tea with biscuits.
4. Two course, served or buffet lunch (including vegetarian option) plus coffee/tea.
5. One service of afternoon tea or coffee with biscuits.
6. Use of one main meeting room appropriate in size to the number of delegates to be available between 8.00 a.m. and 5.00 p.m. on any one day.
7. Availability of an overhead projector (with a spare bulb facility built in) at an appropriate height with a relevant sized screen.
8. One flip chart stand, pad and three primary colour felt tip pens.
9. Table accessories to include an adequate supply of A4/A5 writing paper, writing implements, name cards, sweets, water, glasses, cordials.
10. Three-course dinner offering either a choice at the time of service or from a pre-selected menu (including vegetarian option) plus coffee/tea.
11. No additional service charge percentage to be added to packages. Additional gratuities to be at the discretion of the client.

12. VAT at the current rate to be included. An option to exclude VAT from rates is acceptable but the total amount inclusive of VAT must also be shown.

The MIA 'Standard' Non-Residential Conference Package

This should include items 3 to 9, 11 and 12 from the Residential Package.

Rationale for what is included:

This 'package' does not aim to identify the minimum standard of meeting room facilities such as chairs, lighting, organisers', 'desk tidies', temperature control or services for which an additional charge would not be anticipated, i.e. an efficient telephone/fax messaging service, or lunch served within a specific period of time.

Specifically the rationale in respect of each element of the package is as follows:

1. The majority of clients require rooms with private bath or shower. Venues without this facility in some or all of their rooms need to make this clear to a client.

2. Full breakfast has been included rather than continental breakfast. It meets clients' expectations.

3. There is an argument for including an additional service of tea and coffee on arrival but this would not always be required, particularly for residential conferences over a period of days.

4. Most conferences would want a minimum of a two-course lunch (main course and dessert).

5. It can be argued that the biscuits in the afternoon should vary from the morning service or cakes/pastries should be included. It is not felt that this should be included within an MIA standard.

6. The terminology here is to avoid the need to allocate a room in a package which is far too big for the numbers. The timing must be perceived as the minimum time that a main meeting room would expect to be included within a package. It avoids the situation whereby a client can expect a meeting room from midday to midday within one 24-hour rate. This is obviously open to negotiation. What is included in the package can be enhanced by individual venues.

7. Whilst one could extend this paragraph to state that the lead should be taped down, acetate rolls with pens should be supplied etc., it is not felt that these are appropriate to what is included and required within a 'package'.

8. This is believed to be the minimum standard. The provision of yellow felt tip pens is not to be recommended!

9. This gives flexibility for venues to provide bottled water, pens or pencils and a variety of sweets!

10. This terminology allows delegates either to make a choice at the dinner table, in the case of small numbers, or from a pre-selected menu, for larger numbers.

11. This ensures that there is no additional service charge percentage added to packages.

12. This ensures that, where VAT is excluded from rates quoted, the inclusive figure should also be shown so that accurate comparisons can be made.

Rationale for what is excluded:

Certain items that could have been included within a residential and non-residential package have been excluded as follows:

1. **Complimentary Newspapers** Not necessarily appropriate as residential delegates prefer to choose their own.

2. **Syndicate Rooms** Whilst these are included at certain venues, they should not be included as part of a minimum standard.

3. **Conference Office** This facility is not required sufficiently frequently for it to be included.

4. **35mm Carousel Slide Projector** It is not perceived that this equipment is required to be provided by venues on a sufficiently regular basis for it to be included within the package.

5. **CCTV/Cameras/Television Monitors/Video Recorders** Venues should not be expected to include this in the package.

6. **Photocopying** Whilst some venues include photocopying, it is not perceived as being in the overall interest of clients, who may be paying for the facility when it is not required.

7. **Drinks** Other than refreshments in the conference room and during breaks, it is not recommended that any other drinks are included within the package.

Source: Meetings Industry Association, *Meetings Magna Carta*, pp. 9–11.

Index